Contemporary Theatre in Mayan Mexico

DEATH-

DEFYING

ACTS

Tamara L. Underiner

UNIVERSITY OF TEXAS PRESS, AUSTIN

Portions of Chapters 2, 3, and 4 appeared in "Incidents of Theatre in Chiapas, Tabasco, and Yucatán: Cultural Enactments in Mayan Mexico," *Theatre Journal* 50 (1998): 349–369, published by the Johns Hopkins University Press.

Requests for permission to reproduce material from this work should be sent to Permissions, University of Texas Press, P.O. Box 7819, Austin, TX 78713-7819.

♾ The paper used in this book meets the minimum requirements of ANSI/NISO Z39.48-1992 (R1997) (Permanence of Paper).

Library of Congress Cataloging-in-Publication Data

Underiner, Tamara L.
Contemporary theatre in Mayan Mexico : death-defying acts / Tamara L. Underiner.—1st ed.
    p.   cm.
Includes bibliographical references and index.
ISBN 0-292-70234-5 (cloth : alk. paper)—ISBN 0-292-70250-7 (pbk. : alk. paper)
1. Theater—Mexico—Chiapas—History—20th century.
2. Theater—Mexico—Tabasco (State)—History—20th century.
3. Theater—Mexico—Yucatán (State)—History—20th century.
4. Mayan drama—History and criticism.   I. Title.
PN2315.C46 U53 2004
792'.09725—dc22   2003018258

For Eliana and her friends
—Junajaw, Lucía, Franquito, Marlena,
María Mercedes, and "Ben Aquí"—
who play together in five different languages

CONTENTS

PROLOGUE
Incidents of Theatre in Chiapas, Tabasco, and Yucatán

UNTIL RECENTLY, my husband, Chris, worked in an independent bookstore in St. Paul, Minnesota. One day one of his colleagues asked him about the kind of work I do. "Research on contemporary Mayan theatre," my husband replied. Another colleague, overhearing them, joined in. "Oh, she should talk to my daughter," she said. "She's a professional mime."

It is not unusual for people to mishear the subject of my work. To the U.S. ear, the words "Mayan" and "theatre" don't go together as smoothly or as familiarly as do the words "theatre" and "mime." This is partly a function of critical and historical oversight, for when "Mayan" is understood, most people say, "I had no idea there was such a thing"; some have assumed that the Maya themselves no longer exist. But the confusion has also to do, I think, with my identity as producer of this research: an American woman for whom Spanish is a loved but distant second language and to whom the Mayan tongues are unfamiliar. Friends, family, colleagues, and students, therefore, often ask me how and why I became interested in such theatre. If we have time, I tell them some stories about my hometown.

I grew up in the rural outskirts of the small town of Beaver, Pennsylvania. The received wisdom about this town was that it had been named after the Delaware chief "King Beaver." (In fact, this chief took his name from the Delaware word for the beavers populating the local stream, "Amockwi," now called the Beaver River.) In that part of western Pennsylvania, many place-names record the memory and language (if sometimes in Anglicized form) of its former residents: Seneca and Chippewa Townships, Tuscarawas Road, Blackhawk School District, the village of Sewickley. When I was very young, the huge white barn in the field adjacent to our backyard housed the Chippewa Playhouse, its name oddly contrapuntal to the Broadway musical fare whose melodies wafted across the pasture on long-lit summer evenings. Perhaps, in the peculiar paths of childhood logic, some connection between theatre and Native America was thereby forged in my unfolding awareness.

Sometimes my own "origin stories" take a more literary vein, and I cite the 1963 children's book *Kitten Nell,* whose title character was "a different kitten, a different kind of cat, who longed to be an Indian and wear a feathered hat."[1] Crossing the ocean from her native Europe to America's shores, Nell gets her wish. A monkey greets her and the natives warmly welcome her: "The chief took off his bonnet and popped it on Nell's head. Nell's white, white fur changed almost into a blushy-red."[2]

If Kitten Nell's frankly unreflexive curiosity and desire to "go native" evinced an invitation to me to pursue similar quests, it was my brothers who were best able to actually do so in the imaginary of their childhoods. They belonged to the Indian Guides, a father-son organization sponsored by the YMCA, whose monthly meetings were role-playing extravaganzas in which my father ("Big Tomahawk") and two of my brothers ("Little Tomahawk" and "Tiny Tomahawk") could pretend to be natives of North America as, attired in suede and feathers, they learned these peoples' crafts and survival skills. When it was my family's turn to host the meeting, I would spy on them from the darkness of our hallway to see, as I then supposed, what girls weren't allowed to see.[3]

I believe these kinds of experiences—typical of the childhoods of white U.S. Americans of my forty-something generation and participating in lamentable and gender-inflected practices that helped to recast the myth of the Native American as extinct noble savage—helped to set the stage for what would later become an academic pursuit south of our geo-political border. These experiences were the peculiar manifestations in one little girl's life of her country's complicated relationship with its Native American roots—roots that cannot be ignored because they persist, in place-names and commercial appropriations of native material, but whose power must be channeled through operations of selective celebration and erasure. While official policies regarding Native Americans in the United States have differed from those of Mexico, in both countries European colonization effectively removed natives from their ancestral lands into isolated communities, which have subsequently been fragmented by a variety of social, economic, and political forces. One result is that today, Native Americans in both countries are widely construed as relics of the past, by their compatriots and by visitors from other countries as well. This attitude erects a significant obstacle to truly mutual encounter, an obstacle that the theatre I discuss here exists, in part, to dismantle.

For the Maya, this perspective received a particularly strong charge in the mid-nineteenth century. In 1841 a U.S. diplomat named John L. Stephens wrote a book titled *Incidents of Travel in Central America, Chiapas and Yucatan*. Like his *Incidents of Travel in Yucatan*, which followed two years later, the book was filled with colorful descriptions, maps of the regions, and speculative sketches, by Frederick Catherwood, about ancient Mayan life. Stephens and Catherwood's work introduced—some would say invented—Mayan civilization to the modern world. Their books fired the imagination of readers in the United States and Europe, inspiring an interest in Mayan culture—at least as it once was—that continues to be fueled by international tourism.

As the title of this prologue suggests, the relationship between Stephens and Catherwood's books and my study here is both close and complicated. Their work and all the subsequent discourses that it has generated have, directly and indirectly, determined the course of my own interest in Mayan culture and its expressions. When I first came to this study in the 1970s, most anthropological accounts followed one of two themes: continuity or change. In the first, the goal was to detect lines of continuity between contemporary Mayan life and its pre-Columbian origins. In such accounts, ancient secrets, guarded in stone in a code whose key was long ago destroyed, revealed themselves slowly, reluctantly, to patient researchers in the "Mexican Egypt." Some anthropologists and art historians turned to living Maya for clues, but the focus was often less on the contemporary people themselves than on what they and their customs could reveal about the ancient Mayan past. In a corrective vein, a second line of inquiry then came to focus on the impact of change—including the changes brought by tourism—on contemporary Mayan communities. Despite the efforts of such writing to expose contemporary conditions, often what remained was the subtle implication that something static existed to be influenced: if it weren't for contact with the modern world, there would have been no change, no cultural dynamic, and something authentic might have been preserved. This view, of course, has been significantly challenged in recent years, but I am referring to an earlier strain of thought that had a great influence on my own in the 1970s.

The search for authenticity and the "quest for the Other," to borrow Pierre van den Berghe's coinage,[4] remain prevalent in travel accounts and other forms of popular media. Many newspaper articles, *National Geographic* photo-essays, New Age self-help books, and PBS documentaries invite readers or viewers to muse over the "lost civilization" of the ancient, prophetic, and bloodthirsty Maya. Consider the opening sentences of one recent book on Mayan prophesy: "Lost in the jungles of Central America are the remains of a most mysterious people; the Maya. Who were they? Where did they come from? What message, if any, did they leave for our own times?"[5] Like many popular accounts, this one conflates the ruins in the jungle with the Maya as a people, its consistent use of the past tense leading the reader to conclude that the people, like the pyramids, are a kind of "remains." Similarly, in other accounts, even when contemporary Maya are mentioned, they are portrayed as the scattered descendants of their glorious progenitors—living clues to ancient mysteries—or as the suppliers of collectible handicrafts produced according to age-old traditions. Rarely is the current social, political, and economic situation considered in invocations of these peoples, who are situated squarely within—and interactive with—capitalist systems on a global scale.

In Mexico, the tourist industry in the region is happy to capitalize on the allure of the past; the internationally promoted Ruta Maya (Mayan Route or Way) is a recent incarnation of this appeal. Traversing the archaeological wonders of southeastern Mexico, Guatemala, Honduras, Belize, and El Salvador, it has since 1989 provided travelers of all stripes with an intimate look at the ancient "Mundo Maya."

It was along the Ruta Maya that my dual identities, tourist and researcher, came to intersect, and when people ask me about the origins of my interest in Mayan theatre, this is usually the story I tell. In June 1993 Chris and I were honeymooning on the Yucatán Peninsula, a popular stop along the Ruta Maya, for the express purpose of climbing the pyramids there. Climbing the pyramids was something I had wanted to do since I was a teenager, when I had first learned about the astronomical achievements of the ancient Maya—from a high school anthropology teacher, Harold Howarth, whose interest in and teaching of Mesoamerican civilizations was inspired and inspirational. My first climb, up the great pyramid at Chichén Itzá, turned out to be my only one: gripped by a vertigo I was wholly unprepared for, I had to be helped back down by my husband and a Chilean woman named Yolanda who whispered, "Pobrecita, pobrecita" (Poor little thing, poor little thing), all the way down. An ironic and fitting end to the pursuit of my Kitten Nellish dream: wanting the chance to glimpse the world through the eyes of the ancient Maya, I instead had my own squeezed shut in a mortifying backward crawl down the pyramid's unforgiving spine.

A couple of days later, at the great ceremonial center of Uxmal, I stayed below while my husband made the climb alone. Passing the time in the welcome shadow of its enormous central pyramid, I asked our guide if there was such a thing as "ancient Mayan drama." He told me about the *Rabinal Achí,* a dance drama from Guatemala that predated contact with the *conquistadores* and that was part of a long tradition of performance that had pretty much ended with the arrival of the Spaniards. Having just finished up my master's degree in theatre, I wondered why I had not encountered this before.

On the way back to the hotel, our Volkswagen bus took us through tiny hamlets of grass and adobe huts, all eerily glowing with the blue light of television sets. I began to wonder about the trajectory of indigenous theatre in Mexico, and about how messages broadcast far and wide, both from its urban center and from the United States, have intersected that course. This book is an attempt to follow that trajectory.

From my current perspective, almost a decade after my literal and metaphorical honeymoon in the Mundo Maya, my initial question — Was there such a thing as ancient Mayan theatre? — seems naive, wrapped up in a bundle of romance and privilege. But if my interest sprang originally from the conjunction of several interrelated discourses, many of them the product of unreflexive (neo)colonialism, it continues for at least two reasons: first, because I would like to try to tip the balance away from the Anglo- and Eurocentrism that still consigns the critical study of this performance to the margins of academic inquiry; and second, because of personal relationships I now have with actors, directors, and writers who mean much to me, whose work I respect and wish to make known to more people.

Some of these artists also desire this; others don't really care. In Yucatán, for example, actor-director William May Itzá asked me to tell people in my country that his group, Constelación, "is there and is doing good work." In Chiapas, when my husband expressed admiration for a Mayan poet's published work, telling him that people in our country are eager to know more about it, he received a different kind of response: "That's fine, but we don't care whether you know it or not. We do it for ourselves."

In Chapter 1, I devote a great deal of critical energy to the missionary impulse that fostered much theatre in both the sixteenth and the twentieth centuries. I find I cannot deny something of the same impulse in my own work; I wish to widen the spaces for the inclusion of contemporary Mayan theatre in the scholarly discourse of theatre studies. Taken seriously as art and as action, theatre in Mayan Mexico — an area of cultural contestation, contradiction, and collaboration—can be seen as emblematic of ongoing struggles indigenous artists face in neocolonial contexts everywhere.

I hope that this study will serve others as well, particularly those Mayan theatre practitioners who collaborated so generously with me on its preparation. Many of them still don't quite understand the fascination this *gringa* has for their work. Some, aware of the uses to which some kinds of scholarly interest in local cultures have in the past been put, are a little suspicious of it. But I offer it in a spirit of collaboration and gratitude. It celebrates their successes and, from one point of view north of our increasingly porous border, acknowledges their ongoing challenges. I look forward to following their history-in-the-making of continued encounter and exchange.

—Puebla, Mexico; Minneapolis, Minnesota;
and Phoenix, Arizona 1997–2002

ACKNOWLEDGMENTS

MY PRAYER at the start of this project was that the doors be opened to pursue it, and the full story of how this prayer was answered would constitute a whole new chapter. The doors were numerous, and opened on houses, hearts, minds, resources, theatre spaces, offices, archives, new vistas, other worldviews.

Each listing in the bibliography represents one of those doors. Similarly, each of the hundreds of performers, many of whose names I never learned, provided energetic entryways into new understandings. But there are several individuals and organizations whose contributions I specifically want to credit.

First, if it were not for the groundwork laid by Donald Frischmann, Carolyn Hewko, Punch Howarth, and Cynthia Steele, their published studies and generous sharing of resources, my own work would never have begun. My gratitude for their example and continued support is profound. I also draw deeply on the words, written and spoken, of Barbara Tedlock and Dennis Tedlock, whose ways of thinking and writing about Mayan culture in Guatemala are as inspirational as they are inimitable.

For necessary financial help, I am grateful for a University of Washington Dissertation Fellowship, an Alvord Dissertation Fellowship, University of Minnesota junior faculty research support, a McKnight Foundation international travel grant, McKnight Foundation summer support, and a Herberger College of Fine Arts Research and Creative Activity Grant from Arizona State University. I thank C. Lance Brockman, Margaret Knapp, Cynthia Steele, and Barry Witham for help in making my applications for this support competitive; and Rochelle Emmel, Arlene Hamilton, Shirley Hutchings, Sylvia Kronengold, and Pam Mitman for the administrative support behind the financial support.

To the following friends, colleagues, and acquaintances in Mexico I am particularly grateful—they shared with me their time, expertise, talent, insights, hospitality, and tolerance of my spoken Spanish over the many years of preparation for this book: Domingo Adame, Flor Aguilar Gómez, Pancho Álvarez Quiñones, Yanira Avila Vidal, Igor Ayora and Gabriela Vargas-Cetina, Carlos Baeza Sosa, Liliana Bojorquez, Gladys Casares Priego, Rubén Chacón Salazar (in memoriam), Fr. Richard Clifford, Raymundo Collí Collí, Benjamin Collí Tucuch, Petrona de la Cruz Cruz, Rogelio de la Cruz, María Rosenda de la Cruz Vásquez, Carlota Duarte, Silvia Duartes Rosas, Susana Eckholm, Carminia Eduviges Collí Chim, José Ramón Flores Sarmiento, Israel Franco, Socorro Gómez Hernández, María Luisa Góngora Pacheco, Carlos Enrique Gómez Sosa, Cristóbal Guzmán Meza, Petrona Guzmán Velasco, José Leopoldo Hernández Hernández, María Hernández Jiménez, María Roselia Jiménez Pérez, Susana Jones, Isabel Juárez Espinosa, Miriam Laughlin, Robert Laughlin, Mariano López de la Cruz, Faustina López Díaz, the family of Esteban, Porfirio, and Hermelinda Lopez, Mariano López Méndez, María Alicia Martínez Medrano, William de Jesús May Itzá, Ariel Méndez, Diego Méndez Guzmán, Leticia Méndez Intzin, Candelaria Moreno Hernández, Chip Morris, Alejandro Ortiz, María Francisca Oseguera Cruz, Victoria Patishtan Gómez, Martín Pérez Dzul, Flor de Liz Pérez Hernández, Rafael Pérez Herrera, Anselmo Pérez Pérez (in memoriam), Domingo Pérez Sánchez, María Pérez Sántiz, Roberto Edi Ramirez Méndez, Delia Rendón Novelo and her sister, Celia, Feliciano Sánchez Chan and his wife, Nely, Hermenegildo Sánchez Guzmán, Camilo Sánchez Sánchez, Lucía Sántiz Girón, Margarita Sántiz Girón, María Sántiz Gómez, Alejandrina Selem Bolivar, Kathleen Sullivan, Antonio de la Torre López, Juan de la Torre López, Martha Alicia Trejo Espinoza, Omar Valdés Hernández, Lesvi Vázquez Méndez, Miguel Angel Vásquez Sánchez, and especially the one who opened the first door, German Huet Álvarez, Infante.

I am grateful for the contributions to my emerging thought of students in my University of Minnesota seminars on theatre of the Americas, especially Patricia Ybarra and Natalya Baldyga. Similarly, I would like to thank all my colleagues, friends, and students in Minnesota, Seattle, and Tempe, whose ongoing support and inspiration are deeply appreciated.

For comments on earlier articles and conference presentations that helped to shape the eventual book, I thank Rosemarie Bank, Amelia Becker, Harley Erdman, Donald Frischmann, Jorge Huerta, Margaret Knapp, Michal Kobialka, Loren Kruger, Josephine Lee, Joanna O'Connell, John Rouse, and Cynthia Steele.

I wish especially to thank my earliest manuscript readers—Sarah Bryant-Bertail, Chris Danowski, Katie Johnson, Sara K. Schneider, E. J.

Westlake, and Michael Williams—and those who plowed through drafty middle drafts—Chris Danowski, Sonja Kuftinec, Megan Lewis Schurter, Patrick McNamara, Mark Pedelty, and Matthew Wagner. I also thank my brother Tom for his close reading and gentle eleventh-hour review. A very special note of thanks to Sarah Bryant-Bertail, Chris Danowski, and Cynthia Steele, whose detailed comments on the penultimate draft of this book have improved it greatly. At the University of Texas Press, I am grateful to my editor, Theresa May, for the profundity of her understanding and patience, and to Sheila Berg, Allison Faust, and Jan McInroy for their consistent kindness and attention to detail. And thank you again, Chris, for reading every single word so many, many times.

For assistance with the Spanish translations, I thank Cynthia Steele and Christina Marín. For help with graphics, photos, and permissions, I thank Barbara Trapido Lurie, Joseph R. Higgins, and Alexis Murphy. Thanks to Sherry Anderson and Sarah Becker for their steadily cheerful administrative support.

In the course of this project, I became a mother, and I cannot overstate the importance of trustworthy child care to its ultimate completion. In addition to the campus centers at the University of Minnesota and Arizona State University, I wish especially to acknowledge the "other mothers" in my daughter's life: Lisa Arnold and Hamlin Metzger, Natalya Baldyga and Bill Henry, Michelle and Robert Baum, Mike Danowski and AnGelica Garcia, Kristen Froebel, Barbe Marshall, Karen Martinson, Pam Mitman, Millie Rau, Eric Severson, Alan Sikes, Mary and Bill Upham, Matthew Wagner, and Patricia Ybarra.

My parents, Paul and Donna Underiner, and my in-laws, Jim and Bonnie Danowski, have consistently offered material, spiritual, and child care help, beyond both duty and measure. To my extended families on both sides, I am grateful for a precious sense of belonging and return.

Final thanks, and deepest, go to my husband, Chris, who has walked every step of this journey with me; and to our beloved Eliana, who re-inspired it and has been its sweetest distraction along the way.

Cultura es acción, es hacer, pero un hacer para expresar la idea en la materia.

Culture is action, it is doing, but a doing to express idea in matter.

—Alfredo Barrera Vásquez, 1965

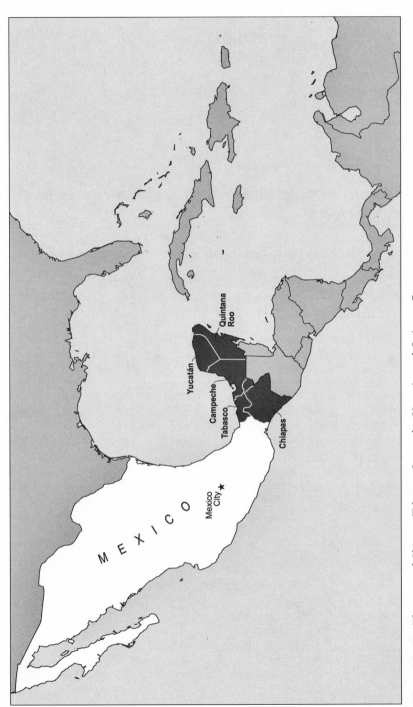

Mayan Mexico. The states of Chiapas, Tabasco, Campeche, Yucatán, and Quintana Roo.

CONTEMPORARY THEATRE IN MAYAN MEXICO

INTRODUCTION

THE BEGINNING of the twenty-first century is a turbid time to be writing about culture, cultural identity, or any scheme by which human beings and our endeavors come to be categorized in some way. We emerge into this millennium accompanied by a cacophony of voices that echo from the street level "up" to the halls of academe, engaged in continuing debates over the nature of human affiliation and how to translate these debates into social and political policy at both the local and the global level.[1]

For example, I call this a book about "contemporary Mayan theatre," but each of the terms in this phrase is, ultimately, both unspecifiable and ungeneralizable within the great diversity of these debates. Each registers my adoption of personal and collective assumptions regarding such ideologically embedded concepts as time, space, and action—themselves central components of any dramatic endeavor. "Contemporary" suggests a togetherness in time of the events discussed and the reader's experience of the current historical moment, but this moment has no precise beginning or end; nor is the term meant to suggest a notion of time proceeding in linear fashion—which, as both the ancient Maya and the more recent philosophers and scientists tell us, is only one way of thinking about and experiencing time. "Mayan" itself is a charged designation in time, geopolitical space, and different spheres of social action, adopted and adapted in a variety of circumstances to a variety of ends. And "theatre" is a word I used at the beginning of my research to distinguish my object of inquiry from both ritual and everyday performances, imagining I could fill a comfortable and familiar role as audience member, my presence sanctioned by the public nature of performances denoted by the term. But neither comfort nor familiarity characterized my numerous research trips to Mexico, and I find it impossible to completely isolate theatrical performance from the other kinds either in my experiences or in my subsequent thinking about them.

Rather than resolve these dilemmas, this book explores many of the contradictions and impasses I have encountered along the way. No grand theory organizes it; instead, it crosses several methodological and disciplinary terrains, drawing from cultural studies, history, performance studies, anthropology, and literary theory to explore the relationship between certain types of cultural performance (named "theatre" by the participants, audiences, and critics) and complex cultural identifications in Mayan Mexico.

Performance, Identity, and Transculturality

The Indigenous Photo Archive of San Cristóbal de las Casas houses a photograph that illustrates the multilayered relationship between performance and cultural identification.[2] It was taken by a young Chamulan woman, its subject her younger sister, shown wearing a jaguar mask and adopting a threatening posture as if about to pounce. It is not a moment of formal theatre, but it registers something of its impulse, recalling Aristotle's insight that imitation motivates human learning and is also at the heart of formal drama.

The girl wears a mask of an animal that is sacred to Mayan mythology and that signifies Mayan cultural identity throughout Mexico, but the mask itself is mass-produced, signaling one kind of negotiation between tradition and modernity. I am most enchanted by her hands, however: drawn up in claws to represent a jaguar on the attack, they remind me of what my young daughter does when she plays monster. I recognize the posture, I can hear the growly sounds that would accompany it, and for a moment I begin to believe that human beings can share more than a pulse.[3] My daughter mimics monsters generated by her culture's collective nightmares, which she accesses mostly by exposure to Scooby Doo and his animated kin. For the young Chamulan actor, the source is rooted in oral and graphic traditions that establish the jaguar as an icon in multiple ways, few of which include commercial cartoons. To my eyes, though the models are different for these two young actors, their individual copies are remarkably the same. This observation trips my utopistic triggers and tempts me to look toward rosy metaphors of performance as the key to world peace and universal understanding. Underneath it all, says my internal eternal optimist, we may be not the same but incommensurably different; still, through performance we can recognize ourselves and find a link to other selves.

In many ways, this has been my experience while gathering the material for this book: I believe theatre and performance have world-changing potential. At the same time, I am aware of the dangers of dwell-

"Li jmuke tey va'al xci'uk sk'oj/Mi hermana está parada con su máscara/My sister is standing with her mask on," by Pascuala Sántiz López, © 1997. Courtesy of Archivo Fotográfico Indígena.

ing too comfortably in such a position, especially as it might add to already intense pressures to homogenize culture across artistic, educational, and geopolitical borders. Thus, this book attempts to situate certain moments of theatrical activity in certain times and places, toward complicating available models of self, other, theatre, performance, culture, tradition, and change. It is especially meant to deessentialize notions of "Mayan theatre" still operative north of the U.S.–Mexico border. At the same time, it addresses the scholarly suspicion of essentialism, which at its extreme can "undermine the concept of culture itself."[4] It explores in specific cases how theatrical performances negotiate these problematics.

Writing about the relationship between performance and identity, John

MacAloon suggests that cultural performances allow us to "reflect upon and define ourselves, dramatize our collective myths and history, present ourselves with alternatives, and eventually change in some ways while remaining the same in others."[5] MacAloon's work is inflected by that of the social anthropologist Victor Turner,[6] who assigns to formal theatre a special role in cultural coherence and change. For Turner, theatre is a particular kind of cultural performance that occupies a liminal time somewhere among the received past, the given present, and the possible future. It almost always occupies a liminal space as well, a space marked off for the special purpose of the performance—a space removed (or transformed) from everyday life but not quite resident in the realm of the divine. Finally, what occurs in that space and time provides, as MacAloon suggests, an opportunity for reflection and redefinition "as a culture or a society," an opportunity to reassert, reclaim, critique, and transform cultural traditions. A favorite professor of mine, whose field is comparative religion, once put it this way: "What theatre *isn't* about cultural identity?"[7]

But the relationship between performance and personal or cultural identity is never simply tautological, and in the case of Mayan theatre in southern Mexico, the cultural identity being performed by various theatre groups can be quite a complicated matter. For example, a Mayan troupe in Chiapas develops its plays collectively but has relied on an urban Mexican playwright to shape them and on U.S. anthropologists and directors to stage them. A Mayan women's collective, also in Chiapas, has chosen to work selectively with non-Mayan women's groups, locally and internationally, to present its work. Another group, begun in Tabasco and with affiliates throughout Mexico, has built an international reputation by adapting the works of Shakespeare, García Lorca, and Mexican playwrights to suit the needs of its largely rural and marginalized urban community members. And several community theatre groups in the Yucatán Peninsula develop plays, based on playwriting strategies developed in training sessions with Mexico City theatre professionals, that reflect and valorize local life and custom. These are then presented in Yucatec Maya in their own communities and, until recently, in regional community theatre festivals. To varying degrees, each of these groups participates in and represents itself as part of a more general resurgence of ethnicity-based cultural activities in Mexico—they call what they do "Mayan" and "indigenous" theatre—a phenomenon that has been described by some U.S. observers as "the Mayan Renaissance."

Reflecting the way ethnicity has long been used in Mexico as one axis "around which cultural distinctions [are] organized,"[8] such labels tend to mask the reality, however, of interest from and conscious affiliation with nonindigenous people and artistic forms in the creation of this theatre. Ironically, then, the labels mark a moment of cultural reclamation and proclamation and in effect allow these troupes to use nonindigenous theatrical styles and techniques to become "more Mayan," or at least more visible as such.

At first glance, this agenda may seem suspect, given emerging understandings of culture as something that cannot be owned, of tradition as a matter of invention, and of authenticity as a nostalgic notion in a postmodern world.[9] The poststructuralist critique of and within anthropology suggests that culture is something ethnographers write, not something that enjoys ontological status in its own right. In the 1980s, following the insights of the anthropologist Clifford Geertz, culture tended to be viewed, therefore, as a "text" to be read and interpreted, a "historically transmitted pattern of meanings embodied in symbols, a system of inherited conceptions expressed in symbolic forms by means of which [people] communicate."[10] In the field of theatre semiotics, and in recent work in cultural anthropology, this cultural text has come to be viewed more dynamically as a "performance text" whose meanings may never be fully interpretable. That is, in recognition of the myriad social exchanges that take place in a globalized environment (and of the fact that this process had already been going on for centuries), culture is seen as dynamic, active, infinitely mutable—and "performed" rather than "borne." Its meanings, therefore, do not reside comfortably within bounded domains of verbal and visual access; as the performance theorist Dwight Conquergood reminds us, these meanings can also be "masked, camouflaged, indirect, embedded, or hidden in context."[11]

Today, in Mexico as elsewhere, local contexts are informed by an increasing globalism that compels mass movements of goods and people across all previously established borders. Thus, the anthropologist James Clifford has reconceived cultural identity as a matter of "routes" rather than of "roots,"[12] building on his insight that "twentieth-century identities no longer presuppose continuous cultures or traditions. Everywhere individuals and groups improvise local performance from (re)collected pasts, drawing on foreign media, symbols, and languages."[13] And as John Kicza reminds us, in Latin America particularly, the exigencies of the marketplace and resultant patterns of migration and return have led many scholars to question the validity of designations such as "Indian community" at all: "As vast numbers of indigenous peoples have become well integrated into the market economies and dynamic cultures of their national societies, they have lost, willingly or not, most of the attributes that had distinguished them from peoples of European or mixed ancestry."[14]

On the other hand, as the examples of pan-Maya activism in Guatemala and the Zapatistas in Mexico illustrate, the critique of essentialism generated by postmodern (often U.S.) theorists does not always serve the best interests of subaltern groups. In the Guatemalan context, as Kay Warren has explored in detail, such a criticism can and has been used to frustrate indigenous political organization, in effect to prevent collective action in service of a continuance of a national culture that excludes Mayan recognition and participation.[15] In Mexico, the Zapatistas (discussed in more detail in the next chapter) have adopted both essentialist and antiessentialist strategies to link indigenous claims to nationalist rhetoric in a way that compels their political recognition *as indigenous*—for perhaps the first time in Mexico's post-Conquest history. As the Latin Americanist James Weil once characterized the early days of the Zapatista movement, "the Maya want their culture back."[16]

But this reclamation project, in which theatre often plays a key part, is not a simple matter of retreating from the rest of the world into a precontact dream of isolated autonomy. Rather, it is a demand for a new kind of power within Mexico: the kind of power described by Carolyn Heilbrun as an acknowledgment of "the ability to take one's place in whatever discourse is essential to action and the right to have one's part matter."[17] In other words, it is a demand for recognition of Mayan and other indigenous contributions to Mexico's plurality in Mexico's emerging democracy and the right to shape that democracy as full participants. In a true democracy, such a demand would be unnecessary. But to articulate it in Mexico is to resist centuries of colonization, both external and internal.

In this environment, indigenous activists and intellectuals are calling for a radical change of perspective, wherein cultural identity is not so much a moving target (to be fixed in the sights of political and academic weapon-bearers) as the act of taking aim. It is in this action, which occurs onstage in theatrical performance and offstage in civic life, that identifications are selected and made visible. Such a conception presumes that identification is a matter of relationship and direction, for the target often determines the stance and position of the one who takes aim, and the one who takes aim in turn has the power to make a point that, literally, sticks—and thereby changes the face of the target as well. Warren reports this happening in Guatemala, for example, when a critic of Mayan activism wrote a spoof on "Ladino [non-Mayan] identity." If it meant to mock Mayan identity politics, it also "helped fuel serious self-questioning among progressive Ladinos about their sense of identity and taken-for-granted entitlement to national culture."[18] In Mexico, the widespread support for the Zapatistas expressed by intellectuals, journalists, and nongovernmental organizations, and, among my acquaintance, many lower- and middle-class Mexicans who find themselves increasingly disenfranchised from the centers of power, suggests a similar reconsideration under way there.

Thus, I am proposing a view of Mayan cultural identity that is transcultural from the start. In using the term "transcultural," I am following a specifically Latin American strain of critical thought, initiated in 1940 by the Cuban anthropologist Fernando Ortiz. He coined the term "transculturation" to describe the cultural changes generated in specific encounters and subsequent instances of cultural expression. For Ortiz,

> the term transculturation better expresses the different phases in the transitive process from one culture to another, because this process does not only imply the acquisition of culture, as connoted by the Anglo-American term *acculturation,* but it also necessarily involves the loss or uprooting of one's preceding culture, what one could call a partial *disculturation.* Moreover, it signifies the subsequent creation of new cultural phenomena that one could call *neoculturation.*[19]

Tracing the migration of this notion through Latin American literary thought and with an eye toward its application for theatre, Diana Taylor notes that transculturation provides three important gains in critical assessment. First, as suggested above, the term marks and maintains the memory of a cultural loss. Second, as it has been developed over time, the notion of transculturation prevents easy assumptions about the equality of exchange implicit in terms, like "syncretism," that suggest an equal coexistence of different cultural elements or systems. Finally, it allows for the possibility of mutual influence and reparticularization, even if that influence is not always immediately discernible. Such a conception of transculturation is particularly useful because, as Taylor writes,

> [it] allows the "minor" culture (in the sense of the positionally marginalized) an impact on the dominant one, although the interactions are not strictly speaking "dialogic" or "dialectical." Transculturation

suggests a shifting or circulating pattern of cultural transference. The measurable impact of the "minor" on the "major" can be a long time coming.[20]

This potential for mutuality is nothing new to native speakers of the thirty-odd Mayan languages in southern Mexico, Guatemala, and other parts of Central America. These languages more easily embed notions of equality and reciprocity between what, in Indo-European languages, are acting subjects and acted-upon objects. For example, what I might think of as the object of an action initiated by a subject is conceived by Mayans, at least in some usages, as another subject existing in relationship to the first.[21] Teresa Ortiz, an activist who works on behalf of Mayan communities in Chiapas struggling for political autonomy, puts it this way: "A Mayan wouldn't say, 'I am drinking this cup of coffee.' Instead, they'd say, 'I and this coffee are in a drinking relationship together.'"[22]

To the extent that cultural identifications are produced through language, it is possible to view the question of ethnic or cultural identity in similar terms of a relationship, dependent on parties and circumstance, that is mutually influential—at least potentially. At the same time, in societies overdetermined by internal colonization, as Mexico has been, it is important to remember that some targets exert more control and resistance to change than others. Under such circumstances, identities tend to coalesce in response. For example, it has often been convenient for the Mexican government to view living Maya as backward peasants in need of a good dose of modernization, or as living artifacts of a glorious past, whose artisan production brings in tourist dollars. Thus, many indigenous groups have strategically adopted a collective identity in order to garner the alliance of international organizations in support of their claims against a government that still denies them full participation in Mexico's emergent democracy.[23]

So, while it can be persuasively argued that "Mayan culture" is largely the result of discursive practices aimed at satisfying non-Mayan touristic desire or, later, constructing a postrevolutionary Mexican nation-state along U.S. and European models, it does not follow that the term is irrelevant for the people so designated. As J. Jorge Klor de Alva summarizes the dilemma, "Many 'organic' or 'native' intellectuals, swept up by the post-structuralist/postmodern tide, are struggling to promote ethnic unity and pride while paradoxically attempting to make out, in the transnational ethnoscapes of their respective communities, nonessentialized patterns of collective identity."[24] "Nonessentialized patterns of collective identity" often find expression through performance, and the performance does not always conform to easy cultural distinctions. As the Argentine-Mexican anthropologist Néstor García Canclini puts it, "It cannot be ignored that even in the most direct and self-managed experiences there is action and *acting*, expression of what is one's own and constant reconstitution of what is understood by one's own in relation to the broader laws of social dramaturgy, as well as reproduction of the dominant order.[25] Offstage as well as on, therefore, culture—"what is one's own," in relation to "broader laws"—is constituted in performance and in the ongoing negotiations between social groups.

Since 1996 I have been an audience member at more than a score of theatrical performances, dozens of rehearsals, and several ceremonies preparatory to performance and displays. I have had the opportunity to interview many of the actors, directors, and advisers involved and have enjoyed social time with some of them after their working hours. To a lesser degree, I have had the chance to mingle with other audience members to get a sense of the works' reception. This theatre works on multiple levels, both as an advancement of local culture and, in many cases, as a nonviolent response to the same kinds of pressures that have provoked armed responses among Mexico's indigenous and peasant populations. One play, in fact, was created a month after the Zapatista uprising and explores some of the roots of that uprising in land and environmental concerns; it ends with both a patriotic anthem and a call for the continued fight of indigenous peoples against injustice.

In other plays, the rescue of local traditions and lore is the focus, with the aim of preserving and valorizing Mayan cultural identity in the face of increasing cultural and economic globalization. A play from the Yucatán Peninsula treats this theme quite literally: when a young man sells a pair of local religious objects to a tourist, who thinks they are souvenir dolls, the dangers of local complicity in cultural commodification are clear. In still others, the performances seem motivated by the joy of making theatre—in plays filled with verbal and physical alacrity and high theatricality, received by audiences so enthusiastic they made my playwright husband envious.

Over the course of my research, I have become increasingly interested in the ways this theatre intervenes in, or participates with, other discursive practices aimed at the production of Mayan identities and alterities. In this study I suggest that the theatre created by contemporary Mayan troupes enacts many of these tensions between identity and identification, authenticity and hybridity. Further, I argue that as a result it is often as "intercultural" as it is "indigenous"—not to essentialize either category but to suggest that nowadays (and to varying degrees this has been true historically as well) both categories are bound up with each other in complex ways.

It may be true that in an ideal world nobody "owns" culture; but in the world Mayans share with non-Mayans, intercultural borrowings and exchanges are frequently informed by inequitable power flows, uneven access to important cultural resources, and differentially charged social interactions. As a result, I find useful the insights of Michel de Certeau, who calls for analyses of "local histories" and "micro-revolutions,"[26] and Gayatri Spivak's notion of "strategic essentialism," which allows for the provisional recuperation and construction of cohesive identities in response to pressures from without to assimilate to dominant cultural paradigms.[27] But in the Latin American context generally and Mexico's particularly, the region's world-historical significance cannot be neatly accounted for in postcolonial theories that proceed from Franco- and Anglophone knowledge centers. Therefore, I find the Mexican social anthropologist Claudio Lomnitz's insights useful and aim, in this book, to answer his call for "grounded theory"—"a kind of theory that flies more like a chicken than a hawk."[28] That is, I hope to show that the "incidents of theatre in Chiapas and Yucatán" that I examine herein merit their own analyses, in all their glorious and messy specificity.

These analyses owe a debt to the work of the Mexican social anthropologist Guillermo Bonfil Batalla, who was concerned to introduce ethnicity into previously class-based models of Mexican social analysis. Specifically, I find useful as a starting point his "theory of cultural control,"[29] for its contributions to assessing the ways power can flow in intercultural encounters.

For Bonfil Batalla, given circumstances of cultural production can be understood by looking at who maintains control over the decisions relating to the cultural elements in play—the production and reproduction of material, the organizational, knowledge-related, symbolic, and emotive elements that belong either to one's own group or to an outside group. Thus, in a specific situation of cultural interaction, what is important is who gets to decide which elements are adopted, imposed, and transformed. From the point of view of a given group, there are four possible outcomes to this interaction:

1) Autonomy—the group retains control over both decisions and elements.

2) Appropriation—the group makes the decisions about whether to adopt another group's cultural elements.

3) Alienation—an outside agency maintains control over the group's own cultural elements, such as occurs in the staging of folkloric dances for tourist consumption.

4) Imposition—the group has control over neither the elements nor the decisions about how they are used, but the results come to be part of the group's culture.

In the case of indigenous and campesino theatre in Mexico, Bonfil Batalla's framework helps us to assess the degree of cultural control exercised by the indigenous performers over their final staged productions, and it is useful in some circumstances for its ability to specify the power dynamics in intercultural exchange. However, the model's rigidly "inside-outside" binary is problematic in a world in which the boundaries between groups are not always clearly maintained; nor does it take into account intragroup power dynamics, some of which are distinctly gender inflected, or strategic alliances with outside groups.

To accommodate these other kinds of social relations, I turn to the insights of Lawrence Grossberg, who uses recent work in spatial historiography to animate inquiry into contemporary cultural politics. He draws on Deleuze and Guattari's notion of culture as emerging "rhizomatically" (here and there, often unexpectedly) rather than vertically (up through a root system to a single, predetermined trunk).[30] "The tree is filiation," they write, "but the rhizome is alliance, uniquely alliance. The tree imposes the verb 'to be,' but the fabric of the rhizome is the conjunction 'and . . . and . . . and . . .'"[31]

A rhizomatic view of cultural transactions thus provides a theoretical move away from persistent notions of the "linear, irreversible and unrepeatable" nature of modern time and toward a spatial logic examining the ways different cultural apparatuses "produce the specific spaces, configurations, and circulations of power. These spaces, configurations, and circulations constitute not only the specific conjuncture or social formation but also the relations between the local and the global."[32] Grossberg also calls for a shift in emphasis from the two available models that Bonfil Batalla's itself seems to draw from—the "colonial model" (oppressors vs. oppressed) and the "transgression model" (oppression and resistance)—toward what he calls "a model of articulation or 'transformative practice.'"[33] According to Grossberg, both models of oppression not only seem inappropriate to the contemporary relations of power but also incapable of creating alliances because they cannot tell us how to interpellate fractions of the "empowered" into the struggle for change in something other than a masochistic (guilt-ridden) way.[34]

Grossberg's reconfiguration offers two important gains. One is that a shift from the temporal to the spatial provides a way out of the time warp imposed on indigenous communities by both their supporters, who wish to privilege a premodern difference from the increasingly modernized world, and their detractors, who assert a Western *telos* of progress, and equate difference with all that is backward. That this time warp still operates is evident in a variety of images that are initially—and sometimes deliberately—discordant. It is becoming more and more common to see, for example, visual images of indigenous people using technology—a photo in Mexico's National Anthropological Museum of contemporary Mayans using computers; a bookstore logotype that features an ancient hieroglyph of an indigenous writer, his writing instrument redrawn to become a laptop; early press coverage of the Zapatista uprising barely concealing surprise that the Indians were using the Internet as a communicative tool. But these images somehow continue—and are meant—to jar; they record the traces of nostalgia for a past uncontaminated with this modern paraphernalia.

Grossberg's insights offer the possibility of micropolitical analysis of groups conceived as living in the same age but in different spaces characterized by differential access to important realms of social and political power. These insights open up a theoretical space for approaching strategic alliances within and across groups, to improve that access by "interpellating fractions of the empowered." To the extent that each of the theatre organizations I discuss collaborates to some degree with various non-Mayan artists, researchers, and financial go-betweens, their collaboration and alliance making need to be taken into serious consideration.

The adoption of a spatial, rhizomatic view of culture and cultural change also follows a certain strain of historiography practiced by Mayans themselves, at least at one time. Though much is made of the complexity of the Mayan calendar and the cyclical nature of time it records,[35] one great text of mytho-history adopts a spatial orientation in its narration of historical and prehistorical events. That is the *Popul Vuh*, which tells a history of gods and humans in the Quiché region of what is now Guatemala.[36] Although virtually all Mayan texts, sacred and profane, that could be destroyed were destroyed by the (literal) flames of Spanish missionary zeal, the *Popul Vuh* survives as a kind of literary hybrid of pre-Hispanic content and colonial form. Originally written in hieroglyphics but transcribed from memory into the Roman alphabet sometime between 1554 and 1558 at the request of Spanish missionaries, "Popul Vuh" translates to "Council Book"—and books were conceived by the ancient Maya as "place[s] *to see*."[37] As Dennis Tedlock, who has translated the text into English, describes its organization, the events it describes

> are presented in two different cycles, with the episodes divided between the cycles more on the basis of where they took place in space than when they took place in time. The first cycle deals entirely with adventures on the face of the earth, while the second, though it has two separate above-ground passages, deals mainly with adventures in the Mayan underworld, named Xibalba. If the events of these two cycles were combined in a single chronological sequence, the above-ground episodes would probably alternate with those below, with the heroes descending into the underworld, emerging on the earth again, and so forth. These sowing and dawning movements of the heroes, along with those of their supporting cast, prefigure the present-day movements of the sun, moon, planets, and stars.[38]

Two things are especially interesting about this text and its provenance. First, the "sowing and dawning" movements of its heroes, while linked to the astronomical bodies that control the Mayan calendar, also act like Deleuzian "rhizomes" in their cropping up here and there on the surface, after periods spent underground. Second, the text comes to us in the Roman alphabet, a form that compels a left-to-right, linear progression of letters-into-words-into-sentences. Nevertheless, the events narrated in the *Popul Vuh* resist this formal linearity and, like its heroes, follow a more undulating pattern; it takes time and effort to force an alien chronology onto them. Thus the original structure, told in the spatial arrangement of hieroglyphs, survives palimpsestically in the version we have available to us. As Tedlock puts it, "Just as Mayan peoples learned to use the symbolism of Christian saints as a mask for ancient gods, so they learned to use the Roman alphabet as a mask for ancient texts."[39] In an important way, then, these texts survive; they are not "lost forever" to a Mayan way of looking.

This insight can also be applied to an understanding of the history of the theatre in which Mayans and other indigenous players have participated. The labeling of contemporary Mayan theatre as a "Renaissance" by some researchers tends to replicate a "linear and irreversible" approach to that history; it suggests the end of a theatrical dark ages ushered in with the Conquest, and narrates Mayan theatre history as one of loss and recapture. I propose an alternate view—that many of the pre-Columbian performance traditions, while interrupted by Conquest, have been rhizomatically cropping up in some form or another, often mixed with or hybridized by other theatrical traditions, since the time of Conquest by the Spanish missionaries. And the forms they now take are neither a Renaissance nor a radically new departure for theatre as a social and artistic medium. Rather, they represent a complex engagement with a continuously changing notion of the relationship between indigenous and nonindigenous in contemporary Mexico.

Each of the troupes I discuss provides a different note in the register of this complexity. Within the microcosms of their own organizations, these troupes, like the revolutionary Zapatistas (whose spokesperson is, in fact, a non-Mayan Mexican intellectual), seek a brand of creative autonomy that does not equal marginalization from the rest of Mexican society and a kind of engagement with that society that does not equal complete assimilation.

Scope of Study

This study begins by situating indigenous Mexican theatre both over time and within various sociocultural spaces. That is, it outlines the long history of intercultural explorations, collaborations, and impositions experienced by native performers and audiences over time and within the rhetorical spaces created by Mexico's larger struggles for a national identity. Specifically, it focuses on how various nationalist rhetorics—notably those of *mestizaje* (an official view of Mexico as a country of mixed European and indigenous races) and *indigenismo* (policies developed to assimilate indigenous Mexicans into a homogenous national culture)—have been challenged by emergent indigenous rights movements, including *zapatismo*. I use the latter term to refer to the heightened consciousness of and mobilization for indigenous rights since the Zapatista uprising in 1994, which took its name from Emiliano Zapata, a key figure in the Mexican Revolution. (Although I use the term to describe the recent movement, it also can refer to the historical aims and followers of Zapata. As Lynn Stephen has recently shown, the ways the two senses of the term intersect and, more specifically, how they are used for purposes of political thinking and organizing differ among Mexico's various discursive communities, indigenous and nonindigenous.)[40] This chapter also treats other sociopolitical forces that inform the ongoing negotiation of ethnic and Mexican national identities, particularly in Mayan Mexico, to provide contextualization for understanding some of the themes and challenges represented by and in the work of theatre artists there.

Chapters 2 through 4 discuss the activities of four theatre groups or networks in Mayan Mexico, focusing on their operating strategies and on analyses of selected texts, each of which illustrates a different aspect of the authenticity/hybridity problematic. Chapter 2 discusses the activities of two rather well-known theatre troupes based in San Cristóbal de las Casas, Chiapas, a key site of the 1994 Zapatista uprising. One, Lo'il Maxil (Monkey Business), was instigated by the desire of Mayan anthropological informants to "take back" their own stories and myths and to use theatre to improve Mayan-language literacy toward that end. These informants have chosen to work closely with U.S. and Mexican anthropologists in forming their organization and securing funding for it since 1983. Eventually, two of the actresses, frustrated by the limited participation it afforded women, decided to form an alternative company dedicated to the contemporary social concerns of Mayan women in rural and urban communities. This troupe, called La Fomma (an acronym standing for "Strength of the Mayan Woman"), has worked closely with the international feminist, academic, human rights, and theatre communities to establish an international reputation. Their very existence points to an interesting dilemma facing many Mayan communities in an increasingly global environment: how to maintain tradition when that tradition often serves to subjugate women and how to reinvent those traditions in order to incorporate new insights brought by a combination of factors, including international feminism.

In other parts of Mexico, a network of theatre troupes that began in Tabasco has established a controversial reputation for "indigenizing" the works of Shakespeare and other European and Mexican playwrights. Chapter 3 discusses this process, through an exploration of the work of Laboratorio de Teatro Campesino e Indígena. This group's stagings of *Romeo y Julieta* and García Lorca's *Bodas de Sangre* (Blood Wedding) have appeared on stages as far away as Madrid, Spain, New York's Central Park, and the Catskill Mountains of upstate New York. The troupe's founder is a non-Mayan Mexican director, who has been accused by many other directors and some Mexican political authorities of teaching her rural performers to forget their campesino roots. This criticism, although directed against cultural imperialism, masks a prevalent desire among many non-Mayan Mexicans to preserve an image of the Mayan peoples as rooted in the rural past rather than to see them as fully participating members of a geopolitical present.

A final example, discussed in Chapter 4, comes from the Yucatán Peninsula, where grassroots theatre flourished during the last two decades of the twentieth century. Although this theatre relies less on the involvement of non-Mayan personnel, it traces its originating impulse to earlier government-sponsored "cultural missions"—groups of urban performers who traveled through the countryside from the 1940s through the 1960s in an attempt to bring rural Mexico into a modernized, mestizized, post-revolutionary present.[41] Later, groups led by local performers trained by these urban troupes would produce theatre in the Yucatec language, covering a variety of themes that include not only the recuperation of Mayan tradition but also its ongoing reinvention.

Finally, I return to the question of "roots" versus "routes" as it applies to the increasing globalization of the very notion of "Mayanness," which I argue has achieved status as a form of symbolic capital for non-Mayans. This representational economy has exacerbated tensions created on the one hand by the desire of the performers for recognition as heterogenous agents of their own history, and on the other by their awareness of the prevalent desire of many non-Mayans to fix this work, and any representational authority it may have achieved, within a tidier scheme of cultural authenticity.

A Note on Terminology and Translations
Maya, Mayan, Maya/n Culture, Maya/n Civilization

As the anthropologist Quetzil E. Castañeda notes, these categories "are not at all empty of meaning or reality," but are "fundamentally contested terms that have no essential entity outside of the complex histories of sociopolitical struggles." Following Castañeda, I use the terms in reference to "heterogenous peoples and societies that nonetheless shared certain religious, historical, aesthetic, social, and linguistic forms in a geopolitical space called Mesoamerica."[42]

In southeastern Mexico, which is the focus of this study, there are regional differences in the ways the people so designated use the terms. In the Yucatán Peninsula, for example, Mayan speakers refer to their language and culture as "Mayan" but often refer to themselves in the present as "mestizo" (which elsewhere in Mexico, by contrast, usually refers to a nonindigenous-identified person). In Chiapas, the identification is first with the community, then the linguistic group (there are more than thirty Mayan languages, each related to one of two major roots, Yucatec and Quiché), and then the Maya. In Tabasco, linguistic group (Chol, Chontal) seems the primary term of identification. The Mexican government also designates ethnicity by first language spoken—a designation doomed to inaccuracy, no matter who makes it, due to historical pressure to speak the language of power, Spanish.

In the past thirty years, there have been efforts among Mayan intellectuals and activists, especially in Guatemala, to develop a "pan-Mayan" identity that spans geopolitical borders in order to achieve greater representation in matters affecting indigenous peoples. In Mexico, particularly since 1994, the call among such activists has been for a pan-indigenous (or indeed, pan-subaltern) sense of affiliation.

Indian, Indigenous, Native

To varying degrees, each of these terms is problematic and, on reflection, not very descriptive. However, they have all attained common usage to designate the descendants—by blood and/or cultural practice—of the peoples inhabiting Mesoamerica at the time Columbus landed and Cortés explored. Where possible, I adopt the designation chosen by the people I am discussing. For more general purposes, I prefer the term "indigenous" in contemporary contexts. I use "indigenous" and "native" interchangeably when discussing the first generation of Conquest. In Mexico, the Spanish equivalent of "Indian," *indio,* is usually very pejorative, comparable to the term "nigger" in U.S. usage, so I avoid use of the word "Indian" unless it appears in quoted material.

Everybody Else

There is no single label, except perhaps "nonindigenous," to describe those who are not descended from pre-Columbian Mexicans in any way, as regional differences abound, and the same term can be used by different people to designate quite different things. In Chiapas and Guatemala, the term *ladino,* which originally referred to the Sephardic Jews exiled from Spain in the fifteenth century and has evolved over time to mean anyone not of indigenous descent, is now widely used in scholarship on the region to signify "nonindigenous." Again, I try to be as specific as the context demands and allows; otherwise, I place "indigenous" or "Mayan" at the center and mark everybody else as "nonindigenous" or "non-Mayan."

Translations

Unless indicated otherwise, all translations from Spanish are my own. The original text of translated material is presented in the notes.

CHAPTER 1.

Indigenous Bodies, Contested Texts

THE *POPUL VUH* records a powerful moment in the prehistory of the human race: before earthly time could begin, it reveals, one of the final deeds of its twin hero-gods was an act of theatrical illusion. In a command performance staged for the lords of the underworld, one twin apparently beheaded the other, cut out his heart, and then brought him back to life. When the delighted lords demanded that the trick be performed on them, the brothers obliged, with one key difference: this time it was not an illusion, and the beheaded lords did not rise again. Thus the twins scored a certain victory over the gods of death: henceforth, they decreed, the lords of the underworld would "limit their attacks on future human beings to those who have weaknesses or guilt."[1]

Because the *Popul Vuh* is in large part the story of how the creator gods and original humans worked together to make the world safe for human habitation, we can see that in the worldview of the ancient Maya the role of theatre and illusion was significant. Not only necessary for the well-being of humanity, it was, literally, a death-defying act.

I use this example not to claim that contemporary Mayan theatre comes from a long, uninterrupted tradition sanctioned by sacred authority, or to suggest that Mayans are, atavistically, theatrically inclined. Rather, I use it as a reminder that in the history of encounters between Mayans and a changing cast of historical others, theatre and performance has always carried a radical potential.

Whatever else "contemporary Mayan theatre" is or does, it always also registers an interaction with other artistic, social, and political forces from both past and present. From the past, it partakes of a rich if discontinuous history of theatricality and performance. From the present, it engages with complex and contradictory social realities that make the very term "Mayan theatre" productively ambivalent. This chapter situates such theatre in both respects—over time, in the history of native theatrical performance; and within the rhetorical spaces created by contemporary sociopolitics. Recalling Conquergood's insight that the meanings of performance can be "hidden in context," this chapter aims to provide historical and contemporary contextualization for the transactions that inform the creation of new work, the adaptation of existing material, and the choice to work with non-Mayan artists and advisers.

The Past Reverberating in the Present

From the pre-Hispanic past, only one "script" of a Mayan performance piece remains—and that text is itself mediated through the interventions of the nineteenth-century French explorer and missionary Charles Etienne Brasseur de Bourbourg. The text is the *Rabinal Achi,* a dance drama from the same Quiché-speaking region (now Guatemala) as the *Popul Vuh.* Its action revolves around a conflict between two Mayan communities, and a key theme is the relationship between cultural identity and geopolitical location.[2] The main character is a warrior-prince from one principality who is captured during one of his many raids on another (Rabinal), in an attempt to break Rabinal's monopoly on resources in the region. Because of his bravery, he is asked to join the ranks of his captor's warriors. His pride and sense of his own local identity prevent him from accepting the offer, and he chooses instead the fate of all such captives: death.

Most researchers have interpreted his end as a ritual sacrifice, arguing that it is both a representation and a manifestation of the ritual aspect of pre-Hispanic performance. But Dennis Tedlock, who witnessed a January 1998 performance in Rabinal, suggests an alternative theory, based on linguistic analysis and his readings of hieroglyphs representing similar events. Tedlock suggests that the death of the warrior is less a sacrifice, with its ritual and religious overtones, than a *political execution,* which in turn casts the play as an early example of sociopolitical theatre. Its performative effect would have been to reinforce Rabinal's imperative to maintain its control over the region.[3]

Outside of Rabinal, the piece has achieved a kind of symbolic currency in a changing set of historical circumstances since its introduction to Europe in the mid-nineteenth century. It has been translated into several European languages, and it inspired a poem by Eduard Stücken that later became the basis for the libretto of an opera by the Austrian composer Egon Wellesz. Premiering in Cologne in 1926 under the title *Die Opferung der Gefangenen* (The Sacrifice of the Captive), the opera presented an exoticized version of a primitive America.[4] Later in the century, in the 1970s, it inspired a play by the well-known Mexican playwright Sergio Magaña titled *Los enemigos* (The Enemies),[5] whose theme alluded to class conflict; this version also introduced romantic rivalry to the military conflict between the two main characters. Magaña's work was in turn adapted in 1994 by a Mexico City theatre company interested in exploring the play's potential from a postcolonial perspective. In this adaptation, a key theme was the limits of European epistemology vis-à-vis native American knowledges and practices. The production introduced the character of Brasseur de Bourbourg into the action of Magaña's text, presenting him not as innocent recorder of the original performance but as complicit in its bloody outcome.[6] Each of these transformations registers a different valuation of the piece and serves also to trace changing notions of the Maya as Other to the European Self, suggesting the power of theatre in their mutual constitution.

Although the *Rabinal Achi* is the only extant example of a pre-Hispanic performance text, the evidence of monuments, codices, and letters sent home by the newly arrived military and missionary settlers in New Spain attests to a theatricality that attended all aspects of pre-Hispanic life. The letters described a variety of performance forms: farces, comedies, jugglers, acrobats, magic shows, puppet shows, clowning, and elaborate spectacles in which wigged, masked, and costumed players enacted ritual stories. In Mexico, such activities were observed in the Aztec societies that dominated the north and central regions, as well as in Mayan communities under their rule to the south and east. So talented were some of them at mimicry that they would be hired by Spanish officers to provide spoofs of the Spaniards for an evening's entertainment.[7]

Spanish missionaries, too, were quick to capitalize on the performing talents of the natives, employing indigenous actors in vast spectacles of missionary theatre that were aimed at converting the latter to Christianity and instructing them in its doctrines. As María Sten has famously suggested, "Theatre was to the spiritual conquest of Mexico what the horses and gunpowder were to its military defeat."[8]

These spectacles generally followed the form of the Spanish mystery and morality plays but incorporated many elements of native theatricality. While Diana Taylor, for example, following Sten, has suggested that the Spaniards "co-opted the indigenous discursive and symbolic apparatus (performative, linguistic, religious) and gutted it,"[9] others have come to question the finality of Sten's pronouncement. Considering an early example of evangelical drama, a Corpus Christi play performed in the mid-sixteenth century in Tlaxcala (north of what is now Mexico City), both

Adam Versényi and Max Harris argue that when indigenous performers acted and danced the Spanish religious texts, the resulting performances generated meanings that exceeded the intentions of the latter.[10] Versényi suggests the result was a "convergence of Spanish and Indian attitudes towards maintenance of hierarchical authority,"[11] with Christian content inhabiting forms dictated by indigenous practice. "Who converted whom?" Versényi asks. "The Indians may have become good Christians but the Spanish became, at their theatrical roots, good Aztecs."[12] Harris argues that this early missionary theatre provides an example of the dialogic nature of theatre to serve

> as a means of communication between conquerors and conquered in the years immediately following the conquest of Mexico, and . . . even today indigenous dramatizations of the theme of conquest in Mexico express the ambivalence of native Catholics towards the conquest that brought them both Christianity and foreign rule.[13]

Harris's study is provocative as a model for "cross-cultural encounter in general . . . that is grounded, figuratively, in the theatrical transaction of offering one's own cherished text for independent performance by another, and of entering as a performer into the world of another's text."[14] This characterization is worth keeping in mind as we approach, later in this book, other kinds of intercultural borrowings and exchanges in latter-day theatrical exchange.

Palimpsest-like vestiges of these early plays still appear in the fiesta sketches, dances, and tableaus repeated yearly in indigenous communities throughout Mexico, and such performances manifest an ongoing negotiation between assimilation and resistance.[15] On the one hand, they serve to reinforce indigenous Catholicism (although this is changing as a result of the effects of evangelical Protestantism and its converts). On the surface, that is, they rehearse the same kinds of saint and Bible stories originally introduced by the Spanish in the sixteenth century, mixed with liberal doses of burlesque and improvisation. On the other hand, as in all Carnival-like events, fiesta performances provide a site for the conventional forms of authority to be overturned, at least symbolically. Thus, in many such sketches the figure of the European is one of ridicule, excess, and lasciviousness—whether that figure is a conquistador or a Spanish bishop.[16] Sometimes the critique may not be so obvious but nevertheless persists in what Harris calls a "'hidden transcript' of resistance [that] has been 'insinuated' into the 'public transcript' of subordination."[17] Harris, who has also studied contemporary performances of "Moors and Christians" dance dramas in Mexico and New Mexico, sees them as "festivals of reconquest," in which the past is reenacted in order to comment in subtle but effective ways on the present. In some performances, he argues, the combination of performative elements—especially in costume and mask—suggests that "the sanctioned narrative of Catholic triumph masks a subtext that invokes the world of the Aztecs in order to challenge current power structures."[18]

This example implies that the power of these performances is not limited to the kind of contained excess theorized most famously by Mikhail Bakhtin. In their studies of Mayan Carnaval celebrations in Chamula, Chiapas, Victoria Bricker and Gary H. Gossen argue that such performances can also provide a site for an alternative historiography to be presented, as they perform a complex, cyclical history of encounters between Mayans and a series of ethnic others.[19] Bricker, for example, shows how Carnaval dramatizes six events in Mexican history, all of them interethnic conflicts, ranging from the Conquest to the Pineda revolt in 1920. All six events are staged, not in a linear sequence, but simultaneously through the combination of costume and action. (An example, though less complex, from the Anglo-American experience might be a staging of Shakespeare's *Julius Caesar* in which the principals would be costumed in the military garb of six different historical periods or nationalities.) All this occurs within the overarching structure of the Passion of Christ, which organizes the surface action and serves as the paradigm for all the other ethnic conflicts also represented. Thus, Carnaval is more than a vestige of pre-Hispanic or evangelical theatre. It is also a complex way of staging both history and the *notion* of history as being cyclical rather than linear, with events repeating themselves structurally if not literally.

Further, within this reckoning, suggests Gossen, Chamulans emphasize that non-Chamulans are their "primitive contemporaries, socially, historically, and morally prior and inferior to them." In his studies of Chamulan belief systems, Gossen has found that "all of us—Europeans, Mexicans, Guatemalans, Afro-Americans, Jews and gringos—are consistently historicized in order to foreground and frame and favor an always-emergent Indian community in the present."[20]

Such historiography is an important act of self-definition, since centuries of political marginalization and a related lack of educational access has meant that it is mostly others who have written Mayan history "for" them. Finally, it is worth pointing out that since Bricker completed her study in the 1970s, Carnaval has attracted increasing numbers of Mexican and international tourists, adding yet another valence to this act of historical and cultural self-definition.[21]

Throughout the twentieth century, starting with the Mexican Revolution and flourishing in a new way at the century's close, a more formal, text-based theatre (as distinguished from the fiesta performances of Carnaval) has emerged from within Mayan communities and in collaboration with non-Mayan artists and audiences. Although in some cases they are designed to reimagine some of the theatrical traditions interrupted by the Conquest, and in others they are colored by contemporary fiesta performance practices, these scripted dramas also emerge from a richly ambivalent confluence of people, movements, texts, and technologies.

Theatre in the Sociopolitical Space of the Twentieth Century: Mestizaje, Indigenismo, Zapatismo

Since the Mexican Revolution, theatre has been a part of many efforts designed to solve the "problem" of indigenous/nonindigenous relations in Mexico, which lay at the heart of attempts to define the new Mexican state. A key term in this definition is the Mexican notion of mestizaje. As contested as it is celebrated, it is a concept that began virtually at the point of contact, when it was used to describe social categories resulting from intermarriages between Europeans and natives. In the twentieth century, the concept achieved a more cultural charge, to suggest the blending of important cultural values as well as bloodlines. It is related to another term in this ongoing national definition, "indigenismo," which refers to the valorization and support of indigenous peoples by nonindigenous Mexicans and foreigners. Both terms, and the policies they generated, have come under increasing scrutiny, and their failures to adequately address indigenous realities are registered in the most recent "ismo" to appear in Mexico—"zapatismo," which attempts to recenter indigenous realities, in rhetoric and in practice, as constitutive of Mexican national identity. In what follows, I discuss the intersections between these social concepts and certain theatrical movements related to them.

Tracing Mestizaje

A famous mural by José Clemente Orozco (1883–1949), created in 1926 during the height of postrevolutionary Mexican nationalism, features the naked embrace of two key figures in Mexican official history: the conquistador Hernán Cortés and his native mistress-interpreter—named

Malinal, christened Marina, known to every Mexican schoolchild as La Malinche, and considered "the first mother of Mexican nationality."[22]

In her study of this important figure in Mexican history and literature, Sandra Messinger Cypess explores the way in which the historical woman has become a sign—variously interpretable in the interaction between her re-creators in literature, drama, and film and the readers and audiences for those media—that "continues to serve as a paradigm for female images in Mexico, for the ways men and women relate to each other."[23] Moreover, the figure of La Malinche, who bore Cortés a son who became symbolically the first mestizo,[24] has come to represent the troubled nature of Mexican political identity for women and men alike. To the extent that La Malinche is viewed as the violated mother, her descendants are born into a country whose very existence is rooted in rape— conquest as violation. To the extent that she is viewed as collaborator with the conquerors, she is a symbol of betrayal that is nevertheless central to the Mexican mind-set: Irene Nicholson goes so far as to suggest that as "sons of Malinche," modern Mexicans "are traitors in their own minds."[25] And to the extent that she is the origin of a mestizo nation—a role frequently invoked during periods of high Mexican nationalism—La Malinche becomes a valedictory symbol of what makes Mexico Mexico: a nation descended from the combined stock of two of the world's mightiest civilizations.

In the first two decades after the Revolution, artists such as Orozco, Diego Rivera, and Frida Kahlo produced work that celebrated Mexico's indigenous past, creating a more positive social value for the notion of mestizaje than had before been associated with it. In the colonial period (before the stirrings of independence in 1810), for example, mestizaje was not at all a matter of Mexican pride but rather one of social control. Intermarriage among natives, Africans imported as slaves, Spaniards (sometimes themselves of mixed European and Moorish descent), Jews, and Asian immigrants created a rigidly hierarchical caste system based on bloodline and national origin. Different rights and privileges attended each group. Because of this and because individuals of mixed blood made up the majority of the population one hundred years after the Conquest, great care was taken to trace heritage, and a whole system of classification and terminology was created to name the progeny of every possible combination. Claudio Lomnitz-Adler lists sixteen such designations; in colonial times, "caste paintings" featuring the visual results of such minglings were popular and betray an obsession with racial categorization that never entirely went away.[26]

The idea of mestizaje as a potentially positive construct did not occur until the middle of the nineteenth century, when nationalist writers began to look to the pre-Hispanic past "not only to incorporate the Indian heritage into the definition of 'Mexican' but also to valorize positively that previously ignored and disdained element."[27] Nevertheless, long after independence from Spain was achieved in 1821, Mexico remained virtually feudal in its social divisions, with wealthy hacienda owners and power brokers of European descent acquiring and holding the best lands, worked by native and mestizo hands.[28] In remote parts of the country, self-governing and self-sustaining native communities remained but always under the threat of land appropriation in the post-Independence climate of property privatization. The excesses and abuses of this system would lead to a number of native uprisings and, eventually, to the Mexican Revolution.[29] Though the Revolution's armed phase was over by 1920, the Mexican government sought to make concrete its ideal of revolutionary change throughout the next three decades of peace (via popular education, indigenismo, and cultural revitalization); through the remainder of the century, its ideals were memorialized in the name of the ruling party—the Institutional Revolutionary Party, or PRI.[30]

Early postrevolutionary administrations did much to promote an official idea of mestizaje, along with a variety of concomitant "mixed" messages still operative today. A key figure in the architecture of mestizaje was Secretary of Public Education José Vasconcelos; his 1925 book, *La raza cósmica*, was influential at the time and is still in print, often resurrected as inspiration during times of ethnic conflict throughout Latin/o America. Vasconcelos envisioned a new "cosmic race" of mixed peoples the world over who would represent the next stage in Darwinian evolution—a stage he was cautiously optimistic would bring humankind into an "aesthetic age." In Latin America, he saw an especially propitious potential for this age to dawn:

> Only the Iberian part of the continent possesses the spiritual factors, the race, and the territory necessary for this great enterprise of initiating a new universal era of Humanity. All the races that are to provide their contribution are already there: The Nordic man, who is today the master of action but who had humble beginnings and seemed inferior in an epoch in which already great cultures had appeared and decayed; the black man, as a reservoir of potentialities that began in the remote days of Lemuria; the Indian, who saw Atlantis perish but

still keeps a quiet mystery in the conscience. We have all the races and all the aptitudes. The only thing lacking is for true love to organize and set in march the law of History.[31]

As Vasconcelos's ideas gained currency after the Revolution, they began to be translated into official policy. Bonfil Batalla, a critic of these policies, describes the "official line" this way:

> The deep roots of our nationality are in the Indian past, the point at which our history begins. It was a glorious past, brought to a halt by the Conquest. Since then the real Mexican, the *mestizo*, has arisen. He triumphs over his history through a series of struggles (Independence and the Reform), which are linked harmoniously until they lead to the Revolution. The Revolution is the final event in the struggle of the Mexican people, the mestizos. It is a necessary fact, foreseen and anticipated by history. After the Revolution, the full incorporation of the Mexican in universal culture will be possible.[32]

This line was supported in fact by new attention to the indigenous past in art and literature and in increased funding for archaeological digs and the museums that showcased their finds. But for Bonfil Batalla and other critics of mestizaje,[33] there is a problem in this for indigenous peoples or mestizos who identify more with their native ancestry and customs: mestizaje as policy, at least as practiced in the first decades after the Revolution, tended to erase that which was indigenous in the very moment of celebrating it. For example, the Revolution may have been successful in the eventual restoration of some lands to native communities. However, traditional ways of farming that land were inefficient for meeting another of the Revolution's goals, the modernization of Mexico. As a result, lands might be returned but only if modern farming methods were adopted. Schools might be built in these communities but only to teach those "universal" (i.e., European) values. Medical services might be extended to them but without recognition of traditional knowledges. Such communities could govern themselves, but local leaders who did not toe the PRI line (encouraged to do so by Mexican politics' legendary graft) did not last very long.[34] In the service of a modern Mexico, natives and mestizo farmers were absorbed into a fictively homogenous campesino class. This class would benefit materially from the Revolution's reforms (particularly during the administration of Lázaro Cárdenas in the 1930s) but at the expense of "old" ways of being in the world—of working the land, of practicing religion, of getting dressed in the morning.

This is not to argue that all "modern" innovations are evil, all the "old" ways better. The tensions between tradition and modernity in Mexico are complex, long-standing, and registered in different ways within and between different communities. In Mexico, however, these tensions are registered precisely because the relationship between tradition and modernity has always been central to Mexican nationalist discourse and operative, therefore, on Mexican bodies.[35] Furthermore, the opposition of the two (tradition is always *versus* modernity) tends to obscure the dynamic nature of tradition itself, which always changes and is always capable of renewing itself via elements from other traditions and not only in a strictly mimetic or subordinated way, as illustrated in the above discussion of Carnaval.[36] Modernity's affiliation with certain types of changes over others (most notably those of a technological sort), coupled with its rhetorical equation to civilizational progress, tends always to cast tradition as backward at worst, inspirational "roots" (but still fixed, unchanging) at best. What I wish to emphasize is that the imposition of a modernity so defined has been assisted by the rhetoric of mestizaje, toward erasing both sign and substance of indigenous custom, in service of a new society in which "[t]he rights of equality [are] recognized, but not the right to be different."[37] Further, when difference is recognized but only as being rooted in a "glorious past," a past interrupted by the Conquest and then subsumed into the same-making face of mestizaje, the result is a valuation of the native past over the native present. From there, it is a too-easy step toward the belief that for these people there is no future as well.

Enter Indigenismo

In its broadest, most generous sense, Mexican indigenismo can be understood as a generally sympathetic stance toward and practice on behalf of indigenous people, held and performed by nonindigenous people. As such, it has existed since the first years of contact, when some Spanish friars (notably the Dominican, Fray Bartolomé de Las Casas) objected to the officially sanctioned abuses and exploitation by Spanish landowners of indigenous laborers and argued (eventually successfully) the existence of the Indian soul. At the same time, it should be noted that these attitudes have always carried problematic aspects. Many early defenses of native Americans essentialized, romanticized, and infantilized them, for example. Even Las Casas himself was not immune to certain of these contradictions: while a secular priest, he supported his arguments against taking Indians into slavery by advising they be replaced with physically superior African slaves, whom he believed had been legitimately taken in war by the Portuguese. (Las Casas would later bitterly regret this advice.)[38] Latter-day indigenismo (like the mestizaje with which it is ontologically associated) is not exempt from its own contradictions and is more complicated in practice than its architects might have intended. And like mestizaje, it has been the target of increasing criticism in the last quarter century.[39]

The decades following the Mexican Revolution saw the country's first consciously indigenist movements. In the postrevolutionary wave of nationalism, argues Lomnitz-Adler, the new Mexico was conceived as having "an Indian soul, a Mestizo body, and a civilized future."[40] However, it was the "civilized future" that often eclipsed the "Indian soul" in attempts to integrate the latter into the former. This was made policy by President Cárdenas, who said in 1940, "Our native problem does not exist in keeping the Indians as Indians; neither, to make Mexico, Indian; but to make the Indian Mexican."[41] Thus, later, in 1958, the indigenist Alfonso Caso could write that "indigenism . . . has as its objective the integration of indigenous communities into the economic, social, and political life of the nation,"[42] without paying significant attention to the effects of this integration on autonomous local development.

The establishment in 1948 of the Instituto Nacional Indigenista (National Indigenist Institute, or INI) helped to solidify and further the modernizing efforts undertaken during the 1930s by the Cárdenas administration. This organization not only served as an important player in matters of official policy but also provided the Mexican government with a corps of anthropologists dedicated to making those policies more effective. It would also serve as the inspiration for a large number of anthropologists the world over who made indigenous Mexico the object of their inquiry.[43] Among those from the United States, probably the most well known is the Harvard Chiapas Project, under the leadership of Evon Z. Vogt Jr. This nearly forty-year undertaking, begun in 1957, resulted in more than 40 books, 180 articles, 2 novels, 2 ethnographic films, and countless unpublished documents.[44]

One of INI's strategies was to employ "cultural promoters" from indigenous communities, train them in the cities, and return them to their communities to become agents of change from within. The idea was that an insider would be more trusted by his or her own people. However, the strategy eventually proved ineffective, as some of these promoters chose not to return, and many of those who did were not welcomed back. Nevertheless, INI was successful in introducing many changes to the daily life of these communities if not in completely reforming them according to its goals. A retrospective of INI's work in the Tzotzil-Tzeltal region of Chiapas (published in 1973 and the first of many such retrospectives) recounts aggressive efforts on many fronts—health, literacy, education, agriculture, technology, community government—all aimed, as its closing words illustrate, at the "integration of Tzotzil and Tzeltal Mayans into national life."[45]

Among those efforts were "Cultural Missions," designed to increase the interdependency of local communities with the larger Mexican national economy, through the production of marketable goods (including tourist souvenirs) and through the purchase and use of various tools of modern life. A necessary component of these missions, linked to rural education programs, was an effort to reduce monolingualism in indigenous tongues and improve literacy in the Spanish language.[46] Significantly, theatre was deployed to serve this last goal, and throughout the 1940s and 1950s such (future) luminaries as the Mexican author and playwright Rosario Castellanos were employed to write plays and puppet sketches to educate the countryside in health, agriculture, literacy, and other modernization issues. Castellanos wrote and commissioned a number of didactic puppet plays for Teatro Petul in Chiapas, for whom she was also director in 1956–1957. During these two years, she and six Tzotzil- and Tzeltal-speaking Mayans toured the state of Chiapas, putting on plays that were written with the Mayans' help. Each of the plays featured a current problem in health, education, or agriculture, and each proposed a concrete and practical solution. Castellanos's reflections on this experience point to the problematic nature of the role of the indigenistas and her Mayan colleagues' roles as cultural promoters:

If for the [Mayan] puppeteers the boundary between the real and the imaginary was imprecise, it had to have been much more so for the audience. As for us (who were we, after all, but a *ladina,* an enemy due to her race, with her performers who were traitors to theirs?), it was possible to view us with distrust and to treat us with reticence. But when they reflected on the fact that we were also the bearers of Petul [a popular stock character], they wiped away their frowns and became hospitable and kind.[47]

Here, Castellanos also alludes to a fundamental difference in world-view that would frustrate relations between the indigenistas and those they hoped to assimilate. When she writes of the imprecision of the boundary between the imaginary and the real for the Mayan puppeteers, she acknowledges what is impossible to ignore when one spends any time in Mayan Mexico: this is a people for whom the spirits of ancestors, earthly powers, Catholic saints, and Mayan deities are as real and often as present as they themselves are; for whom the distinctions between dreamed and waking realities are discernible but not important; and for whom the human soul is viewed as an entity both human and animal, individual and collective, essential and emergent. One result of this complex of beliefs, suggests Gossen, is a "deep skepticism about individual autonomy and the very idea of a 'self-made' individual who is guided only by pragmatic self-interest. In short, these ideas seem to deny the very pillars of Western liberalism."[48] Such a people would be difficult to assimilate into a world intent on keeping the boundaries between spiritual and material, self and other, rather more precise.

In performance, this clash of ideological values was often manifested in patronizing and condescending representations, created by the Cultural Missionaries for the betterment of the indigenous audiences. In an ironic tone, Castellanos goes on to describe Petul as always being "open to the tidings being brought him by his white or *mestizo* friends, thanks to whose intervention the play's climax always led to a triumph of intelligence over superstition, of progress over tradition, of civilization over barbarism."[49]

Evangelical zeal without the religion: the theatrical arm of the Cultural Missions was designed to convert the countryside to the aims of the Revolution. According to Donald H. Frischmann, between 1942 and 1948 alone, the Cultural Missions built two hundred theatres and presented five hundred works, not to mention four hundred marionette shows, like those Castellanos and her troupe staged.[50] Although over the course of the 1940s official support for cinematic "missions" came to eclipse that for theatre and animated cartoons began to take the place of puppets, Frischmann believes that the legacy of the Cultural Missions was important in establishing a precedent in living memory for live theatre in rural areas. This theatrical activity would have long-ranging effects on the re-emergence of Mayan theatre in the past twenty years, as participants in these early experiments would go on to establish their own, community-based theatre groups.

Indigenismo and Its Discontents: *La dama boba*

As suggested by Castellanos's comments, even in its heyday indigenismo was not without its critics. One of the more eloquent and nuanced of these criticisms appears in a play by Elena Garro, *La dama boba* (The Foolish Lady).[51] Like Castellanos, Garro was a Mexican author and playwright involved in the missionary work of theatre. In the mid-1930s, while a student at Mexico's national university, Garro acted with a student troupe that traveled throughout Mexico presenting such educational theatre.[52] Nearly thirty years later, in her 1963 play, she reflected critically on these experiences. Because it explores artistically the ambivalent and conflicted nature of the period's cultural crusades, I describe it in some detail.

La dama boba concerns the fate of the Mexico City–based Theatre for the People, which tours the Mexican countryside with its mobile production of Lope de Vega's play of the same name. Garro's play opens with scene 5 of Lope de Vega's, in which a harried professor is attempting to teach the alphabet to the seemingly simple young woman who gives the play its title. A gathered crowd—almost all the residents of the hamlet of Coapa—follows the action with interest: they and their children have been the recipients of similar efforts, as city-trained schoolteachers have come and gone in state-sponsored efforts to improve Spanish-language literacy.

Suddenly the action of Lope de Vega's play breaks down, when the actor playing the Professor (Francisco) fails to appear in his next scene. While changing into costume for the role of Laurencio, he seems to have vanished into thin air. It is darkly hinted that he has met a fate similar to that of an earlier visiting schoolteacher, who had suffered a "mortal disgrace"—emphasis on mortal—amid widely held suspicions of sexually inappropriate behavior.[53] The remainder of act 1 is taken up by various theories to account for his disappearance—theories that tend to draw lines of contention between the residents of Coapa and those of the city. While the latter assume the former have done something with or to him, the former are certain he has met a more supernaturally ordained fate; the scene's dramatic effect comes from the theatre professionals' frustrations with the locals' resistance to their more "rational" discourse.

In act 2, we find that Francisco has been spirited away, by means unrevealed, to the hamlet of Tepan, which seems to exist in a kind of parallel universe to Coapa: it is virtually identical to the latter, with the exception that its church has *two* towers (made of gold). The reason for

Francisco's disappearance: the mayor of Tepan, whose many petitions for a schoolteacher have gone unheard in Mexico City, has seen Francisco in his role as Professor in the Coapa production and has decided that Francisco is just the *maestro* (teacher) his village needs. Furthermore, the mayor's beautiful and headstrong daughter, Lupe, will set an example by becoming Francisco's first student. Despite Francisco's many attempts to set the record straight, the mayor refuses to see that Francisco is anything but the Professor he is costumed as. Thus, in a Pirandellian manner, the lessons begin—on a set reconstructed to match that of Coapa's *La dama boba*, with Lupe attired as the other dama, and with the whole town gathered round to watch the proceedings. And although Lupe does not know her "lines," a sort of lesson does emerge, with the approval and coaching of her father, who has already seen the "real" thing. The town decides that Francisco is to remain with them for fourteen months—one for each year he himself has spent in school.

The last act takes place at the end of Francisco's first month in Tepan. The first half of the act is taken up in a long discussion among Francisco, Lupe, and her father that further nuances the distinction in worldview noted by Castellano. The Tepanecos tell Francisco that city people like him can only appreciate half of the reality around them—that part illuminated by the light of day. At night, it seems, everything changes; animals change their forms and nature, as do men and, even more so, women. At night, there exists a wholly other reality, as real as day's but hidden. This is a world, however, country people know quite well. Whereas Castellanos suggests the boundaries between real and imaginary were imprecise, here Garro suggests the existence of multiple, incommensurable realities.

Throughout this discussion, the character of Lupe grows in substance. If at first she seemed merely headstrong and given too much to daydreaming, now we begin to see that she is one of the night's most special creatures: a "multiple," capable of being many things at once, the "best kind" of woman there is. Francisco finds himself falling in love with her, just as his troupe, having spent the past month searching, finally catches up with him. On their arrival they marvel at the people of Tepan, who have adopted some of the costume conventions of Lope de Vega's play. The troupe members believe they have encountered a town so backward its people still dress in the style of the seventeenth century—which only renews the troupe's faith in its cultural crusade. And seeing his friends' ignorance in a new light—as incapable of distinguishing imagination from reality as they might accuse their hosts of being—Francisco decides to stay where he is. If Lupe wants him to be her maestro, then he will become his character; after all, actors are "multiples," too, in their ability to metamorphose into other beings. But Lupe has come to mistrust theatrical mimesis, and she has seen how the troupe has claimed him for its own. Neither she nor Garro allows him to stay; as much as he may want to, the play suggests, Francisco will never be able to enter fully Lupe's world. In the end, Theatre of the People forcibly takes him off to Mexico City. Although Francisco vows to return some day, Lupe remains curiously silent as he goes. The play ends with her father resigning himself to yet another letter-writing campaign for a new maestro.

At first glance, *La dama boba* seems to follow the tradition of Mexican indigenista literature—the body of work produced by nonindigenous writers beginning in the 1920s "whose common denominator is a sympathetic representation of the 'indian' and denunciation of injustice."[54] Such literature provided an important impetus for indigenismo as policy. Although the play does not deal with the kinds of injustices Mexico's indigenista tradition critiques, its sympathies clearly lie with the local communities whose worldview it celebrates, essentializes, and, in certain moments, romanticizes. (Cypess, for example, sees in Lupe's character a reincarnation of La Malinche, in her aspect of foreigner-lover.)[55] Nevertheless, it is possible also to read *La dama boba* as a criticism of indigenismo and a register of the tensions that would ultimately render it unworkable.[56]

Clearly, the question of who converted whom is central to the play. Yet the mutual conversion is never complete for either party in the exchange: Francisco can neither remain in Tepan nor take Lupe with him; and although Lupe's father has made a mission of finding a maestro for his town, it is likely that the "forgotten skies" of Tepan will remain so forever. Two models of indigenismo are thus presented and then figuratively rejected. The Cultural Mission arrives in Coapa uninvited, with its play from the conquerors' Golden Age. Not surprisingly, the troupe is received somewhat skeptically by the locals—the same locals who seem to have something to do with the mysterious disappearance of an earlier emissary from the city. In Tepan, in contrast, the mayor *wants* a teacher for his town, but the only way he can get one is to kidnap him, as his pleas to the capital have gone consistently unheeded. Thus, suggests Garro, a politics of invitation is no more effective than a politics of imposition: who is to blame if invitations extended go unanswered? Garro deftly exposes the nationalist illogic underlying indigenismo by linking it to the still unresolved question of indigenous self-representation. For the cultural emissaries in the play, the indigenous communities exist as people to be acted upon; when these people act, as does the mayor of Tepan, they may as well not exist for all the attention they get. But they are not powerless, as illustrated in the figure of Lupe. She is capable of eloquent self-expression throughout the play—until the Theatre of the People arrives in her town. Seeing the troupe (and Francisco's girlfriend Tara), she cannot trust Francisco's sudden desire to remain with her in Tepan. When he begs her to say the word that will allow him to stay, she simply shakes her head, then turns away as he is dragged off.

Here, Lupe chooses an act of silence—an active silence—that eloquently expresses the impossibility of her feelings for Francisco. In this final moment, Garro suggests the impossibility of the whole indigenista enterprise; otherwise, Lupe and Francisco would end the play together, and the story of La Malinche truly would have its modern expression here. This is not to say, however, that what Garro advocates is a maintenance of difference, of rigid distinctions between rural and urban, indigenous and nonindigenous, "night" and "day." It is too late for that: Francisco has savored too much of the "night" to believe in the truth of day, and Lupe has "already learned how to read." If the question of how to resolve the other differences remains open, the play suggests that the only route to resolution will come from the indigenous themselves— whether they choose autonomy, as does Lupe, or collaboration, as does her father.

Recent Developments and Indigenous Movements

Garro's *La dama boba* anticipates much of the subsequent criticism leveled at proponents of indigenismo beginning in the late 1960s. This critique generally focuses on two issues. One is a belief that indigenismo, despite its radical potential, has existed ultimately in the service of a Mexican state, a state that in effect continues to colonize its indigenous citizens. The logical conclusion of this is ethnocide—the eventual elimination of Indian ethnic identity as it is bleached and absorbed into the mestizo national state. The second important issue is that of indigenous self-representation: as O'Connell summarizes it, "one thing *indigenismo* is not is indigenous. Indigenous people themselves have never been its principal promoters or practitioners."[57]

The subsequent history of theatre by and for indigenous communities registers changing attitudes about indigenismo by both indigenous and nonindigenous artists. In the 1970s, for example, the state-sponsored Teatro Conasupo[58] was conceived very much in the model of the troupe in

La dama boba, sending out its own brigades of actors—originally young, college-educated actors from Mexico City—to introduce "great works from the universal repertory."[59] Eventually, the brigades expanded their work to include dramatizations of local myths and legends, as well as original pieces providing critical reexaminations of national history. They established actor training programs in five indigenous languages in central and southern Mexico and incorporated local indigenous and campesino/a actors in their presentations. This in turn prompted many to develop their own collective creations, motivated, as Frischmann puts it, "to participate actively in theatrical activity as a way to denounce and contribute to the transformation of repressive realities."[60]

Although Teatro Conasupo lost financial support with the end of the Echeverría administration in 1976, its concept would continue under the Department of Education's Proyecto de Arte Escénico Popular (Popular Scenic Arts Project). Here, the methods were similar to those of the earlier INI-sponsored cultural programs, but the aims were different. As did INI, the Department of Education recruited maestros from rural communities, who were trained in Mexico City and then returned home as "theatre promoters." Once home, they were expected to form theatre groups, provide theatre training, and work with educators in the development of theatre techniques for bilingual education. "Integration into national life" was a goal now as it had been earlier, but this time it was not to be at the expense of the community's identity. Furthermore, the resulting theatre was not aimed "at" these communities in an overtly didactic fashion but rather at providing them with a new means of self-expression, whereby they could both learn about the larger socioeconomic reality of which they were a part and conceive new ways to transform it. The possible content was virtually unlimited, ranging from social and familial problems to local history to the dramatization of oral legends. However, problems abounded: economic difficulties, decisions over which language to work in, internalized feelings of inferiority that translated into highly untheatrical reserve, the ever-present tension between tradition and progress. Frischmann includes as well the unique dilemmas faced by women in this effort; two Mixe (Oaxacan) actors describe the triple obstacles they face as women, that of "cultural tradition (women's silence), their social situation (the weight of *machismo*) and the racial complex (exposing themselves to the *mestizo* gaze)."[61] But over the six years of its existence, this project helped to extend the participation of campesinos/as and indigenous players in works of their own and others' creation.

Rural audiences have also been the target of theatrical activity sponsored by Mexico's Adult Education Institute since 1983. Although its work tends to focus on promoting Spanish literacy (a controversial topic in multilingual Mexico), Frischmann reports that other values it promotes include solidarity, cooperation, and "women's freedom from the weight of paternalistic tradition."[62] Like its two immediate predecessors, this group trains and incorporates community actors, some of whom devote themselves full time to the effort as touring companies in the nearby regions.

A certain pattern seems to reemerge here, when we compare this latter-day theatrical activity with that of centuries past. That is, an imposed theatrical mission—in this case, evangelizing works of "universal" appeal and high art—has been appropriated and transformed by the people it sought to convert, in the service of their own agendas. Cultural control is neither maintained nor regained but negotiated in an ongoing way.

More recently, an increasing awareness of the limits of both mestizaje and indigenismo has led to movements for indigenous autonomy and intragroup alliances throughout Latin America. Alicja Iwaŋska traces the roots of this phenomenon to the global processes of decolonization after World War II, which awakened similar questions in politically independent but internally colonial states such as Mexico. Writing twenty years ago, she described the situation there as follows:

> All Mexican natives are invited to full Mexican citizenship (which means the European, predominantly Spanish, and recently strongly U.S.-influenced lifestyle). It is assumed that all educated natives [meaning someone born in Mexico] would accept these ideological invitations. If they do not, it is considered an uncomfortable anomaly, something which the majority of Mexicans would prefer not to perceive. The truths of others are not easily recognized.[63]

Over the past three decades, these truths have struggled for both recognition and articulation and have found expression in a variety of ways—religious and social activism, social protest, armed resistance, literature and theatre.

Throughout Latin America, for example, Catholic liberation theology has been of great import to the consciousness-raising of oppressed groups, exerting its "preferential option for the poor" most strongly in the 1970s and 1980s. One of its most controversial supporters has been Samuel Ruíz García, bishop of the diocese of San Cristóbal de las Casas between 1960 and 2000. During his tenure, he worked closely with indigenous communities not only to attend to their spiritual needs but also to address and raise consciousness about their rights to human dignity in the material plane. His "army" of ten thousand indigenous Maya catechists and deacons has built what he calls the *iglesia autóctona* (autochthonous or native church) in Chiapas.[64]

Ruíz's activist theology was part of the impulse behind the First Indian Congress, held in Chiapas in October 1974—the 500th anniversary of the birth of Fray Bartolomé de Las Casas.[65] The congress was attended by hundreds of indigenous representatives (most of them Mayan), as well as some three hundred nonindigenous. Its discussion centered on four themes: land, commerce, education, and health. If these topics seem reminiscent of the Mexican government's agenda in the heyday of indigenismo, it is only because the myriad issues surrounding them had yet to be resolved (which is still true). The more important consideration was that the indigenous people affected by these issues themselves became more involved and represented in attempts to solve them. (In fact, though the government planned the congress, the Mayan participants eventually took over its agenda.) Thus, as the "young Tzotzil" who gave the keynote address concluded, "I believe that if we Indians all organize ourselves we will achieve freedom and do our work better. We all have to be Friar Bartolomé. Then through a common organization we will all defend ourselves. For in union there is strength."[66]

Over the next twenty years there would be many different indigenous responses to the problems outlined in the First Indian Congress, some more radical than others. While the Zapatistas were secretly training Marcos in the jungle, Mayas in Chiapas, Tabasco, and Yucatán were working with other non-Mayan intermediaries to revitalize Mayan culture and its expressions through theatre. Offstage, some of them, along with other indigenous writers throughout Mexico, were coming to the attention of Mexican intellectuals such as Carlos Montemayor, a key figure in the dissemination of Mayan and indigenous literature, poetry, and drama throughout Mexico. Since 1992 he has published nearly fifty volumes of this work, much of it in bilingual editions of Spanish and the local language, helping readers of Spanish to appreciate the diverse written expression of the living cultures of their compatriots.

Still, the pan-indigenous unity called for by the young Tzotzil speaker quoted above has yet to fully develop in Mexico. On the one hand, this could be seen as a manifest if not necessarily intentional resistance to the kinds of homogenization masked by mestizaje and indigenismo. On the other hand, it tends to prevent a necessary critical mass for Mexico's problems in those four areas to be addressed for the benefit of all, indigenous included, in the emerging environment of neoliberal democracy.[67] (And, as I discuss below, this kind of fragmentation has been actively cultivated by the federal government.) With Mexico's turn toward more of a free market economy in the late 1980s, those problems have exacerbated the already poor living conditions of Mexico's poorest communities. But if the combined efforts of agrarian organizers, followers of liberation theology, and Mayan writers and artists did not prevent this turn, they were important in sowing the seeds for what would come to be called zapatismo in the 1990s.

Zapatismo and the Reassertion of Tradition

Beginning on New Year's Day, 1994, a new series of events began to register the fact that mestizaje and indigenismo were not working out on a national scale. On this, the effective date of the North American Free Trade Agreement (NAFTA), an armed force calling itself the Zapatista Army of National Liberation (EZLN) seized seven towns in Chiapas and declared war on the Mexican government. The forces, named after the Mexican Revolution leader Emiliano Zapata, had been training together clandestinely since the early 1980s in Chiapas's Lacandon jungle. They rose up in protest of both NAFTA (for imposing unfair competition on local farmers) and the recent repeal of Article 27 of the 1917 Mexican Constitution (which removed state protection of communally held properties and opened the doors to their takeover by private interests). A charismatic spokesperson, who called himself "Subcomandante Marcos" and claimed he took orders from his indigenous superiors, soon emerged. This Mexican intellectual, identified variously as a college professor, student radical, and former actor, concealed his identity behind a ski mask and his trademark pipe. He quickly captured the world's attention with his eloquent press releases, Web site, and call for solidarity with oppressed people the world over: "Todos somos Marcos" (We are all Marcos).[68]

After thirteen days of fighting, in which an estimated one hundred fifty people from both sides were killed and which the world watched with perhaps more attention than it had ever paid previous "Indian rebellions," the government declared a cease-fire and agreed to negotiate with the Zapatistas. Given the superior strength and numbers of the Mexican military and the ease with which it could have crushed the rebellion, the cease-fire and subsequent peace talks were considered by many observers victories in their own right. The movement attracted the attention and support of artists, activists, and intellectuals within and outside Mexico, who responded to Marcos's call by sending representatives to rallies held in Zapatista communities and by participating in fund-raisers held all over the world.

Significant in the negotiations was the inclusion of Zapatista women and a ten-point women's bill of rights (later expanded to thirty-one). Though their demands and the circumstances that engendered them have become much more visible since 1994, the seeds of gender consciousness were planted much earlier and along diverse paths, as several anthropologists have pointed out.[69] Women grew increasingly active in indigenous movements since the First Indian Congress in 1974, for example. Economic changes compelling men to migrate for wage work in petroleum fields and coffee plantations meant that more power over domestic decisions resided with the women left on the family property; the rise of weaving and other craft cooperatives since the early 1970s became a matter of considerable pride among Mayan women, in addition to giving some of them more economic power than was possible before. Church-sponsored courses and workshops on social injustice and racism, following the principles of liberation theology, caused some women to start questioning gender-based inequities as well.[70] The work of religious and feminist nongovernmental organizations helped to raise consciousness about women's issues in rural communities. And, as I discuss in more detail later, the introduction of theatre in Mayan languages also contributed to a greater awareness of and voice for indigenous women's issues.

This voice calls for change not only to national structures that generate social policy but within newly autonomous indigenous communities as well. Here, the women's agenda does not always square neatly with the general movement: given that this autonomy would be based in the reestablishment of local governance or "customary law" (*usos y costumbres*),[71] indigenous women have been criticized for questioning aspects of that law that, historically, have excluded and oppressed them: "If the recognition of customary law is going to be legislated, it is the women themselves who must decide what should remain and what should be changed as being detrimental to their human rights."[72] Thus, at the same time that many Mayans are mapping out a kind of collective identity based on long tradition, Mayan women caution against an overidentification with that tradition when it is practiced at their expense.

A Postmodern Revolution?

In her 1998 documentary, *A Place Called Chiapas,* filmed during the months preceding the halt to the peace talks in September 1996, the Canadian filmmaker Nettie Wild borrowed the now-famous line that the Zapatista uprising is the world's first "postmodern revolution."[73] She emphasized especially Marcos's adroit self-performance as a romantic, ski-masked, pipe-smoking representative of the cause; his manipulation of the media and Internet technology to spread word of that cause globally; and the Zapatistas' deployment of theatrical props in the course of their public appearances—not only the bandannas and ski masks but also wooden cutouts of the rifles they could not afford to buy. But I would caution against a too-easy use of such a label, which can suggest a merely playful juxtaposition of past and present, tradition and innovation, naïveté and sophistication. As Zapatista spokesperson, Marcos has been the most visible of the Zapatistas, but he has always been at pains to point out that he takes his orders from the Revolutionary Indigenous Clandestine Committee–General Command of indigenous organizers, who themselves operate on a radically democratic basis. His own involvement *as* spokesperson is not only a simple matter of being an expeditious cultural "bridge" between the indigenous and nonindigenous worlds: he spent close to twelve years in the jungle with the Mayans of eastern Chiapas, not so much training them for the revolution, but being trained *by* them for doing it *their way.* In other words, if the "postmodern Indian" is being constructed in and around the discourse surrounding zapatismo, it is not simply being imposed in the same way that mestizaje or indigenismo have been. Juxtapositions of tradition and change are neither the passive result of implacable social processes nor the imposition of a former university professor, political revolutionary, and sometime actor (Marcos). Rather, they are strategically chosen with an aim to redefine not only what it means to be Mayan in Mexico but also what it means to be Mexican at all. National identity is once again at stake, as it was at the height of mestizaje and indigenismo. The difference now is that the calls for change are coming from within the indigenous communities, and the world beyond Mexico is starting to listen.

But I do not wish to leave the impression that the Zapatistas are *the* voice of the Maya in Mexico. Many communities have withheld support for the Zapatistas; many others have sought the same ends but disclaim violence as a means toward them. Land and religious disputes erupt in the region, independent of the general conflict. The government has also exploited existing differences—between 1996, when the Zapatistas broke off dialogue with the Mexican government, and 2001, when the new party took over, the federal government financed anti-Zapatista paramilitary activity and withheld support from Zapatista-friendly communities, with the effect of further turning Mayan against Mayan. A recent report by an international human rights organization accused the current administration of following in the former's footsteps in Mexico's ongoing "war of attrition."[74]

It is important to remember that not every Mayan is a Zapatista supporter, and not every Zapatista supporter is a Mayan. Nevertheless, the Zapatistas remained the most visible representatives of indigenous concerns in Mexico, at least until the recent passage of the controversial "Indian rights bill" (La ley indígena) in April 2001. This bill, Vicente Fox's first official act as the first non-PRI president since the Revolution, was intended to enforce the 1996 peace accords between the government and the EZLN and was considered the key to eventual peace in Mexico. As passed, the bill grants indigenous communities preferential use of natural resources in their lands, guarantees the right to preserve and promote native languages and culture, allows for community governance according to local custom, and prohibits discrimination based on a variety of factors including race, gender, and marital status (or preference). But as passed, it is such a watered down version of the original accords that the Zapatistas, along with the Indigenous National Congress, indigenous organizations throughout Mexico, and numerous intellectuals, journalists, and lawmakers from indigenous-concentrated states, refused to accept it. Particularly, they object to limits to local and regional autonomy represented by the bill's conferral of authority to state legislatures for enacting local customs into state law. In the current climate of intrahemispheric trade and development being fostered by Fox's Plan Puebla Panamá, this authority will be of increasing importance to indigenous communities in resource-rich areas.[75] Further, the bill offers no provision for the disarmament and prosecution of paramilitary organizations associated with counterinsurgency violence. A year after its enactment, the demand for its repeal by more than three hundred indigenous communities and indigenous rights organizations was denied; at this writing, protests have been organized in Chiapas and Mexico City, and there is speculation that violence in the southern states most affected by it will increase.

U.S. and Touristic Influences

Another factor contributing to the complexity of identity formation in Mexico is the pervasive influence of the United States on the everyday existence of many Mexicans. Indeed, the phrase "American way of life" is often left untranslated in Spanish-language discussions of this influence.[76]

This way of life is beamed at Mexicans even in the remotest corners of the countryside, where satellite dishes are now vying with Coca-Cola signs as vivid reminders of the porosity of the border between the two countries. Despite an anti-interventionist distrust of the United States that goes back more than a century, there is nevertheless a strong temptation for many, especially those of Mexico's beleaguered middle classes, to "buy American" (literally and symbolically), even when to do so might be at the expense of homegrown products and producers. As these producers participate more and more in economic relationships outside their own communities, traditional forms of dress—markers of community identity—are being replaced by ready-to-wear in many situations. I mention this not so much to mourn a loss but to make another point: one can be dressed in an A-line skirt and patent-leather pumps and still consider oneself fundamentally "Mayan," despite the pressures of the marketplace to make one feel otherwise. At the same time, the tourist gaze is not the sole or most important reason that donning the traditional *traje* (clothing) makes one feel even more connected to one's roots.

Nevertheless, the tourist gaze is a powerful one, and it should not be underestimated. The Mayan intellectual Jacinto Arias is scathing in his critique of this societal force. In an article tracing forms of conquest in Chiapas and indigenous resistance against it, Arias concludes that the latest challenge to "Indianness" in the region is its new status as a commodity for tourist consumption. In his view, "[t]his gobbling up of Indian products is a symbolic act that reflects the real intention of swallowing the Indian people," a phenomenon he refers to as "indiophagy."[77]

MEXICO ENTERED the twentieth century with revolutionary zeal aimed toward creating a modern, classless society (based on a form of socialism) and away from Mexico's Catholic past (priests were persecuted and churches closed). Today, although the seventy-one-year monopoly of the PRI is at last at an end, it remains to be seen whether Mexico will abandon its virtual oligarchy as well; it is almost certain to remain neoliberal in economic philosophy. Another kind of "revolution" is on the minds of supporters of zapatismo; and the Catholic Church is being challenged not by the government but from within, by divisions between conservative and liberationist elements, and from without, by evangelists of many Protestant and, lately, Muslim denominations. Spanish is still a second language to an estimated ten million Mexicans, who speak one of more than sixty other languages at home.

In such a potentially pluralistic context, is it retrograde to operate under the banner of something as simple as "Mayan" or "indigenous" theatre? As I have tried to find out what people are doing here, why they are dying here, and why they make theatre here, I have come to think it more retrograde to dismiss such labels without giving them long and serious thought.

CHAPTER 2.

"Más que una noticia . . ."

Mayan Theatre in Chiapas

IN LATE SUMMER 1996, several subway stops in Mexico City featured a billboard advertisement declaring: "More than a news item, Chiapas is . . ." Behind these words were pictured all the enticing flora and fauna that southernmost state has to offer: lush vegetation, colorful jungle birds, waterfalls, jaguars, monkeys—and a woman in native dress, weaving on a loom. The billboard assured travelers that Chiapas was still the unspoiled wilderness of exotic creatures—including the Maya—they might have heard so much about, before those irksome Zapatistas came, with their ski masks and their bullet belts, and scared everyone away. Here, the Maya of Chiapas were presented as linked to the natural, uncivilized world of wonders—much as the New World was presented to Europe in the first century after its discovery. Perhaps the most famous and literal example of this was Jan van der Straet's sixteenth-century engraving of Amerigo Vespucci "discovering" America, portrayed as a naked native woman roused from slumber by the European explorer; in the background are portrayed all the natural riches of this virgin territory.[1] The billboard was a modern echo of that sixteenth-century fantasia, the key differences being that the modern woman is caught not asleep but at work and that the subway traveler maintains full control of the "gaze" at her, without having to share it with a sixteenth-century explorer. But now, as then, the female figure does the work of cultural representation and embodiment.[2] She offers roots to the rootless and refuge to travelers from the world of subways, skyscrapers, air pollution, and instant access. As the billboard's tourism board sponsor would have it, she is Chiapas—reprieved from history, linked to transcendent nature, worth a closer look.

And yet many indigenous women see themselves in terms similar to those the billboard implies: bearers of important traditions tied to culture and the land. As they become increasingly involved in the larger economy through the sale of their handicrafts, tradition becomes a source of

"More than a news item." Promoting tourism in Chiapas two years after the Zapatistas' first uprising. Photo by author.

ethnic pride and physical survival.[3] Women weavers who sell their work through artisans' cooperatives or retail shops to wealthier tourists, for example, enjoy benefits ranging from increased income to increased access to government grants, loans, and other services and even, indirectly, to the fine arts markets of museums and galleries. Other women—such as the Protestants expelled from their traditionally Catholic communities in the municipality of Chamula—become street vendors, often with their children in tow, and live in extreme poverty in the "misery belts" surrounding San Cristóbal. Harsh as that life is, it has allowed many women to gain a degree of financial independence they can use to escape abusive marriages.

The combination of increasing economic hardship, generally, and the growing tendency for women to take more control in family financial matters is registered in increasing gender-role tensions, documented by a number of anthropologists. To put it simply, many men, accustomed to being the breadwinners and enjoying greater access to local political positions, are feeling threatened.[4] Thus, the cultural pressure on women to remain "traditional"—that is, to remain at home and economically dependent on their husbands—is strong from both within and outside Mayan communities in Chiapas. At the same time, the increasing hardships facing families have caused women to deploy tradition in the name of social change. As June Nash has pointed out in a larger context, "Women, as caretakers for the young and old, are central actors in the emergent social movements of indigenous peoples in the hemisphere precisely because of their connectedness to the issues of the survival of past traditions and future generations in their own lives."[5] In doing what they can to ensure their families' physical survival, Mayan women at once preserve certain traditions and significantly challenge others.

These challenges go against the grain of practices that have long and deep roots, not only in Chiapas. Mexican women have been allowed to vote only since 1953; according to Nash, indigenous women only rarely did so until after the Zapatista uprising, when the prospect of ending the PRI monopoly began to seem possible.[6] Violence against women, indigenous and ladino, is not taken seriously in Mexico, as illustrated by the following example. In March 2002, the neighboring state of Oaxaca repealed legislation criminalizing the practice of *rapto* (kidnapping a woman in order to marry her or satisfy the man's sexual desire), making it instead a minor infraction. According to a report in the *Washington Post*, a key legislator called the practice "harmless and 'romantic.'"[7] These at-

America by Jan van der Straet, in *Nova reperta* (1638).
Courtesy The Burndy Library, Dibner Institute for the History of Science and Technology, Cambridge, Massachusetts.

titudes are also sometimes embedded deeply in and perpetuated by oral tradition. In her study of female agency in recent Mayan theatre, Cynthia Steele recounts a traditional Tzeltal story about a woman who, venturing out alone to do her laundry in an unknown part of the river, falls into it and drowns.[8] This cautionary tale about the perils of female autonomy was echoed in another one I heard, this time originating among Tzotzil women. In this tale, which the anthropologist Kathleen Sullivan has traced back at least three generations, a man goes to the river and comes back with the knowledge of animal languages. When his wife asks to be let in on the secret, the man consults his animal advisers, who tell him not only not to tell her anything, but the next time she asks, he should also beat her. In this way, she will learn not to ask questions.[9] In a region in which oral storytelling remains a more powerful form of education than the official school system's, these stories demonstrate the strong cultural pressure on Mayan women not only to stay put but also to keep quiet.

The womanly virtues of immobility, invisibility, and silence hardly lend themselves to work in the theatre; indeed, opportunities for indigenous women in Chiapas even to see theatre are practically nonexistent. Nevertheless, some Mayan women do perform, in one of the two Mayan troupes based in San Cristóbal. To understand how this has been possible, it is necessary to explore the emergence of Mayan theatre generally in Chiapas. The story of this emergence is one of artistic intervention against pervasive deculturation. To tell it, I review several performances and play texts that register recent theatrical responses to Mexico's "new world order" and its effects on both local culture and gender roles and relations. This story in turn inspires another one, about how indigenous women are becoming key actors in defining an alternative world order, envisioned theatrically, to be enacted beyond the boundaries of the stage.

Lo'il Maxil and La Fomma

Lo'il Maxil and La Fomma are the two most active and well known theatre-making groups in Chiapas. Both use theatre in their larger programs dedicated to Mayan language literacy and improved sociocultural awareness, Lo'il Maxil as an arm of the nonprofit organization Sna Jtz'ibajom (House of the Writer).[10] Both participate in and represent themselves as part of the resurgence of ethnically based cultural activities in Mexico. Both have nurtured individual writers and visual artists who have become important voices in indigenous art movements. Both work with non-Mayan artists and advisers who provide creative and financial assistance. And both present their works to non-Mayan Mexicans and international audiences as well as in Mayan communities. Whereas La Fomma is an all-woman organization, Lo'il Maxil employs both women and men.[11] Although the two troupes operate independently, their histories are very much intertwined and illustrate the ways in which ethnicity and gender intersect, interact, and conflict in the enactment of cultural identity.

Sna Jtz'ibajom is a writers' collective that since 1983 has worked to improve literacy in Tzotzil and Tzeltal, the dominant Mayan languages in the highland communities surrounding ladino-dominated San Cristóbal.[12] In addition to providing weekend literacy programs, the group is also dedicated to the preservation and promotion of local traditions, and its activities include the publication of stories and poetry, occasional radio broadcasts, exhibitions of photographs taken and developed by its members, and theatre—dramatizations of folktales, Mayan history, and contemporary social issues. (Interestingly, theatrical activity began in 1985 with puppet plays, partly because the father of one of the founding members, Juan de la Torre López, had been a puppeteer in Rosario Castellanos's Teatro Petul, and the puppets were still in the family.) Since 1989, Sna's Lo'il Maxil troupe has staged a new (live) play virtually every year. Some of these plays remain in the repertory and are restaged from time to time. All of the plays have been developed collectively, although some were initiated by an individual member or adviser. They tour to communities in and around San Cristóbal and have been showcased in theatre festivals throughout Mexico, Guatemala, Honduras, and the United States; in 1996 the group also performed for international gatherings of journalists and observers covering or attending the since-halted peace talks between the Zapatistas and the federal government. In Mexico, their work is known through local and national press coverage and has been anthologized in collections edited by the literary historian Carlos Montemayor.[13] Outside of Mexico, accounts of their work have appeared in academic journals and critical anthologies, most notably through the work of Frischmann, Steele, and myself, as well as in such popular venues as the *Smithsonian* and *Ms.* magazines, in articles by the troupe's American advisers, Robert M. Laughlin and Miriam Laughlin. Sna's story is also told, in four languages, on the Smithsonian Web site, "Unmasking the Maya."[14]

The group operates multiculturally, since its members include representatives from Mayan communities that might otherwise consider

The community gathers around a Lo'il Maxil performance of *Cuentos de nuestra raíz/Tales from Our Roots,* in Tenejapa, Chiapas (July 1996). Photo by author, © 1996.

themselves culturally distinct. It also has an intracultural aspect, in that it includes among its aims the revindication of the Tzotzil and Tzeltal languages and regional traditions. Finally, it operates interculturally, through alliances with non-Mayan artists and researchers. As a multicultural organization, it reflects the region's more general movement toward a pan-Mayan solidarity, although, as Steele has pointed out, Tzotzil/Tzeltal power relationships in the region tend to be replicated in the organization.[15] It owes its intercultural aspect to the impulse behind its formation—interest shown in the region by anthropologists over many decades.

Concerned that all their stories and legends were being exported outside their communities, never to return, three Tzotzil men sought the help of the state government to finance an indigenous cultural society that would foster the publication of folktales in Tzotzil and Spanish, the region's lingua franca. When, as often happens, the change in state administration resulted in the end of funding, they turned to Robert Laughlin for help. Laughlin, a Smithsonian curator and anthropologist who had worked on Tzotzil linguistics with the Harvard Chiapas Project, had maintained relationships with some of his informants, who were relatives of the men. With his help, they secured a grant from Cultural Survival, Inc., a Harvard-based organization that supports a variety of grassroots indigenous projects. They continue to be supported by a variety of Mexican, U.S., and international organizations and like many other artistic organizations, constantly struggle to maintain that support.

The group also collaborates with non-Mayans in artistic matters. Key among these collaborators has been Laughlin himself, who not only seeks funding in the United States for the troupe but also arranges and accompanies them on their U.S. tours and serves as interpreter for English-language audiences. Another important collaborator has been Ralph Lee, who has assisted in the shaping and direction of twelve of the yearly productions. Lee, a veteran of Joseph Chaikin's Open Theatre, is the artistic director of New York's Mettawee River Company, which specializes in the staging of indigenous cultural traditions from all over the world. Until recently, Lee would typically spend each February with the group, polishing that year's production. For many years, because Lee knew no Spanish, Laughlin would serve as interpreter and intermediary between the troupe and the director. Two or three of the most experienced members of the troupe would meet with Laughlin to discuss concepts and script development. Laughlin recalls, "I suggested many of the lines in the plays, but they were quick to turn down ones they didn't like."[16] From there, the script would be presented to the whole group for refining.

In 2000, Lee recommended Michael Garcés of the International Arts Relations (INTAR) Hispanic American Arts Center to fill that role. The group has also worked with Amy Trompetter, formerly of the Bread and Puppet Theatre, in the development of masks and puppets. For many years, the ladino playwright and poet Francisco Álvarez Quiñones was a full-time staff member, hired to translate and shape plays written in Tzotzil or Tzeltal. On occasion, both he and Laughlin have written plays for the group to perform, and he has sometimes performed in them (as have visitors from other parts of Mexico). Finally, one of the group's longtime members, Diego Méndez Guzmán, recently completed a course of study with Luis de Tavira, a prolific philosopher of theatre, professional director, and founder of an actors' school near Mexico City. De Tavira is known for staging or adapting works by such European authors as August Strindberg, Heinrich von Kleist, Ingmar Bergman, and Bertolt Brecht, as well as by the Mexican writers Elena Garro, Vicente Leñero, Martín Luis Guzmán, and Ramón López Velarde.

Thus, from the beginning, Lo'il Maxil's work, celebrated everywhere as "Mayan theatre," has been in fact a highly collaborative effort by artists and researchers trained in very different traditions. The performance tradition that is emerging reflects these diverse impulses and influences—

which, in Lee's case, have already been inflected by both Mayan performance forms and indigenous traditions the world over. Anthropological accounts serve as the basis for explorations of the ancient Mayan past in Álvarez's *Dinastía de jaguares* (Dynasty of Jaguars); and Freidel, Schele, and Parker's popular *Maya Cosmos* is a well-thumbed text in the group's library.[17] Official history is critiqued in a play-within-a-play about the imposition of Spanish culture in Mayan religion and education; this technique was suggested by Lee and adopted by the group.[18] Most of the plays feature masks and costume devices not traditional to the region. For example, Lee has often adapted the grotesque half-masks of the commedia dell'arte tradition to mock ladino villains and once used stilts to exaggerate the stature and awkwardness of a German coffee plantation owner in *¡Vamos al paraíso!* (Let's Go to Paradise!). Now, some of the group members conduct mask-making workshops in areas as far away as Florida, where the troupe traveled at the invitation of Florida Rural Legal Services to work with the Immokalee Workers' Coalition, many of whose members are undocumented farmworkers from Mayan Mexico. Mask making was part of the shared theatrical activity, and the workers were inspired to use them in subsequent strikes and protests.[19] As a result, the use of this type of theatrical mask, which is here mediated through Lee's work in European and indigenous traditions, is becoming a new signifier, in theatre, of "Mayan" culture. In matters of plot structure, the plays tend to follow the pattern inciting incident, rising action, climax, and denouement, but they are not so rigidly linear that they do not permit an exploratory episode or two in their progress from beginning to end. Finally, several of the plays have been professionally produced as videos by Álvarez and the professional videographer Carlos Martínez (now famous for his coverage of the Zapatistas), using a technology that is beyond the reach of many Mayan communities.

Nevertheless, Sna is justified in its self-representation as a Mayan organization, to the extent that most of its members are Mayas who control most of the decisions affecting it. One exception has been in the area of publicity and speechwriting, the domain of Álvarez until he left the organization in summer 2002. In these venues, Álvarez frequently invoked the "millennial nature" of the group's work, situating it on a continuum that extends back to the pre-Columbian past and draws strength from the continuance of ancient traditions in the ongoing presence of the colonizer. Álvarez's presentation of the group tended to alternate between Grossberg's colonial and transgressive models, depending on whether he meant to highlight their oppression or their resistance. In his role as intermediary to the educated, Spanish-speaking world, this stance seemed intentionally drawn so as to clearly distinguish Mayan and ladino cultures, with the aim of securing the ongoing support of various publics who in turn see themselves as contributing to the preservation of "lost" Mayan culture. The problematic nature of this position has already been explored in Chapter 1; in the case of Sna, the group's acceptance of the resulting characterizations of their work seems strategic. In a way, Álvarez's relationship to the group paralleled that of Subcomandante Marcos to the EZLN—the educated, eloquent, Spanish-speaking defender of the cause who follows the directives of the group. (Certainly in collective discussions of play development, the Mayan members were not shy about putting the brakes on Álvarez's more grandiose ideas.)[20] After working with the group for more than fifteen years, Álvarez recently resigned and was replaced by a young ladino writer, Antonio Coello, who perhaps will usher in a new era of intercultural collaboration.[21]

Until recently, decisions about the group were made largely by its male members, with women participating in the process only rarely.[22] This was in part a result of the still strong cultural prohibition against young unmarried women having conversations with men; when it happens on the street, for example, it often results in hurtful gossip about the young woman. Very little in a woman's upbringing prepares her for new ways of male-female interaction in the workplace. At Sna, when all-group meetings are held, the women attend and are encouraged to participate. Meetings are conducted in Spanish, the second language of the members. However, in 1996 several of the women told me they were afraid the men would laugh at their use of Spanish, so they were too embarrassed to say much. (Only one of these women was still a member six years later.) But here the weight of tradition becomes another obstacle: it has been far more common for indigenous women to be monolingual in their mother tongue, because contact with ladinos traditionally has been the domain of men. Many women, then, do not feel as comfortable speaking Spanish as they do their native tongue. The tentacles of tradition are long and tenacious, but the situation is changing, slowly, for women in Sna as well as for other working women. During my last visit to Sna in summer 2002, the president of the organization was Leticia Méndez Intzin, a Tzeltal woman from Tenejapa who brought a strong voice to the collaborations and was extremely effective in introducing women's concerns to the group's recent work.

The first women hired by Sna struggled against a more restrictive environment. That they were able to participate at all was due to the fact that both were single mothers, in need of a way to support their children. In a manner reminiscent of household tensions described above, the tensions within the group produced by the conflict between nascent feminism (although the women might not call it that) and Mayan tradition eventually led to a rupture. Isabel Juárez Espinosa (Tzeltal) and Petrona de la Cruz Cruz (Tzotzil) left Sna for a variety of reasons, almost all of them embedded in the pressure of differential gender role expectations and in their own dissatisfaction with their prescribed roles as (passive) bearers of the Mayan culture. Sna's international exposure was a contributing factor: both women were beginning to be promoted in the international press as Mexico's first indigenous women playwrights,[23] and in 1992 one of them was awarded a prestigious state literary prize—resulting in new speaking engagements and a higher profile in Mexican society than is typically enjoyed by Mayan women or men outside of their own communities. But de la Cruz Cruz's groundbreaking play, *Una mujer desesperada* (A Desperate Woman, 1991), which explored in detail the relationship between rural poverty and domestic violence and offered a scathing critique of the traditional structures of male authoritarianism that prevent women's economic and psychological autonomy, was never staged by Lo'il Maxil. Instead, after the women left, the ladina professional women's organization Grupo de Mujeres in San Cristóbal underwrote its production in 1993.[24]

De la Cruz Cruz and Juárez Espinosa went on to form La Fomma in 1994, developing their all-woman troupe in relative autonomy from their former *compañeros* (associates). In addition to theatre, La Fomma also offers special programs for women and children in literacy, art, health, and nutrition, attracting women who have relocated to San Cristóbal for a variety of reasons, including religious and military persecution. They also run a number of small businesses to help finance their operations and provide job training for their *compañeras:* a small convenience store, a bakery, and a knitting mill constitute their business operations. Some of the women who come to La Fomma are married, some separated, some single. Those with children are free to enroll them in the on-site day care and after-school programs, all of which are funded through a combination of Mexican, U.S., and international grants. Like Lo'il Maxil, Fomma invites U.S. theatre artists such as Amy Trompetter to train the troupe in mask making and puppetry; Trompetter's colleagues Denny Partridge and Patricia Hernandez of Barnard College have also worked with them in developing improvisations and new work. More recently, Doris Difarnecio of INTAR has come, like Ralph Lee (with whom she has worked

Members of La Fomma rehearse a scene from their *El mundo al revés/The World Turned Upside Down*, in their San Cristóbal office-rehearsal-performance space. Photo by Miriam Laughlin, © 1996. Courtesy of Miriam Laughlin.

on other projects), to spend a month each year with the group. Difarnecio's method is to work closely with the women through improvisation to motivate the development of story lines for dramatic expression.[25]

La Fomma's growing repertory treats themes specific to the realities women in indigenous communities face. The earlier plays dealt with alcoholic and abusive spouses, poverty, and the dilemmas confronting campesinos who are forced to make their way in the cities—all from the perspective of their effects on women and children. More recent work has explored women's growing participation in international markets, local politics, and domestic culture, revealing the group's ongoing engagement with women's lives in both the public and private realms. In some cases, the founders have spearheaded the development of new scripts for performance; more often nowadays, the women develop them collectively, and they are written down only after the fact if at all. These plays derive from the women's personal experiences, brought to play-crafting workshops and coaxed into dramatic expression by each other and by their collaborators. While the traveling nature of most of the group's work necessitates that they perform in front of a single generic backdrop (a campesino house), decisions about every aspect of production are made collectively and discussed in minute detail. Costume considerations in particular illustrate the group's sensitivity to the power of representation. Throughout Chiapas and in most of indigenous Mexico, the tradition of using dress to mark community identity remains strong, particularly for women. As in Sna, both Tzotzil and Tzeltal women from different communities make up La Fomma's membership. Whether a La Fomma actor should perform in her native dress is a key decision the group must make. Though the results might be lost on a foreign observer, the women of La Fomma are keenly aware that to wear one's own traditional clothing in performance might suggest that the issues the play explores through her character are specific to her community and do not relate to others. (This, in fact, was one of the objections the Sna men had to staging *Una mujer desesperada;* the men from the title character's hometown were afraid they would be held guilty by association. See note 24.) Thus, in many of the productions I have seen, the actors tend to wear generic clothing to prevent this latter interpretation.

In addition to the collective work of the group, both de la Cruz Cruz and Juárez Espinosa continue to write plays individually. De la Cruz Cruz has been collecting ethnographic material from women in many small communities in the highland region, which she then shapes into plays. She recently received a grant to develop this work dramaturgically with the noted Mexican playwright Hugo Rascón Banda and has also participated in Luis de Tavira's directing workshop.[26] This may bring an interesting new dynamic to the group, as it would introduce a very different approach—the director as auteur—to the group's collective work. At present, one of Juárez Espinosa's plays, *La migración* (Migration), has been published in Spanish; a collaboration between the two, *La desconfiada* (The Insecure Woman), has also appeared in print; and de la Cruz Cruz's *Una mujer desesperada* is at this writing scheduled to appear in an English-language anthology of Latin American women's plays.[27]

La Fomma's reputation both in Mexico and internationally has grown, facilitated by their contacts with U.S. supporters, who have coordinated their participation in women's playwriting symposia and arranged performances and speaking engagements in university settings, usually in conjunction with programs on indigenous political and cultural movements. They and their work have appeared in the United States and as far away as Belgium and Australia.[28] As their reputation has grown, so has their network of potential collaborators: for example, three faculty members from Barnard College spent spring 1998 with the group, conducting workshops in storytelling, puppetwork, mask making, and improvisation. The work is also covered from time to time in the Mexican and U.S. press.[29]

Meanwhile, Sna has also continued to build its profile both at home and abroad. In 1999, for example, the organization hosted the Second Indigenous Meeting of the Americas, which brought together intellectuals, artists, and activists from throughout the hemisphere to share indigenous perspectives on topics that included art, language, culture, religion, biodiversity, health and nutrition, education, mass communication, and indigenous rights.[30] As is true of most cultural organizations, funding is a continual concern, but there are other challenges that are more culture-specific. One is member turnover. Men of the group are often required to serve terms of religious and civil office in their communities and so have to take a leave from the group. It is different for the women, whose reasons for leaving are often family oriented: several who have married during their employment with Sna were expected not to work away from the home and have not returned. For reasons that should be obvious by now, it is easier to recruit men to join Sna or temporarily take a role; the turnover of actresses particularly compromises the repertory, because it limits the kinds of stories that can effectively be told or restaged.

In effect, taken together, the two troupes' joint history has followed the pattern that more and more Mayan marriages have taken: as women have either sought or been forced into more autonomy from men, they have found support by affiliating in networks and cooperatives composed of other women.[31] Moreover, their history shows that ethnicity is neither coterminous with identity nor necessarily its primary component: two women left Sna because the group felt they were not "performing" adequately *as Mayan women;* they went on to form a new theatre collective dedicated to the empowerment, through performance, *of Mayan women.* Analytic models of cultural exchange based purely on ethnicity must also take into account intragroup heterogeneity, and perhaps more important, an understanding of who is empowered *within* the group to make its important decisions. Today, nearly ten years after the original split, the groups remain separate, but Juárez Espinosa spoke at the Sna-sponsored 1999 Indigenous Conference, and de la Cruz Cruz's son, Rogelio, has joined the Lo'il Maxil ensemble as a playwright and performer. His play, *El planeta de cabeza* (Mindplanet), was recently staged in Mexico City.

Although Sna's Lo'il Maxil presents itself as more explicitly concerned with ethnicity than gender, its recent productions have featured more overt explorations of women's issues. If in their promotional materials they present themselves as operating neatly within Bonfil Batalla's favored categories of cultural autonomy (they are a "Mayan," not an "intercultural," organization) and appropriation (they selectively appropriate elements of non-Mayan theatrical tradition to further their own ends), in performance their example further complicates this model. La Fomma, in contrast, more concerned with gender than cultural autonomy, in performance blurs easy distinctions by showing how gender and ethnicity inform each other in their particular place and time. The remainder of this chapter is devoted to an exploration of both groups' recent work that illustrates this point.

Unmasking Local Histories: Lo'il Maxil

Lo'il Maxil's repertory of the 1980s and early 1990s, discussed by Frischmann in his overview essay of 1993,[32] established the group's reputation for staging imaginative re-creations of local legends and oral histories (e.g., *El haragán y el zopilote* [The Loafer and the Buzzard] and *¿A poco hay cimarrones?* [Who Believes in Spooks?]). It also revealed the group's emergent sense of theatre's possibilities for retelling official history from the perspective of Mayan subjectivity (*¡Vamos al paraíso!* and *Antorchas para amanecer* [Torches for a New Dawn]) and for exploring recent current events (*Herencia fatal* [Deadly Inheritance]).

In 1994, a month after the Zapatista uprising, the members of Sna developed a play under Ralph Lee's direction that signaled a new direction for the group, one that moved its scope from the local to the national as it continued to revindicate local epistemologies. That play, *De todos para todos* (From All, For All, 1994) and its functional sequel, *Siempre México con nosotros* (Mexico with Us Forever, 2001), explore the roots of the Zapatista uprising and ongoing challenges to politics-as-usual in post-PRI Mexico. Such productions enjoy uneven popularity and are dependent on the politics of the sponsors of the moment. The former, for example, was widely requested for several years after the uprising; the latter, less popular in the current uncertain political climate, has been staged only a handful of times. The group's continuing emphasis on staging local legends thus helps to ensure its continuity even as it runs the risk of being folkloricized by non-Mayan sponsoring organizations and audiences. *Danza para la vida* (Dance for Life, 1999, based on the *Popul Vuh*) and *Cuando nació el maíz* (When Corn Was Born, 2000) are two recent examples. Interestingly, the latter, based on a legend that explains not only the origin of corn but also how ants came to have segmented bodies, had its U.S. premier in 2001 at La Jolla Playhouse, with U.S. actors under Lee's direction.[33] At present it is one of the group's more requested productions in Mexico as well.

In what follows, I discuss in detail *De todos para todos* and *Siempre México con nosotros* because they represent both the group's performance style and its recent engagement with local and national politics.

"Zapateatro": *De todos para todos*

When we lived in Chiapas in 1996, at the height of the negotiations between the Zapatistas and the federal government, and two years after *De todos para todos* had been written, it was frequently requested by nearby communities and nongovernmental organizations monitoring the peace talks. Labeled a "tragicomedy" and dedicated to "the Mayan and Zoque martyrs fallen in the wars of Chiapas,"[34] *De todos* documents the coming-to-consciousness of a rural community displaced into the jungle by the corruption of local land-grabbers who have illegally bought them out of their ancestral lands; it is an analog, in dramatic form, of the roots of Zapatista rebellion.

The ladinos, costumed in the half-masks of the commedia dell'arte tradition that Lee often employs, are both comic and disturbing. Feigning goodwill, one of them, "Don Pompous," pays a friendly visit to a campesino and his wife. His attitude hardens, however, when he informs them he has written proof that their lands, which the family has occupied for generations, have in fact belonged to *his* family since colonial times. He demands to see the campesinos' "papers," which he knows do not exist. For his part, the campesino has no idea what Don Pompous is talking about, provoking the latter's fact-bending outburst:

You uppity *indio!*[35] I am talking about the deed, because you all came and invaded these lands without my family's permission, and now you're going to have to get off of them. I'm giving you one week's time to harvest what you can, so you can see I'm honest folk.[36]

A male member of Lo'il Maxil portrays a ladina secretary in a 1996 presentation of *De todos para todos* in the central square of San Cristóbal. Photo by author, © 1996.

The campesino's only possible recourse is to visit the local land office, run by an official who in some performances was portrayed by the mask of corrupt former president Carlos Salinas Gortari. (Significantly, this mask was never donned in performances in San Cristóbal, for urban and international audiences, but was reserved for village performances.) His secretary is played by a man in drag (echoing centuries of fiesta performances, in which female parts are almost always played by men in order to lampoon them), with full face mask and blond wig. Although he admits the legitimacy of the farmer Petul's claims, the official is more interested in Don Pompous's bribe money, so he settles the matter by offering Petul and the other campesinos land in the jungle. "Maybe it's because we can't read or write," Petul tells the others, "but this is the only option they gave me."[37] Don Pompous has added further motivation by sending out his "white guards," armed plantation employees who are legendary for terrorizing small landowners and pillaging their crops.

Once relocated in the jungle, the campesinos are foiled again, this time by the spirits of the animals who are angered by the slash-and-burn agricultural methods threatening to displace *them* from their ancestral homes.[38] These spirits consult the Earth Lord to develop another plan.

Here, though the ecological message is serious, the scenes are comic, as each of the animal spirits curries favor with the Earth Lord. This figure, costumed in a monklike robe of green and wearing the full mask of a white man, responds by visiting an epidemic of dysentery on the jungle community. Through a dream, a local shaman is given to understand what is happening and is able to temporarily treat the community through his special powers.

Nevertheless, the people remain caught between the vengeance of the spirits and the power of the ladinos, until they can determine for themselves another way out. They seem without recourse, until one of their members, educated in the city, happens to make a visit to the jungle. Although he is able to read and write in the "language of the oppressor," this character, somewhat reminiscent of the figure of Subcomandante Marcos, recommends the more expedient recourse of calling his compatriots to arms, and the play nears its conclusion with the opening shots of the rebellion. Hearing them, Don Pompous and the land official reveal their cowardice by trying to flee to the cover of the nearby caves. The first to fall in battle is the play's only female character, the campesina lead.[39] But she also brings down a white guard as she dies with the battle cry, "This is a fight from all, for all! Even if it means shedding our blood, we want our children to live with justice!"[40]

With her death, and before the battle can escalate into a full-fledged revolution, the characters onstage freeze, and the Earth Lord intervenes with his own plea:

> Earth creatures! Stop this killing! Let no more blood be spilled! Don't you see that you are all brothers? If you wish to live happily on Earth, you must learn to respect each other, and to join together as brothers, and to respect as well the animals and plants. May the great Spirit of the Sun light the way to true peace, if this you do![41]

The play's final moment sounds a deeply negotiatory tone, itself reflecting the uneasy truce that at the time was still being negotiated by the Zapatistas and the federal government. "Long live the fight for indigenous peoples!" is immediately followed by "Long live Chiapas!" which in turn is followed by the Chiapas state anthem. Framed between the Earth Lord's call for brotherhood and the state hymn, the "fight for indigenous peoples" is presented as both revolutionary and patriotic rather than as sectarian, in keeping with the play's title.

De todos para todos represents the difficulties posed by both the facts of life for indigenous peoples in Chiapas and an armed response to these realities: it reflects the same ambivalence that was manifest in the uneasy truce that was operative at the time and which has since been halted. Each performance registers this ambivalence, and the performers must carefully calculate the risks involved. In summer 1996, for example, when the play was staged in indigenous communities, the rebel characters wore the Zapatistas' signature red bandannas. In San Cristóbal (a key site of the original Zapatista uprising) and in the state capital of Tuxtla Gutiérrez (where the play took the state prize for regional theatre), they did not. Clearly, the group changed the degree of overt political resistance in the performance depending on its place, location, and likely audience.[42] Audience response confirmed this strategy. In the villages, the Salinas mask never failed to draw great laughter from the crowds, but this comic bit would be sacrificed in the authority- and ladino-dominated urban centers, where to perform it this way would be to run the risk of an armed attack by PRI supporters. Nevertheless, ladino power is simultaneously staged and subverted through the players' use of masks, drag, and an exaggerated sing-song Spanish: as in much of the Lo'il Maxil repertory, the ladino men are represented as greedy, lustful, corrupt, and cowardly; the women as crude, obsessed with their appearance and with the opposite sex. In contrast, Mayan men and women are portrayed as pragmatic, wise, and brave. These images may be stereotypical and Manichaean, but they challenge the normative representational practices of the Mexican media, which is largely content to leave ladinos unmarked and to overdetermine the representation of indigenous people as exotic, socially underdeveloped, or dangerously revolutionary. By making their own representational choices, the troupe is deploying essentialism strategically.

The Earth Lord is a particularly complex figure in this latter representational practice that, in the context of zapatismo, merits a closer reading. Visually, he is a quotation of the early Spanish missionaries who furthered the aims of conquest; functionally, he is a symbol of authority that predated the arrival of the Europeans. To the troupe members, the figure represents power, and according to Lee, who originally advocated what he calls a "more indigenous look," the troupe members preferred to see the Earth Lord as a green-robed white man.[43] Lee and I speculated, initially, that the Earth Lord was, like many Mexican saints, the syncretic product of Mayan and Catholic mythology, but the figure turns out to be more complicated. For when he appears in a later play, *Cuando nació el maíz,* he does so not as a sixteenth-century friar but as a contemporary

The Earth Lord consults with the animals in *De todos para todos,* San Cristóbal de las Casas, 1996. Photo by author, © 1996.

ladino of some means—dressed in a sombrero, a pair of modern pants, and a neat cardigan sweater.

As Sna president Leticia Méndez Intzin put it, "No one has ever seen an Earth Lord," but they appear often in dreams, and, as confirmed in numerous anthropological accounts, they share certain distinguishing features.[44] Forces for both good (they bring rain, fertility, and wealth) and bad (they enslave their inferiors), they are among the few "totally non-Catholic" supernatural figures widely believed in by Chiapan Mayans—and they are always presented as ladinos. According to the anthropologist Brenda Rosenbaum, Earth Lords are often conceived and portrayed as blond, fair-skinned ladino couples. Such figures "represent transformations of the ancient Earth deity that occurred as white intruders appropriated the indigenous lands, which symbolize sustenance and wealth for Chamulas. . . . They express the power that Ladinos hold over material resources [and] the imposition of Ladino power over the Earth Mother."[45]

If Rosenbaum's interpretation is correct, the Lo'il Maxil Earth Lord reflects more than a simple synthesis of two traditions. Offstage, the Earth Lord may represent an imposition of ladino power, a symbol that is now a fairly accurate depiction of indigenous reality, as if to say "Our gods no longer rule here." In that sense, it is "authentic." Inserted where and how it is in *De todos para todos,* however, it becomes charged with a new kind of agency, one that will bring the end of revolution and the beginning of justice.

The Struggle Continues: *Siempre México con nosotros*

Six years after the Zapatista uprising, Mexico elected its first non-PRI president. But the fight for indigenous peoples called for in *De todos para todos* was, as it still is, far from resolution. In the year the new president took office, Sna developed a new play, under Michael Garcés's direction, that elaborated the critique begun in *De todos para todos.* As its title suggests, *Siempre México con nosotros* demands indigenous inclusion in the new, post-PRI Mexico.[46] It does so through a penetrating exploration of one of the PRI's most troublesome and tenacious legacies: the system of political *cacicazgo.* According to Hernández Castillo, cacicazgo "refers to the consolidated bases of economic and political power presided over by *caciques* (Mafia-style bosses)."[47] The system predates the Mexican Revolution, but under the PRI's one-party rule since then, corrupt caciques represented the local extension of an unbroken party power line from nation to state to village.

The play takes place in one such village, in the highlands of Chiapas. In a production staged in the patio of La Fomma's offices,[48] the playing area and audience area together constituted the village setting: actors emerged from the audience to answer the call of a community organizer to a town meeting, implicating the rest of the audience—including many international visitors—in the action that followed.

This action occurs over ten scenes that anatomize power dynamics within cacicazgo. As scene follows scene, a newly elected municipal president grows ever more corrupt, greedy, and violent. He makes promises he never keeps; bribes municipal agents to support him; falsifies congressional reports to hide the fact that he has pocketed money intended for public works projects; sends some of this money back up the political ladder to his party superiors, with whom he is embarrassingly ingratiating; surrounds himself with menacing bodyguards who terrorize the locals; pacifies these same locals with lies, more promises, and the liberal distribution of soft drinks and alcohol; and has his henchmen ambush his political opponents, going so far as to murder one of them. In the end, several of the villagers are able to provide proof of his perfidy, he is carted off to jail, and a new president of an independent party is appointed by general consensus.

Scene from Lo'il Maxil's *Siempre México con nosotros,* San Cristóbal de las Casas, 2001. Photo by Juan de la Torre López, © 2001. Courtesy of Sna Archives.

The play closes with a powerful epilogue, in which each actor articulates a plank in the platform for human rights in a new Mexico. They include calls for democracy and justice generally, with individual rights under the Mexican constitution. For women, they demand the right to work, to inherit property, to hold religious and civil office, to education and self-expression. They urge a culture of respect for the rights of children to grow up healthy, happy, and learning productively. They call for the preservation and promotion of indigenous rights and culture and argue against the advance of foreign culture in the region. They advocate worker's rights and the right to a bilingual education, with priority given to the mother tongue. They call for local autonomy and argue against state control of resources (an implicit criticism of the Indigenous Rights Bill as passed). They call for an end to racism and proclaim indigenous culture as a source both of ethnic pride and of national development. They ask, in short, that they be taken into account, that there always be a Mexico with, not against, them.

Several aspects of this text and its production help it to escape the confines of a didactic political theatre that relies for its impact on strictly drawn binary oppositions between, say, a bad government and a good people. First, Manuel, the new president, starts out as a basically decent man with honorable intentions, even if that "decency" is marked by a certain casual sexism both toward his wife, whom he dominates from the start, and within the male-bonding drinking rituals he shares with his party superior—a sexism the production seems at pains to point out. He is quickly seduced by his new access to power and wealth and, as the play goes on, increasingly drawn into the party machine, from which he cannot extricate himself. Not that he ever really wants to; the play suggests that once tempted, forever damned, by the seductions of position under the old regime. The hope in this play comes not from his repentance and redemption but from the action—and mercy—of the people, who initially would like to lynch him in revenge but eventually come to see that such an act would only perpetuate the cycle. They opt for legal justice and nonparty governance as a way to break it.

Second, like almost all of Sna's productions, the play features judicious use of humor and suggestive theatrical devices to leaven its message as it furthers it. Crowd scenes feature individual actors carrying four extra puppet heads arranged along horizontal rods, to suggest not only numbers but also the herd instinct that allows the community to be too easily persuaded. In another scene, the candidate Manuel gets so carried away by his own rhetoric that he starts promising things like a new bridge, though there is no river in the community. In the same campaign speech, he promises toys for children who, the villagers remind each other, are too weak from hunger to play with them, or worse. Later, after he becomes president, he dyes his hair light brown to look more like the ladino state politician (played in this case by a visiting artist from Tabasco), who in turn mocks his new look. This use of humor and Brechtian theatrical devices has long been important to Sna's work, not only to provide comic relief and space for reflection, but also because humor especially, says Robert Laughlin, "is the way the Mayas have dealt with their victimization."[49] (Of course, as history has shown, it is not the only way, but it is of central importance.)

Third, as suggested in the crowd scenes, community complicity is also a target of this play's critique. The villagers are shown as being as easily manipulated by the community organizer who is trying to start an independent party as they are by the rhetoric of the official party against whom he rails. Their credulity and the ease with which they can be swayed, born in part of hope in the face of despair, disappoint the community activist; yet this character's existence proves the community has also produced men and women capable of thinking for themselves, in whom the promise of the future resides.

Finally, the "nosotros" (us) in this play, despite the male gendering of the word in the title, includes women in a way and to a degree that few earlier Lo'il Maxil productions can claim.[50] A range of women and their concerns are central to its action. Manuel's wife, Maruch, a traditional woman who kneels on the floor when he takes the only available chair and submits when he tells her that politics is "a matter for men," does so only after she pointedly asks him why he has to conduct his business with the party behind closed doors. Among the villagers he allegedly represents is a young mother of five whose husband has abandoned her, and who, over the course of the play, will lose her youngest to an illness that could easily have been treated had he built the medical clinic he had promised. Another is a member of a women's artisan cooperative, Xunka', who from the start mistrusts Manuel. As she tries to represent the cooperative's concerns to him during his campaign, he interrupts her, saying "Yes, yes. . . . We'll also take the women into account, but we'll see about that later." To which Xunka', furious, responds: "Ay! They never let us talk! They always treat us like that. They don't take us into account!"[51] But the play itself does, in both the domestic and the public sphere of their lives. Further, it clearly links gender politics to national politics by suggesting Manuel's sexism is part and parcel of his (and by extension the whole party's) general corruption.

Still, if *Siempre México con nosotros* suggests that women's issues are beginning to be taken more seriously by Lo'il Maxil and Sna Jtz'ibajom, such concerns are not yet central to the repertory and likely will continue to be incorporated in more general explorations of cultural preservation vis-à-vis the contemporary sociopolitical situation. For the women of La Fomma, on the other hand, the concerns of Mayan women in Chiapas are both the ends of their dramatic explorations and the means by which the group examines and critiques the contemporary sociopolitical situation.

La Fomma: Gendering Neoliberalism

Although the plays that La Fomma has developed are relentless in their exploration of women's issues, they rarely point a finger only at men as the source of women's difficulties. Instead, they more often target the global economic context that forces men to work away from home, in low-paying jobs, for unsympathetic bosses—a situation that is often abusive and always anxiety producing, and which deeply affects the relations and interactions between men and women at home. Another recent strain of the group's dramaturgy uses theatre to help educate women about how to protect their concerns and their children's in this environment; and yet another strain celebrates women's ways and wisdom in communities in which these ways are under stress as the communities themselves fragment.

The plays exploring the effects of neoliberal economic policies on women and children include Juárez Espinosa's *La migración* (1994) and the collective works *La vida de las juanas* (Life of the Juanas, 1998) and *Víctimas del engaño* (Victims of Deceit, 1999).[52] All three show how such policies, which have forced many indigenous men to supplement subsistence farming with migrant work and unskilled labor in the cities, have especially negative trickle-down effects on women and children.

La migración, for example, explores the plight of the family of Catalina, Carlos, and their young daughter, who have relocated to the city where Carlos has decided to follow the example of his friend Mario, a delivery truck driver. Though Catalina would rather stay behind and work their land, as she has been doing while Carlos has sought work intermittently in the city, Carlos rails against her: "You have to go wherever I go, whether you want to or not! As for the land, if I want to sell it, I'll sell it, because it's mine!"[53] No sooner do they arrive in the city, where Carlos rents a few small rooms on Mario's credit, than Carlos loses his job in a general layoff. And here in the city, Mario's friendship amounts to nothing: he has his own job to protect. Thus, with no available options and no marketable skills, Carlos turns to drink. His drunken attempts to find work only compound his humiliation, which peaks when his former friend evicts him from their meager rooms. (Actually, Mario's wife does—"on his orders.") The play ends on a dismal note. The family is homeless in city and country alike, Carlos's only prospect piecemeal work as a bricklayer; Catalina's, work as a domestic servant.

In this play, the villains are not ladinos but ladino values, embodied in the character of Mario. Even though he is Mayan, he speaks the language of the oppressor; he works delivering the merchandise circulating in the era of free trade; not only has he forgotten his traditional loyalties, but, as Catalina puts it, he now "lives off the sweat of his friends."[54] His tragedy may be as great as Carlos's, but Juárez Espinosa clearly reserves her sympathy for the women. Of the three—Catalina, her friend, Lucía, and Mario's wife, Elena—only Lucía is able to maintain a degree of agency in her marriage. Her husband, unlike Catalina's, listens when she objects to moving to the city; but it is also clear that her husband was already inclined to agree with her. Even Elena, who is privileged economically in the play, is forced to do her husband's dirty work against her own friends. Given this kind of gender dynamic to begin with, the

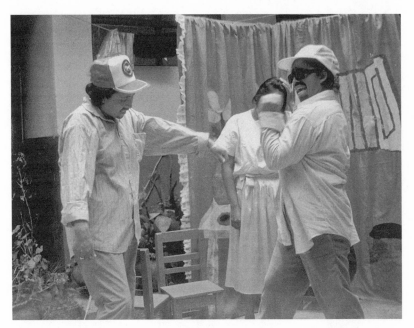

Scene from *La migración*, San Cristóbal de las Casas, 1996. Photo by author, © 1996.

additional pressures on rural families in neoliberalism's wake have particular consequences for women and children. In its disruptive effects on families and communities, the play suggests, neoliberalism has much in common with colonialism.

La vida de las Juanas features another group of "migrants," this time women, all named Juana. Thinking to better their situation through education and work, they exchange their traje for urban attire and head for the city. Once there, their paths divide. One finds work in a governmental office, where she witnesses the sloth of her boss who takes advantage of his bureaucratic position to watch boxing on television and to obsess over his paycheck. Another "Juana" is swindled by two employees of a store who take advantage of her unfamiliarity with the going prices for the goods she purchases. A third "Juana" is humiliated and abused when she seeks work as a domestic servant. In an autobiographical twist, the three come together to form an organization that operates bread-baking and sewing enterprises—and makes theatre. Aleyda Aguirre Rodríguez suggested that here the five women of La Fomma "act out what before they could only suffer and weep over."[55]

It is a powerful and concise acting out, from the title of the play to its

Scene from La Fomma's *La vida de las Juanas,* San Cristóbal de las Casas, 1999.
Photo by Miriam Laughlin, © 1999. Courtesy of Miriam Laughlin.

celebratory close, twenty minutes later. The life (singular) of the Juanas
(plural "Janes," as in the English "Jane Doe") points to an exploration
of contemporary reality from the perspective of a kind of Mayan every-
woman. But it is not Juana, Woman, transcendent above history, but
Juanas, women, precisely located in history, that are the subject of this
play. And it is their collectivity and commitment to act on their own behalf—both materially in the market and representationally on the stage—
that promises a better future.

The final "migration" play I wish to discuss, *Víctimas del engaño,* is
perhaps the most complex of the three. Here, another young husband,
Pedro, is lured to the city from his rural village by the same kind of character and for the same reasons as Carlos in *La migración.* This time, however, the wife refuses to accompany her husband, suspecting the promises
are empty. For a time she is proved right, but in this play, the husband
eventually sets up another household in the city under a false name and
becomes very prosperous by helping to manage his new wife's bakery
business. Meanwhile, circumstances back in the village deteriorate for his
first wife, who has heard (and received) nothing from him since he left.
The couple's land is left untended, as the need to care for her small chil-

dren compromises her ability both to work the land and to seek wage-earning work. The play ends with the new couple planning to convert their house into a retail outlet for the new wife's cakes, in the process providing themselves with a steadier source of increased income and jobs for more of the barrio's unemployed. Meanwhile, the first wife's plight is left unresolved.

Like most of La Fomma's work, this piece explores the effects of social policy and changing economic conditions on women and children, but it is less content to draw easy distinctions between right and wrong, good and bad, victim and victimized. Although it is true that in this piece the male characters are the only ones who practice deception, women are not the only victims of deceit, and three of them—the second wife, a potential employer of the first, and a friend of the latter's in the village—are presented as strong women, self-employed and therefore not dependent on male support. (In fact, for much of the play the second wife supports her husband—a startling image in Mexico, whose film and television industries seem largely content to portray gendered power relations along much more traditional lines.) And the character of the errant husband is compassionately drawn, despite his bigamy. (It is not uncommon for men of all stations to maintain more than one household in Mexico, but it is not formally sanctioned and women do not necessarily accept such arrangements with equanimity.)

Víctimas deals only briefly with the root causes that send people away from their home communities. But for the wife who stays behind, life is not as rosy as it seems to be for those who stay behind in *La migración*. Further, when the husband runs into trouble in the city, there is always someone of goodwill to provide the next meal or bed. In a key scene, the husband deludes himself into believing that under his false name he has won a National Bank–sponsored sweepstakes for a new house. His disappointment on learning the truth motivates him to stop depending on his new wife and to start contributing to the material good of the new household. But the good news of this ending scene—the new couple facing a better future together based on their hard work and not on the charity of the National Bank—is undermined by the disturbing images of the wife left behind in the village to face an uncertain future with her children. Times are hard in the pueblo, especially for a woman alone with children, and the play text does not shrink from presenting this. It is not concerned to valorize the joys of subsistence living according to the old ways; tellingly, before he left, Pedro had supplemented their farming income with handwoven sombreros to sell to tourists. Instead, it is almost Brechtian

Scene from La Fomma's *Échame la mano*, San Cristóbal de las Casas, 2001.
Photo by Patricia Hernandez, © 2001. Courtesy of La Fomma Archives.

in its ambiguity, in its unwillingness to take clear sides on the issue of whether to stay or go, to distinguish the deceivers from the deceived.

In *Échame la mano y te pagaré* (Lend me a Hand and I'll pay you later, 2001)[56] the dangers of entering the international tourist market for handicrafts are explored. It is based on events that happened at the Santo Domingo market in San Cristóbal: a foreign ladina took a large number of weavings from a local artisan, promising to sell them in her country and to provide payment when she next visited Chiapas, which in fact she did. The artisan, made eager by this promising demonstration of income potential, gathered her friends, and together they provided the ladina with a large number and variety of handmade goods. This time, however, the foreign woman did not return, and the women were not paid. Together, the women of La Fomma dramatized this story, adding some lessons that argued for more formality in business dealings, upfront payments from middlemen, the keeping of better business records, and the formation of cooperatives for protection and growth. When a representative from a local savings and credit association happened to see one of the group's San Cristóbal performances, the association financed a regional tour to many communities throughout the highlands.

Here, theatre becomes a means of communicating to large numbers of women some of the risks of entering world markets for their artisanry in order to ease the financial burdens of their families. It does not simply reflect the realities but also provides important guidance, liberally dosed with humor (e.g., the lampooning of the ladina, played by de la Cruz Cruz in a short blond wig). Humor is a key element of the group's recent work, motivated not only by their collaboration with U.S. artists but also by the work itself. When they come together to brainstorm about story lines and scene development, Doris Difarnecio suggested to me, the women tend toward the comedic and the satirical: they have a tendency to find the absurdity in the logic that is supposed to order their lives. Though the earlier plays were less leavened by a lighter touch, they were no less effective for that: melodrama has a long history of effectiveness with popular audiences, serving both normalizing and revolutionary impulses.

Another recent strain in the women's work is a deeper exploration of women's ways of being together and the age-old work they do within increasingly fragmented communities. One example is *La locura de co-madres* (literally, The Madness of Comadres, women whose bonds are social but as strong as blood ties; but it is meant lightheartedly, more in the sense of "Crazy Comadres," akin to "Divine Secrets of the Ya Ya Sisterhood.") It is a gentle but firm call for women to celebrate the traditions they create in the performance of their daily tasks, which require ever more redefinition as societies cease to cohere. As Nash has written about such societies, the bound corporative communities that used to serve so well as objects for anthropological fieldwork are being decimated by religious and political conflicts and increasing economic pressures that result in emigration and drug trafficking.[57] It is often left to women to find a way to keep the social fabric together under these circumstances, and again La Fomma urges coming together, comadreship, and sorority as key to meeting the challenge.

That the concerns of these women is a matter of culture as well as gender is explored in *La conchita desenconchada* (Conchita Comes Out of Her Shell, 2001; the title a play on words that English does not capture). It challenges the notion that so-called traditional societies respect their elders more than technologized societies and links elder abuse to gender abuse and cultural alienation. In *Conchita desenconchada,* an old woman burns the beans one day and is thrown out of her son-in-law's house. She manages to make her way to the city, where her son owns a shoestore, but she fares no better with him: he is ashamed not only of her but also of the family he left behind and the culture they represent. His daughter, however, is intrigued by this, and when her *abuela* (grandmother) uses her knowledge to cure her granddaughter's illness, the latter earns a new

Scene from La Fomma's *Conchita desenconchada*, Jolnajojtík, Chiapas, 2001.
Photo by Robert Laughlin, © 2001. Courtesy of La Fomma Archives.

respect for the ways of her abuela. She offers her grandmother a home
and offers the audience a glimpse of intergenerational sorority that is tied
to cultural preservation. Lest the reader think this is a conservative bow
to cultural nostalgia, consider the last scene—in which Conchita is portrayed learning to drive her granddaughter's car. Neither tradition nor
the bearers of it, the play suggests, can stay still for long.

Offstage, many Mayan women already play roles in tourist dramas:
working at their looms or washing clothes at the river, native women
dressed in ribboned braids and embroidered traje have long been a favorite tourist photo opportunity and travel poster subject. In this environment, the portrayal of native women driving cars and participating in
global tourist economies is significant, as is their performance of all the
male parts their scripts require. When they assume these roles, they do

not do so as a drag quotation of male stereotypes. Born of a necessity created by the all-female composition of the group and played so as not to detract from the plays' serious themes, the cross-gender casting nevertheless presents a startling set of images in a culture in which few women are seen in public performances at all, and in which, during fiesta performances, their roles are traditionally played by men for exaggerated comic effect.[58]

Both organizationally and representationally, then, women of La Fomma have opted for a model of gender autonomy and selective alliance with certain outsiders like Difarnecio; in matters of creative control, each member has an equal voice in the final outcome. Symbolically, their performance as men in many plays reverses cross-gender casting traditions not only in fact but also in style. Onstage, they are able to reclaim for themselves a whole performance tradition that has historically worked to mock and exclude them. Given the pressures on indigenous women in this area to be neither seen nor heard, and the ongoing suspicion (shared by many other cultures as well) that actresses and prostitutes are one and the same thing, this is no small achievement.

EXAMINED SEPARATELY or together, the work of La Fomma and Lo'il Maxil has radical potential. Further, such an examination supports the logic of a spatial rather than temporal metaphor for approaching cross-cultural exchange. Contemporary power relations in Mexican society in general and in Chiapas in particular are now being contested by indigenous groups and by women, both of whom have traditionally been denied access to social, educational, artistic, and economic resources. As the example of both groups illustrates, theatre has become an important site for this contestation to be articulated, both onstage and off.

Because of their high national and international profile and their relationships with non-Mexican anthropologists and artists, both groups have acquired a certain stature and measure of approval in Mexico. Lo'il Maxil in particular is frequently held up as an exemplar of "Mayan theatre" by Mexican cultural ambassadors to the rest of the world. La Fomma too was recently the main feature of a special cultural supplement to the Mexican daily *La Jornada,* in which Ximena Bedregal wrote,

While reflectors illuminate the just dreams proclaimed aloud by ski masks, weapons, wars, commanders, laws of social behavior and militants of the latest new order—silently, invisibly, and peacefully, in a corner of San Cristóbal de las Casas, a group of Indian women is making a noise that few might hear, but that changes the very core of the being and power of many women, by creating scenarios which few attend but where unknown powers are cultivated that no political or military defeat could force into retreat.[59]

In their achievement of such stature and acceptance, both groups run the risk that their work will become circumscribed by the cultural frameworks in which they operate, with every act of resistance subject to co-optation by the powers that be. There is also the risk that they become the latest indigenous cultural "illuminati," a concern one editor raised about their growing visibility on the world stage.[60] But, as Eric van Young has suggested in his review of rural and popular theatre movements in Mexico, much depends on "the respective viewpoints of historical subject and observer."[61] This is a particularly difficult moment for the historical subjects involved in producing this theatre, especially when they stage work that is overtly political.

Through their alliances with other Mexican and international organizations, both groups have found ways, as Grossberg puts it, to "interpellate fractions of the 'empowered' into the struggle for change."[62] Further, theatre has proven to be empowering for many of the women who have chosen to work with both groups. La Fomma members report that their experience with the group has opened the world for them. "I had thought I would always lead a tragic life," said one. "Acting showed me a new way to live." Another said that before she came to La Fomma, she was afraid to talk. Through La Fomma, another came to overcome her shyness enough to confront her drunken husband.[63] This kind of growth was also experienced by at least one Sna actress, Maruch Sántiz Gómez, whose relationship to the troupe was at times difficult and who left the troupe to pursue her work in photography elsewhere.[64] She has gone on to become one of Mexico's most well known indigenous photographers, but while she was a member of Sna, her work with the troupe had been an ongoing source of friction between her and her father. His belief that her work was morally suspect erupted at times into violence and abuse. At last she confronted him, and her story speaks to the power of theatre as a transformative practice: "I used to be very timid, very fearful. But as an actress, I learned how to use my voice better. When I spoke with my father, it wasn't with anger, but yes, he listened."[65]

For women as well as for men, the discipline of the theatre itself can work for change within a culture as well as in the larger world in which it presents itself.

WHEN A SON is born to an indigenous family in Chiapas, tradition holds
that a chicken be killed and a feast prepared. When a daughter is born,
she is given a tortilla as a symbol of what she will spend her life pre-
paring. Between the cooking fire and the loom, a woman's path seems
tightly circumscribed, at least by lore and custom. I want to close this
chapter with a poem, developed collectively by the women of La Fomma,
that provides, at least dramatically, an alternative tradition. It appears in
a play that illuminates the dark side of the tradition romanticized in discourses like the billboard I discussed at the start. *Crecí con el amor de mi
madre* (I Was Raised with My Mother's love, 2001) is a defiant, exuber-
ant critique and celebration that blends satire and poetry to address the
deprecation of women (two of its scenes are titled "When it's a girl, there
is no chicken") and to celebrate their reality, their very existence, in the
face of this disdain. The poem, titled "Rezo de la partera" (The Midwife's
Prayer), occurs early in the play and welcomes a new little girl—another
Juana—to the world of women, men, and the animal spirits that accompany them (*naguales*). I want to reiterate that in this part of the world,
to stage the scene of birth is itself radical and to suggest that women's
experiences as mothers, midwives, and daughters are worthy of dramatic
exploration is even more so, in a larger society where they are routinely
objectified when they are not ignored. This little Juanita may not have her
ritual feast, but here, in this play, she is celebrated and protected by her
mother, her midwife, and the community of women who surround her.

Welcome to this house, to this blessed earth; in her will you pass your
  youth, until you become a woman.
Your heart will be a warrior, curious and strong like the *nagual* of your
  birth. You will fly, enjoying everything that surrounds you, lovely
  butterfly.
Your heart is happy, you carry there the fruit of your belly, which
  flowers like the blossom of corn.
You will be like a goddess full of strength, carried in the footsteps of
  your handsome *nagual*.
Do not allow them to cut your wings: fly over all obstacles and smile in
  your cherished dreams.
Your head held high, you will go forward with steady eyes and firm
  steps.[66]

CHAPTER 3.

Transculturation in the Work of Laboratorio de Teatro Campesino e Indígena

GIVEN THE HISTORY of twentieth-century rural and campesino theatre movements in Mexico, one might expect a group called Laboratorio de Teatro Campesino e Indígena (LTCI), or Farmworker and Indigenous Theatre Laboratory, to have pursued an agenda of theatre for social ends, performed for or with local farmers and their families, aimed at the concerns of small communities in the Mexican countryside. Although this work is part of its activities, it is a small part overall. The term "Laboratorio" provides an equally good clue to the group's work and working methods, calling to mind the experimentation of such artists as Jean-Louis Barreault, Eugenio Barba, Jerzy Grotowski, and Peter Brook, whose theatre laboratories and intercultural work originated in part to urge theatre back to a ritual, performative essence, removed from historicity. But this comparison will only take us so far. If there is a desire in the work of this troupe to recapture a performative essence, it is not a universal, transhistorical one but a specifically local, Mayan aesthetic that combines elements of pre- and postcontact practices. Further, its theatrical explorations of non-Mayan texts, including canonical works from the European tradition, make it an intercultural theatre that is unique in Mexico. The notion of transculturation is useful as a basis for examining the Laboratorio's work, because it offers a theoretical space in which the characteristics of intercultural exchange can be explored in their rich complexity, preventing overreliance on stable categories of culture at the same time that it recognizes elements of cultural specificity.[1]

The Laboratorio's appeals to an authentic indigenous past, I argue, mask a more radical agenda of transculturation in the sense that Ortiz and Taylor recommend it. I begin my discussion with a brief history of the troupe's development, then examine several productions and play texts as examples of its working methods, philosophy, and style and survey the varied reception to its work. The example of the Laboratorio de Teatro Campesino e Indígena presents an alternative set of experiences and practices that shed further light not only on indigenous and Mayan theatre in Mexico but also on available definitions of "intercultural theatre" as it has been discussed and critiqued in European and U.S. theatrical discourses.

The instability of the term "culture" itself produces a lack of consensus about what "intercultural theatre" means for theatre scholars and practitioners. Patrice Pavis, recognizing this, has attempted to delineate its contours by exploring the way in which cultures combine theatrically to produce various permutations—ranging from the precultural through the intracultural to the transcultural, ultracultural, postcultural, and metacultural—and has distinguished six forms of theatrical interculturalism.[2] This precision of terminology nevertheless cannot account sufficiently for its subject, because it remains bound to a notion of interculturalism that keeps as its center the theatrical practices of professional artists from Europe and the United States. Thus, Pavis's use of the word "transcultural" results in a definition that is almost the opposite of the one I cited above. Because Pavis draws his definition from the work of the director Peter Brook, he sees the transcultural in theatre as that which, "indeed, transcends particular cultures on behalf of a universality of the human condition"; directors of this type of theatre are at great pains to remove from their work any traces of cultural specificity at all.[3] In this view, and indeed in Pavis's reader itself, the perspectives of specific, historically underrecognized groups are given short shrift. Fortunately, a growing body of criticism is helping to specify circumstances of intercultural theatre production that originate in areas traditionally considered "other" to the European-American experience, and my discussion of the Laboratorio de Teatro Campesino e Indígena is meant to add one more example to this body of work.[4]

Tabascan Origins

The Laboratorio de Teatro Campesino e Indígena—a loose network of theatre troupes originating in Tabasco and with units in other states to the north and east—has built an international reputation by performing plays by such authors as Shakespeare, García Lorca, and Aristophanes, in addition to works from well-known Mexican playwrights such as Elena Garro and Sergio Magaña and, more recently, pieces they have developed themselves. In Mexico this reputation is equal parts fame and infamy; public opinions about their work have varied widely but are never lukewarm and have as much to do with deeply felt issues of cultural identity as with matters of aesthetic concern. For as its name suggests, the work of the Laboratorio de Teatro Campesino e Indígena has been as intercultural as it is indigenous, and therein lies the source of much of the controversy that has surrounded its history from its earliest days in Tabasco.

Tabasco is a small, oil- and water-rich state on Mexico's Gulf coast, on the western border of the Yucatán Peninsula. Two indigenous groups, the Chontales and the Choles, both of Mayan origin, share a long history in the region. Together, they comprise more than 10 percent of the state's population.[5] Although both groups have always maintained "traditional" community organization and fishing-agricultural lifestyles, it has not been uncommon for their presence to be ignored, even to the extent that there were official "declarations that 'indios' no longer existed in Tabasco."[6]

Like all indigenous groups throughout Mexico, the Choles and Chontales were subjected to strong pressures for integration and assimilation in the years following the Mexican Revolution. In the 1920s and 1930s, for example, then-Governor Tomás Garrido implemented educational reforms aimed at "castellanizing"—making Spanish—the native Tabascan population.[7] In addition, during this period indigenous peoples of Tabasco were enjoined from wearing their traditional dress and trained to adopt mechanized methods of agriculture, as part of the process of "de-Indianization" noted by Bonfil Batalla. As a result, on the surface it appears that there are "no indios" in Tabasco: indigenous populations seem to have been successfully assimilated into the mestizo-campesino class. No one wears traditional traje, and one is hard pressed to find native speakers of Chol or Chontal. However, the traditional languages did not die out; as Laboratorio maestros discovered, many elders as well as many of the younger generation have remained fluent, although it is necessary to develop trust within the communities before they are willing to share this fact.[8]

So, despite efforts aimed at eliminating them, according to the anthropologist Rubén Vera Cabrera, many indigenous groups continued to practice traditional customs, while others took selective advantage of integrationist programs to improve their living conditions. Still, Chontales and Choles of Tabasco, like their indigenous counterparts in all of Mexico, suffer from ongoing governmental and, more recently, corporate privatizing efforts to deprive them of their best lands and their ancestral territories.[9]

The discovery of petroleum brought prosperity to Tabasco and indeed to all of Mexico in the 1970s and with it, significant changes in the Chol and Chontal regions: oil work came to replace fishing and agriculture (which were threatened anyway from environmental pollution from the oil industry); youths migrated from the farms to the oil fields; and income distribution grew ever more uneven. However, as Vera Cabrera also points out, these "aggressions against Chontal culture" have been mitigated to some exent:

> [S]tate and federal development programs [are designed to] support basic self-subsistence, schools for children and literacy projects for adults. Similarly, they emphasize the construction of roads, housing, the improvement of health and a strong impulse toward rescuing its cultural traditions; all this at the community organizational level and the participation as such in the process of autonomous development.[10]

It was as part of this emphasis on community development, during the administration of Tabascan governor Enrique Gonzáles Pedrero, that the Laboratorio de Teatro Campesino e Indígena came about. In 1983 the prominent novelist Julieta Campos, the governor's wife, was in charge of the state's family services programs.[11] She hoped to establish a theatre component aimed specifically at community development in a program initially reminiscent of some of the Cultural Missionary work of the 1940s and 1950s. Toward this end, she solicited the assistance of María Alicia Martínez Medrano, a well-known theatre director.

Martínez Medrano had built a reputation adapting the techniques of Stanislavsky and Meyerhold (as introduced to Mexico through the Japanese director Seki Sano)[12] in theatre workshops for campesinos and campesinas and other workers in Michoacán and Yucatán since the early 1970s. Campos wanted Martínez to organize similar workshops in Tabasco to help campesino communities throughout the state develop plays based on social and family themes. Martínez Medrano had other ideas.

In 1983 she and a team of graduates of her Yucatán theatre workshops came to Tabasco and conducted a statewide survey of communities to determine whether they wished, as a community, to participate in Campos's program. Backed by a virtual blank check from Campos, the team was able to offer free workshops to children, youth, and any adults who could spare the time. Oxolotán, a small pueblo of approximately fifteen hundred residents located several hours from the capital of Villahermosa, was the first to agree, in May 1983; by July six other small communities throughout the state formed a network of LTCI troupes.[13]

According to an early public report, in each community the teams pursued four broad objectives:

1) To develop teachers, actors, directors, producers, dancers, scenic designers, musicians, and other theatre workers;

2) To recover theatrical values in indigenous and campesino towns and communities;

3) To build a theatrical repertoire;

4) To participate in national and international presentations and conferences in theatre.[14]

Students followed a three-year program consisting of twenty-two courses of study, including acting, voice, diction, memorization, text analysis, genre study, playwriting, dance, Meyerholdian biomechanics, pantomime, stage makeup, costuming, production, music, theatre history, Tabascan and Mexican history, and the study of indigenous cultures throughout Mexico. In the first four years of its existence, LTCI graduated more than 2,200 students, and since then that number has grown to more than 17,000 nationwide in five "generations" of alumni, many of whom have gone on to lead other Laboratorios in urban and rural settings throughout Mexico. As Martínez Medrano once told me, her life's goal is to spread the Laboratorio system "throughout the world."[15]

From the beginning, the Laboratorio avoided didactic works on social problems. Instead, it produced the works of well-known Mexican playwrights (including Garro's *La dama boba*); García Lorca's *Bodas de sangre* (Blood Wedding), adapted for Chontal audiences; and several works developed as a collaboration between Martínez Medrano, her maestros, and the communities. In its first four years it staged eleven such works in vast open-air theatrical spaces donated by and constructed in each community by the Laboratorio participants and named for famous international theatre figures. In its first six months, it developed the production for which the Laboratorio is most well known: García Lorca's *Bodas de sangre*, "Oxolotecan version." While this may seem reminiscent of what Garro critiqued in *La dama boba*—the use of theatre to "civilize the country-side—this production, like many others, is more complicated.

Bodas de sangre, bodas de culturas

LTCI's staging of García Lorca's play would become the signature production for the entire Laboratorio network over the next decade and a half. Martínez Medrano and a cast of literally hundreds of Oxolotecans took García Lorca's original tragic tale of passion and vengeance and

An LTCI performance space in Tucta, Tabasco. Photo by author, © 1996.

transferred it from the Spanish countryside to the Tabascan cornfields. Significantly, local history—long ignored in official Tabasco, as it had been by earlier Cultural Missions—was recuperated in this production in several ways. The Oxolotecan version is set in a time before Garrido's Hispanicizing programs worked to erase such signs of Indianness as traditional dress, ways of farming, and the native language. These signs reappeared in the Oxolotecan *Bodas:* traditional traje was worn by both women and men; machetes replaced the knives that play such a key role in the original; and songs, composed and choreographed by the members of the community, were performed in a mixture of Spanish and Chontal, as was much of the text.[16]

The mise-en-scène created by Martínez Medrano for this production of *Bodas de sangre* would become a familiar hallmark, employed in other productions and as far away as Mexico City, Spain, and the Catskill Mountains of upstate New York. In Oxolotán, the communal lands donated for the "Constantin Stanislavsky" outdoor theatre space featured a vast expanse of field, with distant trees providing a cyclorama of nature as a backdrop. A raised wooden platform in the center of the area was used for all interior scenes; it was flanked on one side by a tower, constructed by the locals of tree trunks, which enabled varied playing levels for the subsequent action.

Although the published version of the script appeared in Spanish, it was performed in a mixture of Spanish and Chontal.[17] The production remained generally faithful to the action of García Lorca's text, but Martínez Medrano distilled some parts and added others, most notably an overture called "The Presentiment of Death." In the LTCI script little more than the entrance of "La muerte" is noted, but in fact this overture comprises more than a quarter of an hour and serves as a thematic prologue. The Mexican critic Tomás Espinosa described its effects in performance:

> [T]he overture presents the whole pueblo, in the situations, work and roles they play in the tragedy. The characters remain in *estampa* [frozen in place] more than fifteen minutes, with a virtuosity that can only be achieved by well-trained and disciplined actors, those who know what it is and how it is to be consumed in organic concentration. They form a great mural, careful in plastic composition unto infinity. Flute music and Chontal drums . . . interrupted by Death, on horseback, in black cape, a mask of pallor, full head of hair, roving in search of plunder, tracing figures, searching, enveloping the people, circling the protagonists. It leaves. With this were woven all the threads of the plot, and the characters and symbols painted in: before the entrance of Death there appeared four *arlequines* [harlequins] mounted on horseback, dressed in motley and kerchiefs, subtly made up; they are happiness, the tranquillity of life and of the earth.
>
> In one moment the entire play is captured. They fight against Death, they flee it. In this frieze of life, María Alicia dares to present the bridegroom and his rival together on top of one of the structures, the result of which is intense and perfect, since in the end they will return together under the Earth.[18]

Similarly, when the critic Gloria F. Waldman saw the 1986 production of Bodas de sangre in the Catskills, she wrote:

> [D]irector María Alicia Martínez Medrano is one who knows that an audience must be hooked from the first moment. There are no second chances. This Oxolotecan version is all detail: long flowing hair, perfectly placed skirts, hanging saddles and religious icons adorning plasterboard walls of simulated *casitas* [small houses]. . . . Whatever follows must live up to this spectacular entrance which caused audible intakes of breath in the public. [19]

Death makes a spectacular reappearance in the final scene, replacing the Beggar Woman and Moon, which symbolize death in the original, as the literal sign of itself. Death's cape is spread in two wings of a nearly thirty-foot span, which it passes over the pueblo and the bodies of the two rivals. Like the original, the play ends with a chorus of weeping women. But these women are from Oxolotán (in every respect), and the wedding they have come from celebrated music and dances born there as well.

In production, then, the García Lorca text and the Oxolotecan mise-en-scène constitute a hybrid performance, in which (recalling Max Harris) the (Oxolotecan) performance text exists in dialogic relationship to the (European) play text, and the result is neither purely one nor the other. Further, it is a performance that puts the European text in service of a local culture and its history by recuperating in signs—music, dance, costume—what had been officially suppressed before. This recuperation of local history, and national history from the local perspective, is a key strategy of the troupe's dramaturgy, seen even more clearly in its production of Shakespeare's *Romeo and Juliet*.

Romeo y Julieta in the Yucatán and New York

In 1990 the Laboratorio based in Sinaloa[20] presented its adaptation of Shakespeare's classic. The troupe transferred the setting from seventeenth-century Verona to the Yucatán henequen plantations of the early twentieth century, where indigenous laborers were employed in the harvesting of agave fiber for the manufacture of rope and woven fabrics (now effectively replaced by Mexican petroleum products; many of the old haciendas have been converted into posh hotels). Further, LTCI resituated the conflict between the original's semiaristocratic families to two Mexican indigenous groups—the Maya of Yucatán and the Mayo of northwestern Mexico, who were of different language, bloodline, and custom from the Maya.

Throughout most of the nineteenth century, the Yaqui and Mayo of northern Mexico actively opposed their treatment at the hands of the new leaders of independent Mexico, and in the latter days of the Porfiriato (that is, the administration of Porfirio Díaz, before the Mexican Revolution), movements for indigenous self-sufficiency and autonomy in the region had led to a kind of indigenous "state within a state" that the government would not tolerate.[21] Díaz's policies against this self-governance led to rebellion and guerrilla warfare. In response, he deported and dispersed large groups of insurgents throughout Mexico. Some Yaqui and Mayos were sold as slaves to Cuba; more found themselves working as slaves in the Yucatán's henequen plantations. There, they encountered the resistance of the Maya who were already there and whose jobs they seemed to threaten.

In the Laboratorio's adaptation, set in 1908, Juliet was Maya, native to the Yucatán, Romeo and his family were immigrating Mayos, and the action took place in the open-air theatre representing the henequen plantation.[22] As with *Bodas de sangre*, the LTCI *Romeo y Julieta* maintained the basic elements of the original plot but brought setting, costume, and custom closer to home. It was performed in three languages, Spanish, Maya, and Mayo. The figure of Death—reminiscent, as in *Bodas de sangre,* of the Mexican Day of the Dead character—made a reappearance here, cape included. So did "ancient" elements of the Mayo culture that had not yet "succumbed to the dominant culture."[23] In the party scene there were fanciful and grotesque characters that one reviewer noted might have had nothing to do with indigenous culture at all. But overall, the content was very much linked to an overtly political message specific to Mexican history:

A voice, which interrupts at various moments in the work, announces that the Mayos and the Mayas are united neither by their belonging to the same country, nor by the land itself. What unites them—assures the voice—is their hatred and rancor toward one cacique: Porfirio Díaz.[24]

Once again, LTCI produced a hybrid performance text, this time of "Shakespeare in tongues he surely never heard."[25] In *Romeo y Julieta,* as in *Bodas de sangre,* the Laboratorio took the canonical European text, inserted it in a local setting, and through its manipulation of time and space created a different chronotope that provided, in effect, another register of the performance's hybridity. First, the spatial and temporal adaptations of the play—the transfer from Verona to Yucatán and the move forward three centuries—created a new *Romeo and Juliet* that was as much intercultural as interfamilial in its central conflict. One important effect of this is to remind the audience (Mexican and non-Mexican, for the New York production) that there is no single, essential, and homogenous "indigenous Mexico." Second, not only was the play's European setting manipulated, but so were the chronotopal conventions of modern European theatre: it took place in a vast, outdoor space that rendered the results as much like pageantry as drama; the long, slow prologues and dance passages occur in a kind of ritual time rather than in a dramatic time marked by numerous events and scenes. In fact, the pacing was the only thing the New York critic Wilborn Hampton complained about when he saw the production in Joseph Papp's 1990 Festival Latino in Central Park. At three hours, he felt that much of the production should have been trimmed.[26] At three hours, though, it was as long as any uncut production of a Shakespeare play in the original language; and by local standards in a Mexican pueblo, where fiesta performances can last for days on end, it could have been twice as long and still acceptable. But Willis's criticism was a quibble compared to some Mexican reviewers' opinions about the Laboratorio's work and, indeed, its very existence.

Critical Reception

When *Bodas de sangre* traveled to Spain in 1987, it was greeted quite favorably by the Spanish press.[27] Martínez Medrano likes to refer to this experience in terms borrowed from one reviewer, "the re-conquest of Spain." On the one hand, it is quite possible to see the group's manipulations of the classics as an appropriation of Western dramatic texts so as to revindicate indigenous cultural texts (clothing, dance, music, custom). On the other hand, it is just as possible to see both cultural imposition and alienation at work: the former, in the fact that the group's nonindigenous Mexican director chooses the repertory and actor training techniques; the latter, in the placement of indigenous elements outside of their original domestic or ritual contexts.

These perspectives have varied among Mexican theatre critics and theatre professionals, other Mayan theatre artists, and the troupe members themselves. In general, critical commentary in the Mexican press, even when supportive, has tended to follow three strains of thought. One, manifested more frequently in reviews of their early work—especially among admiring critics—reveals the difficulty some reviewers had believing that a group of rural peasants could competently manage the likes of García Lorca and Shakespeare. The second is more complicated and at times more insidious, targeting the social outcome of such work over its aesthetics: this view holds that the theatrical activities of the Laboratorio keep the participants away from their "true work," which is to till the fields. The third strain of criticism reveals the uneasiness mentioned above: the repertory masks an agenda of hegemonic cultural imposition. Because these responses point to the complex nature of the sociopolitical context in which the Laboratorios operate, a brief sampling of examples follows.

Among the first group of critics, who were surprised at the troupe's competence, were those who tried to rationalize this by pointing to the ritual or fiesta nature of the performances. For example, in a review of *Bodas de sangre,* Arturo García wrote:

> And the production becomes a ritual, and the actors do not act, they are themselves, as they live: simple and dignified, giving life to what they are. Imagination, professional honesty, cheer. Virtues that surround each expression, each dialogue, each movement, each chorus and each song. They are not actors, they are themselves. They march, dance, run, recite, and sombreros and skirts catching the breeze, turn the production into a revel.[28]

García Hernández's review echoes early indigenismo in its paternalistic portrayal of native purity and childlike simplicity; it takes pains to insist that the indigenous and campesino/a participants "*do not* act" (though they do recite), thereby implying that they cannot because they are indigenous. Aware of the racism inherent in this review, LCTI's assistant director, Delia Rendón Novelo, responded:

> Many critics think . . . that the indigenous are incapable of representing a theatrical work well, because they believe that Indians don't know anything about theatre. We consider this situation to be an advantage, because we can train them without running into the obstacle of bad habits that many other actors have, and are difficult to break. These people are "fresh," they are raw material, without pretensions other than to live together and defend their culture; they can be molded and educated before they develop bad habits.[29]

Rendón Novelo's comments are telling for the way they reveal how difficult it is to talk about these issues in Mexico without falling into essentializing discourse. She was one of Martínez Medrano's actor-maestros from the early days in the Cordemex workers' theatre group and has been associated with LTCI since its beginnings. She and Martínez Medrano share a fierce belief that indigenous actors can, in fact, "act," and her respect for and commitment to the communities she works with is deep. Still, she refers to them as "raw material," unfettered by dramatic training in psychological realism. In the condensed form of a newspaper interview, however, this "freshness" comes to sound more like an ethnic trait than one resulting from a lack of access to the very educational institutions that would give them not only bad acting habits, but, possibly, more social power.

Cartoon accompanying an article announcing the production of LTCI's *Romeo y Julieta* in the 1990 Shakespeare Festival in Central Park. Artwork by Jesús Castruita, for María Elena Matadamas, "El teatro campesino, a Nueva York," *El Universal* (Mexico City), July 13, 1990, C1. Courtesy of María Elena Matadamas, © 1990.

For many others in Mexico, what the indigenous are essentially already shaped *for* is the work of the plantation and cornfield rather than the passions of the stage. At its worst, this view holds that theatrical work has given the participants inflated ideas of their abilities and falsely raised the peasant consciousness. Such opinions gained currency in the troubled years following the change of administration in Tabasco in 1988, when the new governor, Salvador Neme Castillo, slashed funding for the group in an effort to distinguish himself from his predecessor, a common phenomenon in Mexican politics.[30] In 1990 one particularly virulent critic, Reynaldo Zuñiga, criticized the former governor for wasting so much money on

> this amorphous group which, protected by a supposed cultural activity aimed at recovering values at the hands of the campesinos, has been made accomplices in the ill use of finances and the degeneration, even, of the campesino groups of Oxolotán, Tabasco. . . .
>
> The fact is that the LTCI group spent more than 500 million pesos to stage "Bodas de sangre" and on the trip to Spain—including horses even—to mount the work with "campesino actors," who are none other than the inhabitants of Oxolotán who, in exchange for a little bit of food, do what the "intellectuals of campesino theatre" ask them to.[31]

Claiming that LTCI had bribed critics to review their work favorably, this one went on to lambast the group for corrupting youth, turning campesinos/as away from their traditional occupations, and even introducing serious diseases into the communities due to their exposure to foreign climates. More recently, as reported by Gerardo Albarrán de Alba in *Proceso,* when the Oxolotecans were negotiating LTCI's new budget with state officials, the state public relations director, Francisco Garrido, taunted them, "So . . . you're going around deceiving yourselves that you're artists? What you all need is to take up your machetes in the field and work the land." Albarrán de Alba continues: "Joking with Neme Castillo's private and general secretaries, Francisco Garrido told them that he still needed 20 peons for his ranches, and offered them 10,000 old pesos a day."[32]

Zúñiga's and Garrido's overtly racist sentiments were echoed in the words of an otherwise sympathetic professional theatre director, a former director of Mérida's Teatro Daniel Ayala. He told me he thought the LTCI groups were "contaminated" by their trips abroad—not literally, as in Zuñiga's unspecified diseases, but in terms of expectations and perhaps occupation. Given their ongoing difficulties in financing, he wondered, "What happened when they returned to their pueblo and their *milpa?*" suggesting that any disillusionment on their return was a tragedy easily avoided. When I asked if he thought LTCI would have been better off if they had never had those experiences, he replied, "They should have stayed in Oxolotán, among their own people, who could understand it [their work] better."[33] Other Mexican researchers with whom I spoke shared the concern that such experiences may have led the participants to dream of careers in Mexican film, television, and professional theatre, where institutionalized racism would have been a considerable obstacle to their acceptance. This protectionist view, I think, proceeds from a focus on the titles of the works the Laboratorio had become famous for rather than on the community revitalization that both motivates and results from their work, especially recently.

First, the concern about "contamination," however well intended, runs the risk of colluding with the Mexican imaginary in its suppression of indigenous voices. It reflects a desire for purity at all costs and pleads a forced authenticity that, at minimum, compels such communities to stay "occupied with the Savior's concern," as Trinh T. Minh-ha has described the ways in which a "return to roots" rhetoric can operate as both a product and a tool of hegemony.[34] In other words, this view exerts an ongoing pressure on these communities to be the kinds of indigenous it is convenient or desirable for them to be, from the perspective of nonindigenous cultural power brokers. It festers at the core of the belief that LTCI activity ruptures traditional community ways of life: if everyone in the small community is involved somehow in the theatre, and is compensated for that involvement (as happened in the days in Tabasco when the budget was unlimited), then theatre effects a material change on traditional livelihoods. Reflect for a moment that it was acceptable for the petroleum industry (and now, with the Plan Puebla-Panamá, virtually any transnational corporation) to disrupt traditional ways of earning a living but not for theatre to do so.

Second, the concern about contamination implicitly denies the possibility of community agency and decision making in the matter, as though the LTCI participants are the passive receptacles of changes wrought by exposure to the larger world through its dramatic texts and the troupes' travels to perform them. Although it is true that the Laboratorio did not emerge of its own accord from each of the communities in which it is now situated, neither did Martínez Medrano simply descend on them and proceed without their permission and cooperation. In fact, at times that permission has been denied or difficult to obtain. In the dedication to a published version of LTCI's first original work, *La tragedia del jaguar* (Tragedy of the Jaguar), the Oxolotecan coauthor, Auldárico Hernández Gerónimo, wrote:

It is one thing to bring us the means to produce good things (even the most modern means); and the information to educate us in sciences, technology, and multiple disciplines that compel us to evolve economically, and show us the ways of life of other cultures, in particular that of the West; it is another thing to crush the indigenous cultures.

I asked permission of the elders, in order to have their consent, because this work obliges us to describe ceremonies that are sacred to us Chontales.

On the other hand, we have heard so many promises that in the end turned out to be lies, and therefore I didn't believe in the Laboratorio de Teatro Campesino e Indígena. As time passed, I realized that the Laboratorio is serious. Because I saw it, among children and young people of our communities. I lived it. It does attempt to revalidate our culture. Not like other institutions that only assist in ethnocide, that absorb our leaders, trapping them in bureaucracy and turning them into renegades and traitors; they corrupt our leaders, who in turn try to corrupt others. That is also why I asked permission of the elders, to have their consent and their trust.[35]

La tragedia del jaguar was developed over eight months of interviews with these elders, and it remains in the network's repertory. It is a synthesis of Chontal lore and ritual, the story of a young woman murdered by her brother for loving the wrong man—tellingly, a conquistador whom she feels she has been destined to love "since forever" and to whom she submits herself to be "owned." The brother kills her lover as well, after the Chontal community has surrounded and killed the other conquistadors. Meanwhile, the title character, Jaguar, symbol of Chontal as well as all Maya culture, sustains grievous injuries but is left alive at the end. Even though "they say that the Conquistadores killed all the jaguars," this play stages an alternative history and interrogates Mexico's ongoing dependence on the rhetoric of mestizaje.[36] In this uniquely Chontal version of the La Malinche story, she is both traitor and protagonist. But here her historic destiny is forestalled: both she and the conquistadors die, the indigenous endure, and a brave new racial mixture does *not* emerge, as it does in Vasconcelos's fantasia, to serve as history's consolation prize.

This recentering of local custom and lore, in interaction with that of a larger world, is characteristic of the majority of LTCI's work and working methods, even when that work starts with a text from the canon of "universal art" (Martínez Medrano's words). In those Laboratorios carrying on the original design of the program (three years of training in acting, voice, directing, movement, and theatrical and political history), the Laboratorio takes the place of college for most of its young participants. In poor rural communities and urban neighborhoods that LTCI usually draws from, these young people would most likely have quit high school, or left school even earlier, to go to work. If they are lucky enough to attend university, there they would be subject to even greater Europeanizing pressures, without an equivalent valorization of their own traditions, which LTCI is at pains to provide (even as it risks essentializing and exaggerating some of them in performance).

Recent Work and Cultural Returns

In May 1996 the group announced its "rebirth" with its own festival of theatre—featuring *Bodas de sangre* as the centerpiece—and called on artists and intellectuals throughout Mexico to lend their support. Since then, the work of the group has taken several different directions. The X'ocen (Yucatán) Laboratorio restaged *Romeo y Julieta* in Mexico City in April and May 2002, but there has been just as much effort in recent years to celebrate and "recapture" (*rescate,* Martínez Medrano's word) local traditions and to combine them in other kinds of performances for urban audiences and tourists in the capital and on the Yucatán peninsula.

For example, on a Sunday afternoon in May 2000 the Laboratorios collaborated in staging *El árbol de la vida* (Tree of Life) in Mexico City's Zócalo. This spectacle brought together forty-five indigenous communities to blend the traditional and the invented: theatricalized rituals performed by members of the LTCI workshops served to ceremonially open and close the event; groups from distinct communities danced and performed comic sketches; and the whole was linked together by the virtuoso neo-Aztec dancing of the Concheros, a professional troupe.[37]

"Arbol de la vida" refers to a folk icon with a long tradition in Mexico —ceramic Trees of Life, which themselves are interesting intercultural texts blending central Mexican Nahuatl mythology with Christian themes. Their branches are covered with leaves and flowers, on and under which can be found such biblical figures as Adam and Eve, the Holy Family, and Noah and his menagerie. Further, they can be "read" as stories from bottom to top and at the same time as a historiographical interpretation—the blooming of Christianity on the existing Nahuatl tree. According to Chlöe Sayer, a specialist in Mexican art and popular cul-

El árbol de la vida, Mexico City, May 2000. Photo by author, © 2000.

ture, latter-day sculptures can tell many other stories as well, drawn from Mexican history and tradition, for example, or from the artist's own life or even, in the case of commissioned work, from customers.[38]

LTCI's version of *El árbol de la vida,* whose staging area covered almost a city block in the Zócalo, featured an enormous central pyramid, which over the course of the event would become covered with examples of artisanry—pottery, painting, textiles, and other crafts—from throughout Mexico. The participants performed both on the Zócalo floor and on the various levels of the pyramid. The audience was seated in bleachers facing one side of the pyramid. After they performed, all the groups came together to allow the public to take photographs. At the end of the day, Martínez Medrano made a speech of thanksgiving that had more than a hint of a political thrust, as she called on fellow Mexicans never to forget the source of their culture in the living indigenous, significantly mentioning those of Chiapas.[39] This performance took place at the height of the presidential election campaigns that would result a few weeks later in the overthrow of the PRI, so I view this speech and, more important, the event itself as a pointed call to the contending powers to take Mexico's indigenous into account.

Other Laboratorios based in the suburbs of Mexico City have worked with Martínez Medrano to present, on the one hand, indigenista works by Mexican writers looking back to the past and, on the other, dance performances I read as engagingly postmodern. The former include a production of Sergio Magaña's *Moctezuma II,* which attempts a retelling of the story of Conquest from the indigenous perspective (and in one production near Mexico City also featured the Conchero dancers).[40] In fall 2000, another Laboratorio based near the capital brought together seventy-two young dancers in homage to the Cuban composer and exile to Mexico, Dámaso Pérez Prado. The dancers, many of them recent immigrants to the city living in working-class barrios, adopted rural dances to the mambo beat of the border-crossing Prado, who himself was known for irreverent adaptations of such classics as Tchaikovsky's *Nutcracker Suite.* The result is an energetic and highly eclectic mix of Afro-Cuban, Mexican, and indigenous music, rhythm, and movement, an embodiment of transculture in action.[41]

Finally, the Yucatecan Laboratorios in X'ocen and in several Mayan communities near the state capital, Mérida, have developed two performances based on the *Vaquería.* This traditional ceremony-fiesta predates the Conquest but since then has been mixed with Spanish dances and dress among many Yucatecan Mayan communities. (The name is based on the Spanish word for "cow," but the fiesta is nothing like a rodeo.) In X'ocen, home to one of the oldest Laboratorios, the performance is titled *La Vaquería;* in Ticopo, where the Laboratorios stage a similar production in which the Vaquería plays a central role, it is titled *Siete momentos en la vida do los maya* (Seven Moments in the Life of the Maya). There are important tonal differences in these productions, based on their different histories with LTCI and different participant-audience relationships: although both are designed to draw in tourists, X'ocen, near Valladolid, is a bit more remote, and its audiences are largely from surrounding communities; Ticopo is close to the capital city, and *Siete momentos* is featured prominently on the "Yucatan Today" tourism Web site, so it attracts larger numbers of non-Mayans.[42] Nevertheless, they share enough similarities to merit discussing them together.[43]

Martínez Medrano, Delia Rendón, and a team of LTCI maestros spent

La Vaquería, X'ocen, Yucatán. Photo by Mary J. Andrade, www.dayofthedead.com, © 2001. Courtesy of Mary J. Andrade.

several years researching the week-long fiesta and its ceremonial and ritual performances, different portions of which survive in different towns throughout the peninsula. They distilled the results into a seventy-minute performance that includes more than four hundred local participants. This gives some idea of the scale of the performances, which take place in large, open fields.

An overture includes a blessing of the space and presents an idyllic version of life as it is lived in a typical Mayan pueblo: children play and chase each other, the men go off to work on the land, the women gather around cooking fires, making tortillas during the entire performance. A comic but realistic interlude involves a group of *borrachos* (drunks) who weave their way through the scene. (Fiestas are often seen by outsiders and religious missionaries as excuses for male drunkenness, but one Mayan writer told me such behavior is no indication of the depth of reverence for what the fiestas celebrate.)[44] The scenes that follow present certain performative aspects of the original fiesta—all removed from context, some very deliberately reconstructed and theatricalized. There is a ceremonial planting of the sacred ceiba tree, a kind of Mayan tree of life, to which offerings are presented; the procession of the *gremios,* or guilds, who sponsor certain sacred offices and whose appearance would inaugurate each fiesta day's events; a presentation by all the participants (men, women, and children) of the *jarana,* a quick-stepping dance popular throughout the peninsula; and a danced version of a bullfight, beautifully incorporating some of the dance steps recaptured by the LTCI team's research efforts. The program closes with a blessing and breaking of bread, a sharing of tortillas between the participants and the public, and the affirmation, "Los Mayas: Aquí estamos y esto somos" (The Maya: Here we are, and this is who we are).

The target audiences for these conscious restagings of tradition are tourist groups drawn to the region. In X'ocen, which is about one hundred miles from both Mérida and Cancún, the group found that just as often its audiences were from nearby communities (men, women, and children of all ages, allowed to attend for free). This local interest spurred the development of dance classes in their communities and in a number of small towns near Mérida, which in turn developed *Siete momentos*. Buses bring tourists from the capital, and, as in X'ocen, friends and families of the performers crowd the stands (locals are admitted free of charge). LTCI is working with community officials and state tourist authorities to establish this as a permanent performance site, which would make possible other business enterprises for the town and nearby communities, such as concessions and crafts markets.

Taken alone, LTCI's increasing penetration of tourist markets raises the question of self-folkloricization, whose risk is to both essentialize and to freeze the culture so represented. Certainly, life in the pueblo is not always as idyllic as it is presented in *La Vaquería* and *Siete momentos,* and by trying to recapture an older tradition in danger of disappearing, the performance effectively invents a new one in the name of the old. But taken in the context of LTCI's history, in particular the artistic vision of the non-Mayan woman who drives it, these activities are just one strategy in a campaign that exists on multiple fronts to compel more respect for indigenous people in Mexico. This is registered in responses by the participants themselves, who gain a cultural self-respect through the opportunity to perform in these productions. In some cases, the community dance classes have led young people to begin wearing again their traditional clothes. In a region where U.S. gang-style attire has become increasingly popular for young men, this represents a clearly different strategy for displaying cultural affiliation through dress.

Despite the storms of identity politics LTCI's work has generated, Martínez Medrano continues to pursue a combined indigenous-nonindigenous performative aesthetic operating on a rather spectacular scale. As she once wrote in a document accompanying funding requests,

[B]eginning with the Conquest, the elites in power have withheld the right to enjoy and learn about what they have named "the fine arts": European and mestizo arts with sources and codes that are more European than indigenous. . . . It is enough to see indigenous architecture, sculpture, painting, dance, theatre, and scenic design to understand that this legacy forms part of the "fine arts."[45]

LTCI's work is distinguished from that of the other theatre groups discussed in this book by the scale and scope of the productions, which incorporate texts from various theatrical traditions, music, visual spectacle, and dance, and by the almost military discipline with which Martínez Medrano runs the organization, classes, and rehearsals. Her view is that community self-expression through amateur theatre, while important for individual communities generally and the performers specifically, ultimately keeps them bound to retrograde conceptions of indigenous talent among culture brokers in the urban center who fund such efforts. For her, quality and attention to the last detail is everything; that is why her ideal training course takes a full three years. Further, it is the discipline of theatre itself (in her own Stanislavskian–Meyerholdian–Seki Sanoan incarnation) that will unlock the participants' creativity and lend the quality that the indigenous components deserve.

Despite its name and perhaps because of its vision, LTCI is not universally accepted among Mayan scholars and artists. Martínez Medrano's greater access to cultural brokers and their funding gives her Laboratorios more visibility, which is a source of frustration to some of the amateur or "popular theatre" troupes I met in the Yucatán. One Mayan writer-director objected that her strict discipline was foreign to the Mayan way of life; another criticized LTCI's *La Vaquería* for being too synthetic and abstracted from the fiesta and ceremonial context of the event; almost everyone I spoke with expressed concern over the community participants being used as "extras" in the spectacle, with the maestros having the central performing parts.

What is generally missing from most of the discussion of the work—indeed, the very existence—of LTCI is a legitimating sense of the porosity between worlds. More important, the debates about whether and how much colonizing is still going on take too little account of the participants themselves as subjects of their own evolving histories; as Grossberg would put it, their "positivity" is ignored.[46] But LTCI maestro Martín Pérez Dzul, who was a member of the first LTCI generation from the Yucatán and who continues to work with a new Laboratorio based there, takes his own aim at these debates. "Here in the Yucatán," he told me, "we are used to hurricanes. An entire harvest can be wiped out in one storm. We don't have time for regrets. We know how to keep going. And we do."[47] Pérez Dzul is not advocating a romantic stoicism in the face of cultural change but rather engagement with that change, as the communities themselves grow ever more imbricated in newly global realities. Further, Pérez Dzul's comment places the responsibility for action squarely with "us," the communities and the theatrical participants themselves.

ALTHOUGH MARTÍNEZ MEDRANO remains the driving force in LTCI, and for some observers her characteristic style is too evident, every year new graduates emerge to take over leadership positions in labs all over the country. Each of them lives in the community in which they work and trains subsequent generations to do the same. Herein lies the potential for the transformative spiral of creative endeavor, for new participants to explore the theatrical expression of cultural identity. Herein also lies the potential for a true transcultural theatrical experience, in the sense Carl Weber has envisioned it: "Eventually, the model 'dis-appears' in a new text or technique, which gains its own identity of form and of content."[48] In the case of LTCI, the model can be a play by Aristophanes or Shakespeare or García Lorca, by Magaña or Garro or Tomás Espinosa; or it can be the residual trace of a once-vibrant fiesta tradition. Whether "universal" or radically local, the model does not disappear. It dis-appears, the hyphen suggesting the preservation of an important memory at the same time a new form or expression is emerging.

Intercultural theatre, especially as it is discussed in works like Pavis's, has tended to maintain a Euro-American theatre tradition as its center and frame of reference. In the last century, its practitioners have sampled the performance traditions of Asia, Africa, India, and sometimes even Mexico (as did Artaud) to find new ways to animate theatre for audiences at home.[49] Another strain of intercultural theatre, for audiences abroad, proceeds along the lines of "Shakespeare in the bush," to borrow the anthropologist Laura Bohannan's term.[50] Here, works from the European canon cross cultures and are presented, usually by Westerners and often with adaptations, to and for audiences of non-Westerners for their edification and betterment. In this latter case, Western theatre is a means toward an end that itself is rather Westernizing (even though the audiences for this theatre, as Bohannan points out, actively translate its meanings into their own terms of cultural understanding); in the former, Western theatre is the end in itself.

It is where the center of textual authority is located in LTCI productions that distinguishes it from both of these kinds of intercultural theatre. Canonical and Mexican indigenista texts may be the starting point, but they do not stay put as centers of gravity in the final productions. Local traditions and tempos may highly inflect (or overshadow) the works but not with an eye to whipping some life back into old warhorses for their own canon-weary audiences. Nor does Martínez Medrano arrive in town with a troupe of professional actors, perform a play or a series of plays for the general improvement of the audience, hold a few after-show discussions, and then leave for the next culturally underprivileged pueblo.

Instead, indigenous experience and participation takes center stage, in its own right, and over the textual authority of nonindigenous works. If the result is interesting, beautiful, and powerful theatre, what is perhaps more telling is the incredulity with which it is still greeted by many who see it, especially in Mexico, where it seems it is easier to believe in introducing indigenous actors and audiences to canonical texts than it is to believe they can master them and make them their own.

CHAPTER 4.

Theatre and Community on the Yucatán Peninsula

ALTHOUGH THE Yucatán peninsula first came to the world's attention through excavations of its ancient past, in all of Mexico it is perhaps the region most oriented to the postmodern present, with its tourist-friendly mix of beaches, resorts, ruins, and Old World charm. But geography, politics, economic history, educational systems, and theatre also factor into the peculiarly Yucatecan cultural mix. This chapter examines the relationships among these factors, focusing particularly on grassroots theatre in the Mayan language as it has come to articulate new ways of understanding cultural belonging on the peninsula.

Since the eighteenth century, the Yucatán peninsula has often been the first stop in Mexico for European business travelers—and theatre companies—on their way to the capital.[1] Regional entertainment and cuisine reflect a blend of European taste and local flavors. The Yucatán enjoys a stronger regional theatre tradition than do other parts of Mexico because of the historical presence of several theatrical families, most notably the Herreras, and a significant number of professional playwrights. The *Enciclopedia yucatanense* notes that there is a theatre space in almost every Yucatecan pueblo, and the fare offered at least superficially reflects the region's multicultural makeup:

> Although at times characters from the highest social classes take part in the dramatic action, the true heroes belong to the pueblo, are Indians from the haciendas and "mestizos" of the towns in the state's interior or from the barrios of Mérida. Other characters include Chinese and Arabs, the latter often called "Turks." It may seem a bit unusual that an essentially regional theatre would feature so many foreign characters, but in this case it should cause no surprise, as the foreigners represented have been settled in Yucatán for many years and been mixed with (though not mistaken for) the popular masses. These characters are always drawn with a comic slant, and with the exaggeration of caricature.[2]

Although this description is now twenty-five years old, the foreign characters remain familiar, in popular variety shows and revues and in local television programming that has taken their place in recent years. And although the "heroes" of the pieces may be "Indians," chances are good that in the professional regional theatres they will not be played by Mayans from the haciendas.

The reasons for this should by now be familiar, as the Yucatán shares much of Mexico's colonial and colonizing history, as well as a troubled identity crisis on a regional scale. For a time the region was independent of Mexico, in the same way Texas once was. With the publication of John L. Stephens's *Incidents of Travel* books in the mid-nineteenth century, Quetzil Castañeda suggests, intellectuals from the peninsula were quick to claim the Mayan past in the service of an independent Yucatán nation—much as the Aztec past was claimed by central Mexico's criollos to achieve independence from Spain. At other times in the nineteenth century there were movements aimed at annexing Yucatán to the United States.[3] Economics was a key factor in that relationship. Until the mid-twentieth century, the region's henequen production made it an important supplier of rope and twine to the world's largest agricultural producers. Among these producers was the United States, who lent money to *hacendados* (landowners) on a grand scale, until it found a cheaper supplier after World War II. This contributed to an economic crisis in the region from which it is only now, through citrus farming and tourism, beginning to recover.[4]

Despite or perhaps because of Yucatán's historical traffic with the rest of the world, its Mayan populace has yet to enjoy full participation in that trade; for most of the region's modern history, peninsular Mayans have been consigned to its worst lands or to working on someone else's in virtual serfdom. As a result, the region is also known for its history of indigenous rebellions, the most well known being the Caste Wars of 1847–1853.[5] And for many the neocolonial situation continues: the remotest communities are also the poorest; economic opportunities continue to be unevenly distributed according to ethnicity; and many Mayans (from Yucatán and, increasingly, from other parts of Mexico as well) serve as the exploited underclass in an exploitative tourist industry, working as guides at the archaeological sites, producing handicrafts for sale in and around tourist destinations, and performing with folkloric dance troupes in and near the tourist hotels.

In the Prologue, I mentioned being intrigued by the bluish light of television sets leaking through the adobe walls of many Mayan houses on the road between Chichén Itzá and Mérida. Since that trip in 1993, satellite dishes and cable technology have extended the reach of programming from Mexico City, Spain, urban centers in South America, and the United States. Mexico City television programming—particularly its advertising and *telenovelas* (soap opera–like series that last about six weeks each)— helps to constitute viewers as national subjects, in the sense of a virtual nation created by televised recourse to national symbols and norms of social (especially heterosexual romantic) behavior. These norms may be far outside the lived experience of its rural viewers, but not all of them reject these models, for they appeal to many women and young people.[6] The varied responses to the other worlds Yucatec Maya come into contact with, whether real or mass mediated, play as important a role in the formation of Mayan identity (how they see themselves) as they do in the production of Mayan alterity (how they are seen by others). Increasingly, with the growth over the past twenty-five years of community-based theatre activity on the peninsula, Mayan-language theatre is a site where both these processes of ethnic and social distinction are explored and enacted.

In Chapter 1 I discussed briefly the trajectory of state-sponsored theatre for rural and indigenous audiences in Mexico—theatre that generally began with an agenda of cultural indoctrination but led to homegrown programs that became autonomous expressions in their own communities. In other words, theatre became one of those processes of and for cultural identification, produced in the context of relations between the local and the national.

In the Yucatán, community-based theatre has generally followed this same spiral from the cultural imposition of theatre imported from Mexico City through adaptation and appropriation to a form of theatrical autonomy. As early as 1931, theatre in the local language was used to extend state and federal social improvement programs. The library of the Universidad Autónoma de Yucatán contains a fascinating document that provides a trace of this early work. A collection of school plays printed only in the Yucatec Mayan language, it was compiled by Santiago Pacheco Cruz, a Yucatecan playwright working as a federal school inspector in the state of Yucatán. In his Spanish-language afterword to the work, he wrote that the collection was motivated by his desire to resolve a "biological mystery": the fact that in the propagandistic plays sponsored by the Secretariat of Education and its affiliate agencies, the women of the pueblos were not getting the jokes—because they remained monolingual in Yucatec Mayan:

So this is how I resolved the enigma of that biological phenomenon: writing these playlets and others that I publish in this pamphlet, taking as basic arguments those of the [national indigenous and popular pro-education] campaigns: antialcoholism, literacy, and Spanish-language instruction (*castellanización*)—the same that the Secretariat of Public Education is determined to realize.[7]

Monolinguism is still common in remote areas of the peninsula, especially among women, which makes theatre in the Yucatec language an important factor in cultural preservation and promotion. If in 1931 Mayan-language theatre was used in service of postrevolutionary Mexico's plans for a unified Spanish-speaking country, in later years it was appropriated for more local purposes and ends. In the late 1970s and early 1980s, the Proyecto de Arte Escénico Popular was active on the peninsula, but soon groups in cities and small communities began to work more or less independently, sharing their ideas and results with each other in peninsula-wide festivals, or *encuentros*. I had the opportunity to attend the 1996 Encuentro Peninsular de Teatro en Lengua Maya, which was organized by the Yucatecan poet and playwright Feliciano Sánchez Chan. The Encuentro in general and the work of Sánchez Chan and his fellow Yucatecan María Luisa Góngora Pacheco in particular provide interesting examples of how theatre participates in ongoing definitions of community and cultural identity in the region.

Teatro Comunitario in Yucatán

In some ways, community-based theatre[8] in this region can also be seen as an outgrowth of theatrical activities in its primary and secondary schools. As Frischmann points out,

Mexican school teachers are routinely trained to engage their students in some form of theatre for holiday observances; in many cases, however, neither teachers nor students have ever actually seen a nonscholastic play performed. This gap is precisely the point at which theatre undergoes a process of transculturation or cultural syncretism, freely incorporating whatever elements the author, director, or artists deem desirable. . . . [T]his results in an inseparable blend of contemporary Mayan worldview and age-old indigenous performance modes (ritual and historic drama, social and political satire, dance) with Western theatrical structures (drama, comedy, farce).[9]

Where do the "Western theatrical structures" come from? There are at least three sources: exposure to professional regional theatre, the legacy of such programs as Proyecto de Arte Escénico Popular and the training they provided, and the increasing presence of cable and satellite television. The career of Sánchez Chan illustrates the way these influences converge and diverge in Mayan community theatre in the Yucatán.[10]

Sánchez Chan was born in Xaya, a small community of about one thousand people in the southern part of the state, and was raised to be a farmer, which remains his first love. However, as a young man he was recruited to be a theatrical "promoter" by the Proyecto de Arte Escénico Popular, just before this project was terminated in 1982. Thus he received training in Mexico City and returned to Yucatán's capital city, Mérida, where he and several others who had performed together in school theatricals formed a Mayan-language theatre troupe based in the local Office of Popular Culture.

In addition to collectively developing and touring their own theatrical productions, which he describes as simple affairs developed out of group improvisations with ready-to-hand props and costumes, they also affiliated with other groups on the peninsula that were doing Mayan-language work. Eventually, this led to workshops sponsored by the Office of Popular Culture, run by theatre professionals from Mexico City, to train the groups in crafting plays and directing and acting in them. However, both funding and enthusiasm seemed to follow a cyclical pattern. Although the groups did not require much in the way of technical support, money and vehicles were necessary to tour the shows from community to community, and the towns themselves were often too poor to provide help. As a result, a great deal of work went into putting together a production, only to have it staged three or four times; spirits were dampened, people dropped out, and continuity was compromised.

To address the problem of maintaining continuity in touring community-based theatre in the region and to encourage permanent theatre groups in communities, Sánchez Chan developed a basic theatre manual. Funded by the National Council on Culture and the Arts, the manual drew on his earlier training and work with several members of the Mexico City–based Experimental Theatre Workshop.

This how-to guide is an interesting and, I would argue, intercultural document. It represents an attempt to negotiate an array of competing impulses: aesthetic versus social, amateur versus professional, troupe collectivity versus directorial authority. Moreover, the manual represents Sánchez Chan's attempt to negotiate two different discourses: the "age-old" performance tradition of Mayan communities, which he invokes to legitimate the current work, and more modern theatrical models, implicitly inflected with the theories of Aristotle, Freytag, Stanislavsky, and a touch of Boal. For example, Sánchez Chan cites René Acuña's 1978 study, *Farsas y representaciones escénicas de los mayas antiguos* (Farces and Dramatic Scenes from the Ancient Maya) to provide historical justification for taking seriously contemporary local theatre. The latter theorists I mention here are not named in the manual, but their influence is discernible, as I discuss below. Sánchez Chan also cites contemporary Mexican scholars and practitioners concerned to develop a model of the homegrown actor—the kind of actor, as Alejandro Ortíz put it, who is not interested in "achiev[ing] a certain fame, interpreting the great roles of the universal stage," but in learning from life itself.[11] The latter models of dramatic structure and acting are employed not to "rescue" the former Mayan performance traditions but to find new ways for community theatricals to articulate present realities, using their own resources:

> By *teatro comunitario* we mean that done by groups who do not confine themselves to conventional spaces with lots of scenography, properties, lights, and special costumes and who do not necessarily express themselves through the works of great authors but rather with texts created according to their own needs and starting with their own problems and reality—be these groups indigenous, campesino, popular or community. . . .
>
> Teatro Comunitario is an artistic-cultural activity that a given group of people develops, based on its own reality and creativity, utilizing elements from everyday life to express its own viewpoint on a given situation in its own community, inviting everyone else in the community to reflect on those themes.
>
> Teatro Comunitario, normally spoken in the mother tongue (Maya), demonstrates our way of life, signaling on occasion what we do like and what we do not, even proposing ways we can change things.[12]

The above passage mirrors the philosophy that theatre is an important mode of cultural enactment, providing, as John MacAloon suggests, "occasions in which as a culture or a society we reflect upon and define ourselves, dramatize our collective myths and history, present ourselves with alternatives, and eventually change in some ways while remaining the same in others."[13] The manual's suggested themes are drawn from the experience of the existing groups and range from the local to the global: children's games, alcoholism in individuals and families, the pueblo's oral storytelling traditions, the abuses of teachers who do not allow their students to speak Mayan in school, agricultural rites and traditional fiestas, inconsistent electrical service, communal land management, the commercial concerns of farmers, land scarcity and the resulting overuse of existing fields, the emigration of youths to the cities, the effects of television on children, "etc., etc., etc."[14]

Once the theatre group has selected a theme to pursue, the manual provides advice on how to shape it into a play, proposing a common structure that is "found almost invariably among community theatre groups in the State." This structure bears remarkable resemblance to "Freytag's pyramid," which described a particular kind of theatrical realism operative originally in the bourgeois theatre of the nineteenth century and still recognizable today. In Freytag's schematic, a play begins with an expository scene or an inciting incident, which leads to several scenes of rising action, ultimately culminating in a crisis or climax, followed by a falling-off, or denouement. The community theatre paradigm follows this structure, adding its own local variations:

1) Introduction of the main theme, characters, and setting; the setting is usually a farmer's home, specifically, its kitchen.

2a) "Everyday scenes," which follow the theme and deepen it and introduce the central problem in concrete terms, through one of the characters. This is typically followed by a series of

2b) "Parallel scenes," showing how the theme plays itself out in other areas of local life and how competing interests in the community create the central conflict.

3) Establishment of the conflict through the direct confrontation between or among competing parties, each of whose interests are given a chance to be heard.

4) The climax, when the conflict reaches its strongest moment and some course of action must be decided on.

5) "Unraveling" (*desenlace*) or "finale," in which a solution to the problem, among many considered, is finally chosen—the more important point being to compel reflection about those alternatives rather than to advocate the solution.[15]

I include this information about dramatic structure and its similarities to European and U.S. drama neither to reify that structure as the norm nor to suggest, because it is "found almost invariably among community theatre groups in the State," that these groups somehow independently discovered the same, "universal" structure. Nor am I suggesting that a form of cultural imposition is at work, through the forcing of native content into Western structures. Rather, this how-to-structure-a-play information suggests that grassroots theatrical expression on the peninsula is informed by exposure to a variety of other theatrical forms and training programs, as well as to television. More to the point, it illustrates how local artists and their concerns in turn reshape those structures to suit their purposes. The number and pacing of the parallel scenes from everyday life are an important example.

In many Mexican communities, indigenous and mestizo, a typical fiesta dance-drama (such as the Dance of the Moors and the Christians) can last six hours or longer. Television and its plot structures may have "invaded" the Yucatán countryside, but audience attention spans continue to be conditioned more by the conventions of communal performance than by the interval between television commercials or the typical length of a telenovela.[16] When presenting a drama of contemporary social concerns, there is virtually no limit to the number of "parallel scenes" the group and its public are willing to explore and accept, and plays, like dance dramas, can also go on for hours. All the complexities of a given problem can be explored, allowing for an eventual resolution that is educational without being didactic, because it is not based on simplistic notions of right and wrong or good and bad. Further, the quotidian nature of the scenes—their content drawn from the everyday life of the people—provides the audience with something they very rarely see on Mexican television. Three recent plays provide an illustration of how Mayan communities in the Yucatán use theatre to re-create local identities, both through and apart from external referents that may be foreign to local norms and practices.

Community (Re)action: *Los aluxes*

Los aluxes (1996) was the collective creation of the community theatre troupe Chan Dzunu'un (Little Hummingbird) in Oxkutzkab, a community of some twenty-seven thousand inhabitants in the state of Yucatán. It was developed under the coordination and direction of Góngora Pacheco, who, in addition to writing essays, plays, and short stories, now

Scene from *Los aluxes* by the group Chan Dzunu'un, in front of the common backdrop of the plays staged at the Encuentro Peninsular de Teatro en Lengua Maya in Tecoh, Yucatán, August 1996. Photo by author, © 1996.

also works as researcher and adviser for the state's Office of Indigenous and Popular Culture.[17] I saw a much-shortened performance, in Yucatec Maya, during the 1996 Encuentro Peninsular en Lengua Maya in Tecoh, Yucatán.[18]

As did almost all of the more than one dozen plays presented at the Encuentro, this play opens on a typical country home. (In fact, such a home was depicted on the permanent backdrop provided by the Encuentro's organizers, so that almost every play was staged in front of it.) Two families are represented: an older couple, who maintain the traditional customs; and a younger couple, in which the husband, Marcelino, has abandoned the traditional ways largely because of the influence of television.

Marcelino's inability to perform and adjust to his traditional responsibilities as a new householder provide most of the play's humor: he can't tell corn from grass, doesn't know how to eat tortillas (and doesn't like the way they taste, anyway), can't maintain his balance on the low wooden chairs that most families use, and can't properly conduct himself during a planting ceremony: he demands to be shown where the gods they are propitiating are, since he cannot see them himself. The jokes revolve around a culture clash and crash headlong into the scatological when he has to learn how to use a corncob for purposes of personal hygiene. (These episodes are among those parallel scenes in which the problematic of tradition versus change is explored, in this case, in a not very

The title characters from *Los aluxes*. Photo by author, © 1996.

nuanced way; few rural families really resort to corncobs, for example. Rather, the scenes were played for maximum laughs, which they consistently got.)

The action of the play turns on Marcelino's decision to sell two *aluxes* to a tourist from the United States (played in this case by the light-haired Góngora Pacheco herself). Aluxes are legendary beings, similar to the fairies of European lore, who benefit those who believe in them and torment those who do not. They exist in both the spiritual and the material realm; for believers, statues and figures of aluxes are not treated as representations but as real. They are widely believed in throughout the peninsula, though some think of them as more devilish than beneficial. In this production, they were played by two children, a boy and a girl. Marcelino has not believed in them but begins to once he becomes the victim of their nighttime pranks: on three separate occasions, they come to steal one shoe, hide the other, tickle his ears, and generally prevent him from getting a good night's sleep. Between the second and third visits, the husband sets out a calabash for them to take, specially scented so that he can trace them the next day. When he finds them asleep in a field, he kidnaps them and ponders how he can turn them to his own profit.

At this point in the performance we witnessed, a bit of impromptu monologue recalled us to an acute awareness of the piece's improvisational origins. During a speech in which the young husband considers selling the aluxes to some gringos he has heard were sighted in the region, the actor paused and said, "I wouldn't have believed it possible, but there are two of them right there!" Then he suited the action to the word and pointed straight at my husband and me, easily the only gringos in a twenty-five-mile radius, seated before him in the front row. Some of the audience simply laughed, but most were more interested to see what we would do. Startled by this sudden reversal of the conventional observer/observed relationship, the most we could manage was a pair of sheepish grins and a kind of mea culpa gesture, after which the show went on. If I had hoped, somehow, that in my research project I could occupy a sanctioned role as audience member to make my observations in anonymous solitude, as I so often do in my own country, this moment recalled me to other truths. Such a luxury is neither possible nor, I think, desirable in these kinds of intercultural encounters. The gaze always turns back; the researcher is always implicated in the scene.

Eventually, through an intermediary, Marcelino finds a buyer for his aluxes—the American tourist, who thinks they are attractive souvenir dolls and buys them both for U.S. $75. But it is clearly dirty money: soon the young couple becomes deathly ill. The older pair take them to the *jmen*, or *curandero* (healer), who is able to cure them but demands the return of the aluxes. Repentant at last, the young man is able to overcome the intermediary's objections and convince the tourist to sell them back. But the unrepentant intermediary, so willing to turn his culture into an easy profit, remains an ongoing threat to the community, and here the play sharpens farce into critical self-reflection.

Los aluxes is a play that is manifestly about the cultural negotiations produced in the transaction between local practices and external pressures. The young man's values and attitudes have been informed too much by a media that promotes an urban if not global culture; the tourist embodies that culture and represents the potential for material power to trump cultural and spiritual power (the protection provided by the aluxes). In this play, the encounter between the local and the foreign does not result in equitable cultural exchange but in a change of ownership of cultural and spiritual wealth; the young man's personal gain comes at great cost to him and his family and eventually endangers the community as well. It is clear that its members "want their culture back," in the form of the sold aluxes. But it also clear that the play does not simply advocate a return to a mythical cultural purity, with ground zero being some point before television, or before the community's "discovery" by tourists. The uneasy, ambiguous moment at the play's end is telling in this regard: the community has its aluxes back, but it is also stuck with the unrepentant middleman, who it seems will sell anything. Thus the order restored at the end of the play is only provisional; the ending is not as happy as one might expect, despite all the laughter the preceding scenes generated. Instead, the work sounds the warning that the processes and problems of cultural change are not going to go away and, more important, are the responsibility of the community itself to manage.

Communities in Action: *Las abejas* and *Las langostas*

Community autonomy and accountability is a recurrent theme in the published works of Sánchez Chan as well. In 1993 many of his plays were anthologized in a multivolume series of Mexican indigenous literature, published in bilingual editions (Mayan languages and Spanish).[19] Most of these plays were developed in group improvisation by his troupe in the mid-1980s and only written down in Yucatec Mayan after they had been toured throughout the peninsula and in other parts of Mexico. It is no small feat to record a play in any language; it is even more difficult in Mayan, as the opportunities to learn written Mayan are few and far between. In fact, it was the experience of trying to capture the essence of the plays, Sánchez Chan told me, that motivated him to teach himself to learn to write in Yucatec Mayan rather than in the Spanish he already knew. Today, as coordinator for the Institute for the Development of Maya Culture in Mérida, he is using his position to increase programs in Mayan-language literacy.[20]

Like the offerings in the Encuentro where *Los aluxes* was staged, Sánchez Chan's collected works include both legendary-mythological material and explorations of contemporary problems. Although Sánchez Chan believes the "soul and poetry" of the original Mayan texts are completely lost in the Spanish translations, these translations maintain their effectiveness as theatre, and two are particularly appropriate for the ways they address certain tensions between cultural preservation, on the one hand, and transculturation, on the other.

Both plays, *Las abejas* (The Bees) and *Las langostas* (The Locusts), were written by Sánchez Chan alone and before rehearsal with actors rather than developed collectively through improvisation. As their titles suggest, both rely on allegorical figures, a device he frequently uses for both artistic and educational ends: because community-based theatre attracts audiences of all ages, Sánchez Chan frequently uses animal figures as a way to intrigue the youngest members of the audience.[21]

In *Las abejas,* the bees of the title are both an important symbol of cultural identity and the prism through which a particular view of history is refracted. In the first scene, the character Native Bee (that is, a bee indigenous to the peninsula) recounts his recurrent dream:

> I've been dreaming that my lord Jobnil Bakab was coming to visit us, and that all my friends captured and ate him. I leave my hive and see the field totally dry, its trees dead, and out of nowhere come these giant bees that chase me. I close myself up in the hive and when I feel I'm about to suffocate to death, I awake. I don't know why I dream such horrible things.[22]

The dream is, in essence, both an allegory and a prophecy of the Spanish Conquest, and the rest of the play treats the subsequent human history of that event in episodes that span four hundred years. An early scene shows the conquered people giving native bee honey to the conquistadors in the hope that it will appease them, but it only inflames their greed. Later, a cunning hacendado figures out how to get more yield from imported European bees, which he raises to curry favor with the Spanish crown. If it means more work for his Mayan workers, no matter: they are easily "pacified" with gifts of alcohol and the promise of a reduction of their debt to him. As the story line approaches the present day, scenes depict independent farmers deciding to make the transition—supported by the Mexican government—from native to European bees, even though the native honey has superior flavor, curative power, and ceremonial efficacy. Finally, the arrival of yet another strain—African killer bees—threatens bee and human population alike, and while the government experiments with crossing the two non-native varieties as a way to control them, the community votes to salvage their knowledge of native bee keeping and apply it to increasing their yield.

Although the general impulse in this play is to valorize the native over the imported—in bees as well as in other cultural elements—it also maintains an ongoing critique of native complicity in its own devaluation and consistently calls the community to account. Following his manual's advice, Sánchez Chan is generous with scenes in which difficult choices are explored and their consequences revealed in a way that is reminiscent of Brecht's *Lehrstücke,* or teaching plays.[23] The scenes' variations on and progression of the central theme are anticipated in the opening dream passage: Native Bee's own kind have captured and eaten their own lord, who abandons them to the arrival of giant foreigners, who in turn lay waste to their land. But the dreamer bee's response to this—hiding away in his former home until they pass—is tantamount to death by suffocation: a retreat to the precontact past is clearly not a safe option. By the end of the play, what is a viable option for the human counterparts is a blend of autonomy and cooperation: working in tandem with the government, they will use new technologies to increase the yield of native bees while the government worries about how to control the invaders. In the process, they will also regain the curative and ceremonial powers they lost when they abandoned the old bees. So if hybridity is here to stay, as the play suggests, it is up to the community to define and defend its ongoing position rather than to let other groups—including the Mexican government—do it for them.

In *Las langostas,* Sánchez Chan again blends history, myth, and contemporary social commentary to take on, among other things, that overdetermined icon of global culture, Coca-Cola. Taking as his starting point a plague of locusts that decimated the Yucatán in the 1940s, Sánchez skillfully weaves a series of scenes to suggest that junk food and cola are modern-day locusts, effectively starving the region's children to death. The message—to eat more healthily—is not a new one: even Mexican television commercials for Coke and snack foods carry similar advice, subtitled at the bottom of the screen or hastily tagged on to the narration. What is more interesting is the way Sánchez Chan situates the responsibility for the problem squarely within the community's "response-ability" to it and enforces that message theatrically through powerful local symbols.

The play opens with two prologues: one aural, one visual. In the first, flute and drum music provide the background to an unseen voice intoning the mythical history of the Mayan peoples, based on the epic *Popul Vuh.* It seems to start in medias res, in the middle of the creation story that ends with the formation of humans from maize. The narration continues through the prophecy of Conquest and its aftermath, the enforced marginalization of the Maya who, forced to speak their language and perform their rites in hiding, soon began to forget both. Abandoning their gods, they were in turn abandoned by them. This prologue ends with an introduction to the play proper, which will recount "how the inhabitants of the rural zones of Yucatán live."[24]

The second, silent visual prologue is a rear projection that shows a

field of healthy corn in silhouette. Suddenly swarms of locusts descend
and in moments leave nothing behind. Also in silhouette, the figures of a
man and a giant locust appear. They fight, and the locust flies off. Even
without the first prologue, the second provides a powerful image that no
one in this corn-growing region is likely to dismiss. But coupled with the
first prologue, the connection between past and present is made more
clear and the symbolic association between historical and modern locusts
anticipated: locusts consume corn; humans are made of corn; therefore,
locusts can consume humans as well.

In the first two scenes, the plague and its aftermath are presented
through the experiences of several villagers: a couple who decide to leave
to find work on a coffee plantation; an old man who decides to stay and
most likely dies of starvation; and a widower who returns later to the village, having lost his wife to malaria on the coffee plantation. When the
action switches to the present day, the locusts take on human size and
symbolic import. In one scene, for example, two of them appear in the
dreams of a young boy, a scene enacted by two masked dancers who surround the sleeping boy and his brother. They move "very mysteriously
and begin to make gestures and magical figures around the boys, like a
dance of enchantment in which they make strange sounds."²⁵ When the
little boy wakes up, he refuses to eat the tortillas and beans his mother
has prepared for him, demanding money from his mother to buy soda
and snacks instead. Soon a neighbor appears and reveals that she routinely gives her children money for such fare as a way to keep peace in
her household, because they demand it so often. Furthermore, the snacks
are cheaper than milk and meat, more convenient than caring for a gar-
den and livestock, and allow her the freedom to watch her afternoon telenovelas—which are sponsored by the soda and snack companies.

A parallel scene deepens this debate, as the situation is discussed between the boy's parents and with a close family friend, who reports the
success he has had raising his own produce and thereby providing his
family with healthy food. Meanwhile, the neighbor's infant has developed a severe stomach problem from having been fed Coke instead of
milk. They decide to follow the friend's example and raise their own nu-
tritious food, but no sooner do they begin to work their land than they are
visited by the Modern Locust—an actor in a locust mask and a costume
composed of hundreds of soda cans and junk food wrappers. Husband
and Locust struggle and fight; the wife calls the rest of the community
together; and the community fights back with the tools of their farming
trade. Leaving the Modern Locust for dead, they declare in unison: "A

The Modern Locust in the last scene in *Las langostas* by Feliciano Sánchez Chan. Photo by Feliciano Sánchez Chan, © 1986. Courtesy of Feliciano Sánchez Chan.

PUEBLO THAT PRODUCES WHAT IT EATS WILL NEVER BE MANIPULATED."[26] In the end, however, the Modern Locust has the final moment: cursing the public and making rude gestures at them, he bursts into laughter and runs off.

If this Modern Locust has the final moment, does he have the play? Is the community defeated without even realizing it? How should this ambiguous ending be taken? An answer lies in the play's beginnings; its ending serves as a structural counterpart to the first prologue. The play begins in Mayan prophecy and ends on another prophetic note: the battle between community self-sufficiency and global absorption, the play accurately foretells, will go on and on. Again, what is most important is the community's role in its own defense and definition. The final moment is less a defeat than a call to continued vigilance.

Quetzil Castañeda's "Coke theory of culture" has relevance for a discussion of *Las langostas* in particular and Yucatecan grassroots theatre in general. In Castañeda's view, Coke and Culture are produced in much the same way: goods (coca leaves and cola nuts) are shipped in from the periphery, made into a product and transformed into a commodity through the alchemy of marketing, then shipped back to the periphery, where Coca-Cola "variously supplants indigenous beverages in contexts ranging from recreation to ritual."[27] Much of the cultural imperialist critique, which tends to view Coca-Cola's spread as something like small-pox, misses a major point: "the natives in the periphery of capitalism have incorporated Coke into their life as part of their own reality (often) without any contradiction in their own eyes, just as they have done with countless other Western artifacts and ideas."[28] To see this phenomenon at work in Mexico, one need only look at people's smiles: Coke-contributed tooth decay becomes transformed into a kind of status symbol, cast in gold and silver dentalwork. In terms of cultural analysis, the question often becomes whether to focus on the glitter or the rot. Critiques from and of the center that focus only on the decay (the erosion of cultural practices) tend to see the periphery as passive victims of global culture. In Castañeda's view, what is called for instead is "a historical analysis of the complex apparatuses that produce, market, distribute, disseminate, and consume both Coke and its concept."[29] This kind of historical analysis operates poetically and dramatically in the work of Sánchez Chan and Góngora Pacheco, who resituate Mayan cultural practices as central and use their own culture's modes of historical analysis (for example, the Mayan prophetic tradition) to assess the complex current state of negotiations between the local and the global. If they focus on the "rot," they also focus on the complicity of the locals in its spread, refusing to deny local agency and responsibility for determining what form and direction their own future will take. Further, the forms this theatre takes, liberally incorporating structures and styles from Western drama, suggests that Western theatre itself has become one of those "artifacts" that Mayan performers have transformed to their own ends.

Nevertheless, even in these plays and certainly in the others staged at the 1996 Encuentro, it is hard not to notice a certain sense of curatorship over tradition that could easily be interpreted as nostalgia for a utopian past, a belief in culture as something that can be (literally, in the case of *Los aluxes*) "owned." I have chosen to focus on those instances in which this nostalgia is resisted or subverted as a way to demonstrate the perpetual state of tension between hybridity and authenticity that this theatre both registers and enacts. I saw this tension made manifest more conservatively, in the discrepancy between the active participation of women as directors, actors, and writers and the more passive portrayal of female characters in the plays staged in the Encuentro. While offstage they seemed to enjoy parity with the men in terms of troupe responsibilities, onstage they were rarely the main characters and still less frequently portrayed as the agents of change. In the serious plays, they were usually the bearers of tradition and repositories of cultural information;

in comedies, they were usually the long-suffering wives of stupid or lazy husbands. There were a few exceptions to this general rule. One was the Encuentro's only Spanish-language play, which was an adaptation of a short story in which a young woman, pursued by three brothers, cleverly outwits them all. The other was a piece of forum theatre in the manner of Augusto Boal, presented by a young professionally trained actor from Mérida and her educational theatre troupe. In their presentation, a woman trying to supplement her family's income by joining a women's work cooperative met extreme opposition from her husband. The audience was asked to provide a series of solutions, a challenge it only half-heartedly met.

In representing gender roles, far more typical was a play called *La triste realidad del campesino* (The Sad Campesino Reality), in which a young woman ventures with her brother into the city to seek work as domestic servants, only to be murdered by an urban gang. Though the young woman appears again onstage after death, her spiritual resurrection could not mitigate the conservative thrust of the play, which strongly suggests that women are better off within the confines of their small communities. Ironically, the "sad reality" offstage for the young woman who played this role is that her father has since forbidden her to participate in the local theatre troupe, which Sánchez Chan confirms is not uncommon among young women under parental control and among wives and younger mothers subject to the gendered division of labor still common among Mayan households. According to William May Itzá, by day a researcher in bee biology at the University of Yucatán and in his free time a director-playwright for the group Constelación (based in his hometown, Kimbilá), none of the women in the photograph of his troupe is still acting, for similar reasons. As these on- and offstage practices suggest, consciousness-raising proceeds unevenly. A group may be sensitive to issues of ethnicity but not interested in exploring the intersection of ethnicity and gender. In fact, to the extent that the women in these plays become the signs of the culture, I would argue that, onstage at least, gender does a good deal of the work of ethnic consciousness-raising in the theatre in this region.

ANOTHER MEMORY PERSISTS, a gentler reminder of the researcher being implicated in the scene of interethnic encounter. On the first day of the Encuentro, my husband and I were having lunch with several members of Constelación who were slated to perform later that afternoon. We were talking and laughing together when suddenly, for no apparent reason and

Cast of the production of *Sac Nicté*, Grupo Constelación of Kimbilá, Yucatán. Photo by William May Itzá, © 1996. Courtesy of William May Itzá.

from no apparent cause, one young actor fell off his chair. "This happens every year," said another member, looking meaningfully at us as though he meant to share a deep secret. "It is our custom."

A split but perceptible second of silence followed before the whole table erupted again in laughter at this piece of improvised satire. In this parody of the anthropological informant at his most romanticized, Chris and I had simultaneously been interpellated in the role of foreign re- searchers, performing this role for an audience of performers. We would experience the profundity of that split second again later when we were singled out in the improvised dialogue by the young lead in *Los aluxes* and again made keenly aware that offstage has become onstage. Whatever cultural nostalgia appears in the theatre of the Encuentro, offstage understandings of the performativity of culture and interculturality are quite sophisticated, as this self-conscious play of identity and alterity illustrates.

Sadly, a variety of factors have prevented the Encuentro from being held again since 1996. Since then the old problems of underfunding, lack of transportation, and diminished organizational energies have re-emerged to dampen the enthusiasm for developing, staging, and sharing new work. The turnover of women participants is also a problem, as are increasing numbers of young men and women emigrating from their communities to jobs in the tourist industries in Mérida and on the Caribbean coast and to the United States and Canada. I am concerned that in this vacuum, Mexican television will have nothing to challenge its hegemonic symbolic economy, in which peninsular Mayans (and indeed any indigenous Mexicans) have yet to see the reality of their lives explored in a serious way. Mayan theatre on the peninsula has provided an alternative view, a space for reflection and reconsideration of those realities. Sánchez Chan told me that if I were to travel to the communities who had sent work to the Encuentro and ask them about their theatre, they would tell me that the group was still together and planning a new project. This was confirmed in my later interviews with May Itzá from Kimbilá and Góngora Pacheco from Oxkutscab, who spoke of both future projects and present difficulties. At the time I am writing, they are no doubt more concerned with the aftermath of Hurricane Isador, which was devastating to the peninsula. I am reminded of how Martín Pérez Dzul invoked the metaphor of a hurricane as a symbol of resilience. As communities rebuild in the wake of the all-too-real Isador, perhaps Yucatecan theatre will also become reanimated. The impulse to continue it is strong, the obstacles familiar. I look forward to seeing what the next cycle will bring.

EPILOGUE
Routes and Returns

ABOUT A YEAR after my first research trip to Mexico, I had dinner with a U.S. dance scholar working on similar issues of performance and community. At the end of a long conversation about our respective projects, she fixed me with a hard look and asked, "So. After all that, where do you think the *real* Mayan theatre is happening?"

This book has been an attempt to address that question by situating "real Mayan theatre" within the very discourses of cultural desire the question itself reflects. I have argued the focus should not be so much on the target—a definition of "real Mayan theatre"—as on the action of taking aim at its ongoing redefinition by people historically denied such actions in the past. In Chapter 1, I suggested that this disempowerment in the twentieth century came from alternating policies that attempted, on the one hand, to deny cultural difference (mestizaje) and, on the other, to reify or even fetishize this difference before it disappeared entirely in the wake of Mexico's postrevolutionary modernization programs (the effects of indigenismo and tourism, for example). More recently, the publication of indigenous literature in indigenous languages and the staging of plays in those languages throughout southern Mexico have, as has the rhetoric of zapatismo, participated in a general movement to take back the discourses of Mayanness that have largely been produced by non-Mayans empowered to do so.

Yet this taking back and taking aim does not necessarily represent a retreat to a precontact utopia of uncontaminated purity, although the temptation to do so remains great for many of the artists I met. As I also argued in Chapter 1, Mayans and other indigenous peoples of Latin America have always collaborated with foreigners in the production of culture. To be sure, since contact with Europeans, these collaborations were more often than not enforced rather than voluntary. Nevertheless, if we look, as Matthew Restall has, at the historiographical documents produced by Mayans themselves in the era of Conquest, we see that in the Yucatán at least powerful Mayans viewed the Spaniards as "new political players in the peninsula that might be of use in the pursuit of long-standing rivalries."[1] This viewpoint reminds us that from the first moments of contact, Mayans strategically chose their alliances as subjects of their own history. This attitude did not disappear in the intervening four hundred years, much as "official" history might have liked it to; it appears and reappears in a variety of indigenous cultural expressions, not the least of which were the evangelical dramas of the sixteenth century, in which text and performance worked in dialectical relationship to each other, and the latter-day dance dramas of Carnaval, which stage a complex alternative historiography from a Mayan point of view.

The scripted dramas that have emerged from within Mayan communities, or have been adapted by them from Western sources, represent the most recent upsurgence of this attitude of strategic alliance and awareness of the positivity of the Mayans' place in world history. They have not emerged organically or evolutionarily from a long and uninterrupted theatrical tradition that extends forward from the pre-Hispanic period, for that tradition was interrupted by Conquest, when theatrical practices were redirected in the service of conversion. Nor do they spring logically from fiesta performances like Carnaval—the closest thing to a continuous theatrical tradition indigenous Mexico maintains—although from time to time various elements of such performances are incorporated into the plays. Rather, as I suggested in Chapter 1, these dramas emerge in a moment in Mayan history particularly informed by the crossings of cultures, ideas, people, texts, and technologies. I believe the example of zapatismo provides an instructive metaphor for understanding theatre's role in the way some Mayans are taking aim and staking claim to their own constructions of cultural identity rather than allowing this to be done "for" them in the discourses of others. As in the rhetoric of zapatismo, sometimes this takes the form of a return to roots, a celebration of the traditional ways of doing things. At other times, it means an unflinching look at how Mayans and indigenous peoples participate in the severing of those roots, with results that are not necessarily entirely negative. And at all times, there is a strategic decision to work with non-Mayan outsiders but in new kinds of relationships that refuse to replicate the old ones of domination and submission.

This is not to say that my colleague's question is irrelevant to the theatre practitioners who work in what they would call "Mayan theatre," for each of the troupes I have discussed has a stake in proclaiming such an identification. Each would answer it differently, both in theory and in practice, and a comparison of the varied activities among them reveals a surprising range of texts, artistic approaches, working methods, and performative results. In Chiapas, for example, the mixed-gender Lo'il Maxil uses theatre to valorize Mayan traditions and to explore and critique contemporary realities arising from conflicting social agendas. Theatre is just a part of their overall activities, which also include community education and outreach in Mayan-language literacy throughout Chiapas, the hosting of international conferences on indigenous affairs, artistic and documentary photography and videography, radio programming, and the publication of bilingual editions of local lore and original essays and fiction, as well as attending to the ever-present demands of fund-raising and fiscal reporting. Theatrically, their repertoire consists of a blend of local legends adapted for the stage and original dramas and comedies. Developed collectively, often with the collaboration of non-Mayan artists from Mexico and the United States, these works are almost always bilingual, signaling the multiplicity of target audiences for whom they may be staged: local rural communities, theatre festivals in urban centers, tourists from all over the world and representing a range of ideological leanings, and academic visitors and guests. The Spanish-language versions have borne traces of Francisco Alvarez's writing style, as their production style—which features simple sets and costumes and not so simple masks—testifies to collaboration over the years of work with Ralph Lee of the Metawee Theatre Company, Amy Trompetter of Bread and Puppet Theatre, and, more recently, Michael Garcés of INTAR. Offstage, Lo'il Maxil has worked closely with Robert Laughlin to secure international attention and, thereby, funding, which is never guaranteed from year to year. That the troupe is now approaching its twentieth year is a testament to the strength of these collaborations and the interest in this part of Mayan Mexico that their work both registers and cultivates. If funding is difficult, so is attracting personnel who are willing to get up and act—especially if they are women, who are discouraged from public performance by a variety of tacit cultural and traditional restraints. Many who join the troupe leave after they marry and have new domestic obligations that are seen to outweigh the salary provided by Sna. (As a recognized nonprofit cultural organization, Sna Jtz'ibajom pays all its members a regular salary.) Finally, performing for the stage may be part of the job description, but the training has to occur on the job. Aside from fiesta, there is little chance to perform or to learn how to, nor is there a culture of theatregoing beyond what Lo'il Maxil itself can provide. Thus, actor training takes place in workshops throughout the year, as the workload allows, and during rehearsals for the annual new production. As a result, the productions are energetic, thought-provoking, vital, and often highly theatrical, but they are not "slick" by the standards of most professional theatre in the United States and Europe. For this reason, this theatre has yet to appear on the radar of professional theatre criticism and has been of more interest to academics whose leanings are as much anthropological as artistic.

Much of this description of Lo'il Maxil can also be applied to Chiapas's all-woman La Fomma: theatre also forms but a part of its overall activities; the work is collectively developed and staged for a variety of audiences; members are paid a salary; and artistic results are mediated to some degree by the artistic, financial, and scholarly contributions of non-Mayans. There are three important differences, however. One is in the degree of collectivity achieved among the women of La Fomma, who conduct their decision making in all matters along radically consensual lines (whereas Sna members tend to defer to the stronger personalities, who are usually men). Another is in the underlying motivation to produce theatre as well as all the other activities La Fomma is involved in, from literacy workshops to knitting mills: whereas Sna's activities are dedicated to the preservation and promotion of Mayan culture generally, La Fomma's is less concerned about preserving or presenting tradition and more concerned about improving Mayan women's material realities, whether through providing a means of income (or the training thereto) or through education about women's rights and their options for escaping untenable domestic situations. On-site day care—an innovation still woefully uncommon in my own supposedly more civilized region of the world—makes it possible for La Fomma women to blend the multiple facets of their identities as Mayan women. La Fomma's emphasis on contemporary women's realities translates into the third key difference— that of the theme, content, and style of their plays, which also favor those realities over staged explorations of legend and lore. Women and children take center stage, literally and figuratively, in the work of La Fomma in a way that is unparalleled anywhere else in Chiapas and perhaps most of Mexico as well. These explorations are unflinching in their examinations of the difficult contradictions of life for these women; each of them is a confrontation and a poem.

In other parts of Mexico, the Laboratorio de Teatro Campesino e Indígena has built a (controversial) reputation for turning small Tabascan and Yucatecan communities into virtual theatre towns, where the works valorize a mixture of Mayan and European cultural and theatrical traditions.

Over the years, the repertory has alternated among staging the works of professional Mexican and European playwrights, developing original new work such as *Tragedia del jaguar,* and theatricalizing local performance traditions such as *La vaquería.* Their work has not escaped the notice of professional theatre practitioners in other parts of the world: until his death, Joseph Papp was a strong supporter of their work. Indeed, of all the theatre troupes discussed here, LTCI operates on the grandest scale. Laboratorios exist throughout Mexico, run by alumni of María Alicia Martínez Medrano's theatre courses. Productions directed by Martínez Medrano and her closest associates favor large open outdoor locales in which actors and horses perform together; even in indoor spaces where no horses appear, in an LTCI production one senses the heart of a great mythical beast pulsing behind the precisely articulated speeches delivered by the well-trained actors. LTCI training is long and rigorous—"militaristic," as one Yucatec Mayan writer put it—and the core personnel have completed the full three years of body, voice, movement, and analytic training. If Martínez Medrano's approach is influenced by her background, a peculiar mixture of Mexican, European, Russian, and Japanese influences, it is also true that she derives aesthetic inspiration from local performance traditions as well, and it is with the aim of recapturing these traditions that her maestros are now involved in ethnographic and performance research in Mayan communities throughout the Yucatán peninsula. Her work and that of LTCI over the years demonstrates the inseparability of ideological and artistic perspectives. Inspired by the beauty of indigenous cultural contributions to Mexico's mestizo past, Martínez Medrano went on to create theatre that has sparked strong ideological opposition throughout the past two decades. Many representatives of official Mexico have found it hard to consider theatrical performance a viable manifestation of "Mayan tradition," unless it operates within a folkloric scheme that does not include the staging of more literary texts by non-Mayan greats. On the other hand, some Yucatec Mayans I spoke with expressed distaste for the theatricalization of local performance traditions as being too synthetic. It is a kind of *Riverdance* phenomenon: like that theatricalized version of traditional Irish dancing, *La vaquería* and *Siete momentos* in the Yucatán produce equal parts of local pride and local and external criticism. Martínez Medrano negotiates this double bind by refusing to concede that this is the only kind of performance Mayans are "good for"; the emergence of this latest aspect of the work has to be considered not only in the context of LTCI's larger history of involvement with Shakespeare and Aristophanes but also in the context of Mexico's increasingly tenacious and widespread tourist industry.

Finally, among other practitioners in the Yucatán, the question, What is Mayan theatre? is often interpreted as a linguistic one. The result is domestic dramas and social comedies developed and enacted by, for, about, and in Yucatec communities—and called *teatro en lengua maya*. Unlike the theatre in Chiapas, Yucatec grassroots theatre is not formalized in a "House of the Writer" or a complex housing women's educational and income-producing activities. It is a free-time activity that proceeds according to the inclination and availability of people, resources, and local funding. These groups do not have the "pull" of LTCI or the international connections enjoyed by the Chiapas troupes (although I am aware of several European and Mexican doctoral students now exploring this work). This theatre in particular suffers from gender trouble, as young women rarely think of continuing this "leisure time" activity after they start families. Older women often choose to return to this kind of work after their child-rearing days are past, and this would provide a fascinating cross-cultural perspective to add to the growing field of intergenerational theatre studies. Like the other troupes discussed here, the history of cultural missions in the region and the long-standing tradition of regional theatre in Mérida mean that Yucatecan grassroots theatre has always already been mediated by non-Mayan forms of dramatic—including televised—representation. But of all the theatrical activity discussed herein, from an academic perspective, this is the most evanescent as an object of study. The texts are rarely written down, and if they are, not necessarily in Spanish. The performances too are usually in Yucatec Mayan, making it impossible for nonspecialists to appreciate the complexity of the verbal aspects of the entertainment. Time and again, the men and women who acted as interpreters when I attended the last peninsular encuentro of Yucatec Mayan theatre would stop in frustration at the difficulties of translating a particular pun from Mayan into Spanish. Thus the linguistic emphasis of the designation "Mayan theatre" is, for these troupes, not at all arbitrary or merely convenient. The performances depend for their effect on a verbal alacrity that is lost on anyone not from there. What Shakespeares might the world lose because most people on the Yucatán peninsula are not taught how to read and write in their native tongue? Such a context makes the emergence of intellectuals and writers such as Feliciano Sánchez Chan and María Luisa Góngora Pacheco worthy of serious academic attention.

Each of the troupes I have discussed in this account struggles to maintain, or negotiate, a position on the roots/routes spectrum identified by James Clifford as being a hallmark of contemporary cultural identifications. At one end of the spectrum is a temporal urge: a desire to return to the past, to reenergize an enervated present; at the other, a spatial one in which contemporary Mayan–non-Mayan interrelationships—and the power inequities embedded therein—are explored, exposed, and, with hope and time, transformed. The criteria each uses to make its claim as indigenous or Mayan theatre differ from troupe to troupe, and sometimes within troupes, based variously on the participants' community or ethnic identification, the themes explored in the works, and the language used. As the examples of all these groups suggest, the staging of Mayan cultural identities is a complex matter of local identification within an increasingly global and intercultural field of operations. If in response to this complexity their repertoires reflect a kind of strategic essentialism, to use Gayatri Spivak's term, it is also true that the results bear a different stamp from region to region and troupe to troupe. It is not that there is no such thing as "real Mayan theatre" so much as there is no *one* such thing.

Onstage and off, so many actors, directors, organizers, and supporters answered this question similarly: Here, in my troupe, in my community, we are doing Mayan theatre. I think about what it takes to say something like this, what it might cost. Historically, the official response to such self-proclamations has been to co-opt their power, to folkloricize them or assimilate them in ways both subtle and forced. Theatre becomes a way to intervene in these processes, to articulate identities that are very much in-the-making, as are all identities in the world we share: when the Zapatistas celebrated their fifteenth anniversary as an organization, they did so with an extended theatre piece enacting the EZLN's history.[2] And now more than ever, as Mexico is making its halting transition to democracy and decentralization under a new party leadership that is giving more power to local *municipios*,[3] issues surrounding who gets to represent whom—both politically and theatrically—are gaining increasing urgency.

Yet it remains difficult for these troupes to be taken seriously by much of the non-Mayan world. They are variously tokenized, ignored, or denigrated for being "amateurish" (it is rarely recognized that most of the participants in such theatre have not attended school beyond the middle grades); essentialized on the one hand or criticized on the other for not being Mayan enough. Further, they do their work in an environment in which modernist urges for an encounter with an exotic other (tourism) compete with an international postmodernism that celebrates the cause—or perhaps more significantly, the rhetorical and representational style—of both zapatismo and the ancient Maya. At the same time that the Zapatistas' cyber-charged "postmodern revolution" has both empowered local communities and compelled global attention, their strategies have fed a kind of logic among a new type of tourist class that thinks it is "cool" to ally with the rebels. Marcos once encouraged this himself: when the French critic Regis Debray suggested that Marcos's "superstar" status was going to turn him into a tourist attraction, he replied, "'Zapatour'? So what. Marcos loses face, but the indigenous gain security. That's what matters. They'll have more likelihood of eating, and fewer threats besides. So we welcome the famous."[4]

It was two years before the border performance artist Guillermo Gómez-Peña, uncomfortable with all the hype surrounding zapatismo, "succumbed to [his] own curiosity about it":

> Though I was fully aware of the postmodern media strategies of the zapatistas and their masterful manipulation of the media, the idea of one of my performance characters shaking hands (or rather exchanging props and performance tips) with the rebels just seemed too hip and opportunistic for my taste.[5]

But, disguised as eco-tourists, he and his performance partners visited a community of Zapatistas in the jungle, only to be "humbled by their political intelligence" and startled by a reversal of the anthropological gaze:

> [The] exoticizing gaze slowly turned through 180 degrees toward us. And in the end, they were clearly in control of the gaze, of the context, and of the terms of the communication process: they clearly knew more, much more, about us than we knew about them.[6]

Taken together, both Marcos's and Gómez-Peña's comments suggest a certain inevitability of the tourist gaze to all things Mayan—and also the possibility that such a gaze can be manipulated and reversed. Nevertheless, the representational economy remains unbalanced. Like the discourses of traditional tourism, New Age spirituality, and millennial consciousness movements that know no geopolitical borders, zapatismo is also at risk of constituting a kind of vicarious Mayanness for non-Mayans.

If one thinks of Clifford's "routes" in term of vectors of representation

Stereo components marketed via neo-Mayan architecture in Phoenix, Arizona.
Photo by author, © 2002.

as well as of people's movements, it has become possible, especially in
the past thirty years, to speak of a "Mayan diaspora"—not only of immigrants, but also of symbolic capital that serves a multiplicity of purposes
in a wide variety of contexts. If it is cool to be associated with the rebels,
it is also useful to associate with the ancient Maya, through belief in their
prophecies, collection of the imitation artifacts created by their descendants, and participation in ceremonies linking them to a new cosmic consciousness. Such a ceremony was held during the 1999 spring equinox,
at a "Prophets Conference" in Tulum, Yucatán. Participants stayed in a
nearby five-star hotel and were bused to the ancient sites.[7] In my new
hometown of Phoenix, Arizona, a concrete and frankly commercial example of this has arisen not far from my house: an ersatz Mayan pyramid now houses a new Fry's Electronics Superstore, built according to
the same design as an earlier store in San Jose. Apparently, the owners
and designers believe that the cachet of the ancient Maya will attach itself
to the sale of stereo components in the U.S. Southwest. The popular recent film *Chocolat*, based on Joanne Harris's equally touted novel, depends for its plot, theme, and characterization on the magical properties
of the sweets sold in the shop Chocolat Maya, which help the residents

of a small hidebound French village to release their pent-up passions. The heroine's dark secret is revealed to be the legacy of her mysterious Mayan mother's wanderlust. The film does nothing to mitigate a romanticized, essentializing notion that indigenous peoples, like the Maya, are the privileged repositories of something important now lost to the modern, Western world. Such examples indicate that if one were to redraw the map of "Mayan territory," tracing the routes this kind of symbolic capital has traveled over the past century and a half particularly, virtually no developed nation would be unshaded. As a result, much of the world already thinks it knows what it is to be (or to have been) Mayan.

To the extent that Mexican and international tourists and scholars make up part of the audience and that Mexican and international foundations supply part of the financial support for the theatre I have been discussing, these expectations exert a powerful pressure on the troupes to produce a readily readable "indigenous" or "Mayan" brand of theatre. Again, the power of theatrical representation becomes a political matter as well, no matter the overt content of a given work. In this environment, the troupes who say "We do Mayan theatre" are saying something bold, impossible, and altogether necessary.

NOTES

Prologue

1. Dick Bruna, *Kitten Nell*, trans. Sandra Greifenstein (Chicago: Follett, 1963), 6.
2. Ibid., 24.
3. For a fascinating study of such role-playing in U.S. history, see Philip J. Deloria, *Playing Indian* (New Haven: Yale University Press, 1998).
4. Pierre L. van den Berghe, *The Quest for the Other: Ethnic Tourism in San Cristóbal, Mexico* (Seattle: University of Washington Press, 1994).
5. Adrian G. Gilbert and Maurice M. Cotterell, *The Mayan Prophecies: Unlocking the Secrets of a Lost Civilization* (Rockport, Mass.: Element Books, 1995), 1.

Introduction

1. I use scare quotes around "up" to call attention to the way class privilege in academia is itself made visible in many street- and field-level critiques. See, for example, Dwight Conquergood's recent essay, "Performance Studies: Interventions and Radical Research," *TDR: The Drama Review* 46, 2 (summer 2002): 145–156.
2. The Indigenous Photography Archive is part of the Chiapas Photography Project, begun in 1992 with the intention of equipping Mayans in the region—themselves so often the object of the photographic gaze—with cameras and the power to record their experiences via the photographic medium. Since 1995, more than two hundred Mayan photographers from the state have contributed to a growing archive of photographs, some of which have become available in postcards and book publications. See Proyecto Fotográfico Chiapas at www.chiapas photo.org.
3. This was a favorite expression of my late theatre professor Michael Quinn, who was passionately interested in the things that connect human beings across time and space.
4. Edward F. Fischer, *Cultural Logics and Global Economies: Maya Identity in Thought and Practice* (Austin: University of Texas Press, 2001), 11.
5. John MacAloon, ed., *Rite, Drama, Festival, Spectacle: Rehearsals toward a Theory of Cultural Performance* (Philadelphia: Institute for the Study of Human Issues, 1984), 1.
6. Victor Turner, *From Ritual to Theatre: The Human Seriousness of Play* (New York: PAJ, 1982).

7. Michael Williams, graduate seminar in Comparative Religion, University of Washington, December 1993.

8. Claudio Lomnitz, *Deep Mexico, Silent Mexico: An Anthropology of Nationalism* (Minneapolis: University of Minnesota Press, 2001), 274.

9. The Nigerian playwright Wole Soyinka, for example, once responded to critics who claim he "transgresses" when he incorporates ethnic rituals in his work: "They have no right. Culture is not their property. Culture is universal" ("Art, Exile, and Resistance," *American Theatre* 14, 1 [January 1997]: 26–29). Similarly, Julie Stone Peters writes, "Who owns a culture? Who inherits it, from the moment of celebration to the documents of barbarism? Nobody, of course. . . . That perplexing 'right to culture' . . . is the right to as much of it as we can participate in, without any of it being taken away from anyone else" ("Intercultural Performance, Theatre Anthropology, and the Imperialist Critique: Identities, Inheritances, and Neo-Orthodoxies," in *Imperialism and Theatre: Essays on World Theatre, Drama and Performance*, ed. J. Ellen Gainor [New York: Routledge, 1995], 199–213). For critiques of the notion of authenticity from a subaltern perspective, see Trinh T. Minh-ha, *Woman, Native, Other* (Bloomington: Indiana University Press, 1989); and Deborah Root, *Cannibal Culture: Art, Appropriation, and Commodification of Difference* (Boulder, Colo.: Westview, 1996). Finally, Eric Hobsbawm and Terence Ranger provide useful insights into the strategic construction of authenticity in their *Invention of Tradition* (Cambridge: Cambridge University Press, 1983). For an earlier historiographical perspective on how the Americas were invented in European discourses and the epistemological work therein of the trope of "discovery," see Edmundo O'Gorman, *La invención de América: El universalismo de la cultura del Occidente* (México, D.F.: Fondo de Cultura Económica, 1958).

10. Cited in Diana Taylor, "Transculturating Transculturation," in *Interculturalism and Performance*, ed. Bonnie Marranca and Gautam Dasgupta (New York: PAJ, 1991), 61.

11. Conquergood, "Performance Studies," 146.

12. James Clifford, *Routes: Travel and Translation in the Late Twentieth Century* (Cambridge, Mass.: Harvard University Press, 1997).

13. James Clifford, *The Predicament of Culture: Twentieth-Century Ethnography, Literature, and Art* (Cambridge, Mass.: Harvard University Press, 1988), 14.

14. John E. Kicza, *The Indian in Latin American History: Resistance, Resilience, and Acculturation* (Wilmington, Del.: Scholarly Resources, 1993), xxv–vi.

15. Kay B. Warren, *Indigenous Movements and Their Critics: Pan-Maya Activism in Guatemala* (Princeton: Princeton University Press, 1998).

16. James Weil, discussant's comments on the panel "Sociocultural Formations" at the 1995 conference of the North Central Council of Latin Americanists, Ripon, Wisconsin, October 28, 1995.

17. Carolyn Heilbrun, *Writing a Woman's Life* (New York: Norton, 1988), 18.

18. Warren, *Indigenous Movements and Their Critics*, 201.

19. Cited in Taylor, "Transculturating Transculturation," 61–62. The original source is Fernando Ortiz, "Del fenómeno social de la transculturación y de su importancia en Cuba," *Revista Bimestre Cubana* 46 (1940): 272–278. I distinguish my use of the term from the way it is used in U.S.-European theatre discourse

to describe a universal or transcendent kind of theatre not reducible to cultural specifics, which I discuss in more detail in Chapter 3.

20. Taylor, "Transculturating Transculturation," 63.

21. My thanks to Donald Frischmann for introducing me to this insight during his presentation, "La construcción del sujeto poscolonial en el discurso escénico maya contemporaneo de México," during the meeting of the Asociación Mexicana de Investigación Teatral, March 25–27, 1999, UNAM, Mexico City. Frischmann follows the work of Carlos Lenkersdorf on Mayan languages in Mexico: *Los hombres verdaderos: Voces y testimonios tojolobales* (México, D.F.: Siglo XXI, UNAM, 1996) and *Cosmovisiones* (México, D.F.: UNAM, 1998). Lenkersdorf's observations pertain particularly to Tojolobal speakers in Chiapas; according to the Smithsonian linguist Robert Laughlin, Tzotzil and Tzeltal speakers commonly use subject-object constructions as well (personal interview, June 26, 2002). According to Feliciano Sánchez Chan, a Yucatec playwright and poet, in the Yucatán the intersubjective use is more common in ritual contexts than everyday conversation (personal interview, June 15, 2002). Thus, I use this example not to make a fetish of the grammatical construction but as an imaginative entrée into another way of viewing human subject–object relations.

22. Teresa Ortiz, comments made during a visit to my seminar "Theatre of the Americas," University of Minnesota, April 30, 1999.

23. For an interesting anthropological-historical perspective on the relationship of discourse to such collaborations in the Yucatán Peninsula, see Paul Sullivan, *Unfinished Conversations: Mayas and Foreigners between Two Wars* (Berkeley: University of California Press, 1991).

24. J. Jorge Klor de Alva, "The Postcolonization of the (Latin) American Experience: A Reconsideration of 'Colonialism,' 'Postcolonialism,' and 'Mestizaje,'" in *After Colonialism: Imperial Histories and Postcolonial Displacements,* ed. Gyan Prakash (Princeton: Princeton University Press, 1994), 242.

25. Néstor García Canclini, *Hybrid Cultures: Strategies for Entering and Leaving Modernity,* trans. Christopher L. Chiappari and Silvia L. López (Minneapolis: University of Minnesota Press, 1995), 204; my emphasis.

26. Michel de Certeau, *Heterologies,* trans. Brian Massumi (Minneapolis: University of Minnesota Press, 1986).

27. See Gayatri Spivak's "Can the Subaltern Speak?" in *Marxism and the Interpretation of Culture,* ed. Cary Nelson and Lawrence Grossberg (Champaign: University of Illinois Press, 1998), 271–313. I should note that Spivak herself has come to criticize the "fetishization" of this term, in cases in which it is deployed unscrupulously (see Bart Moore-Gilbert, *Postcolonial Theory: Contexts, Practices, Politics* [London: Verso, 1997]).

28. Claudio Lomnitz, "Nationalism's Dirty Linen," in *Deep Mexico, Silent Mexico,* 127.

29. Guillermo Bonfil Batalla, "Lo propio y lo ajeno: Una aproximación al problema del control cultural," in *Pensar nuestra cultura: Ensayos* (México, D.F.: Alianza, 1991), 49–57.

30. Gilles Deleuze and Félix Guattari, *A Thousand Plateaus: Capitalism and Schizophrenia,* trans. Brian Massumi (London: Athlone, 1987).

31. Ibid., 25.

32. Lawrence Grossberg, "Cultural Studies and/in New Worlds," *Critical Studies in Mass Communication* 10 (1993): 8.

33. Ibid.

34. Ibid.

35. See, for example, Barbara Tedlock, *Time and the Highland Maya,* rev. ed. (Albuquerque: University of New Mexico Press, 1992).

36. The geopolitical border separating Mayan peoples into Mexican and Guatemalan citizens was created in the nineteenth century. Guatemala is adjacent to Chiapas.

37. Dennis Tedlock, *Popul Vuh* (New York: Simon and Schuster, 1985), 23; my emphasis. As books were also conceived of as "seeing instruments," the use of the word "place" above includes the connotation as a *site from which to see,* as well as an object *of sight.*

38. Ibid., 35–36.

39. Ibid., 27.

40. Lynn Stephen, *¡Zapata Lives! Histories and Cultural Politics in Southern Mexico* (Berkeley: University of California Press, 2002).

41. These cultural missions, discussed further in the next chapter, traversed all of rural Mexico.

42. Quetzil E. Castañeda, *In the Museum of Maya Culture: Touring Chichén Itzá* (Minneapolis: University of Minnesota Press, 1996), 13.

1. Indigenous Bodies, Contested Texts

1. Tedlock, *Popul Vuh,* 46.

2. Despite much scholarly controversy over its provenance, Brasseur de Bourbourg's 1856 transcription is generally accepted as a relatively faithful record of a drama that was originally created in the latter half of the fifteenth century. An English translation by Richard Leinaweaver appeared in *Latin American Theatre Review* 1–2 (spring 1968): 3–53.

3. Dennis Tedlock, "The *Rabinal Achi*: Continuity and Change in a Mayan Dance Drama," presentation given at the University of Minnesota, October 8, 1998.

4. See Anita L. Padial and A. M. Vázquez-Bigi, "Estudio comparativo del Rabinal-Achi y la tragedia clásica griega," *Cuadernos Americanos* 249, 4 (July–August 1983): 159–189; and Caroline Cepin Benser, *Egon Wellesz: Chronicle of a Twentieth-Century Musician* (New York: Peter Lang, 1985).

5. Sergio Magaña, *Los enemigos* (México, D.F.: Editores Mexicanos Unidos, 1990).

6. This work, presented by La Compañía Nacional de Teatro del Instituto Nacional de Bellas Artes under the direction of Lorena Maza, is discussed in detail in the April 1995 issue of *Gestos* by Armando Partida Tayzan ("Interculturalidad: Deconstrucción de un texto y construcción escénica del *Rabinal-Achí,*" 101–117) and Becky Boling ("Language and Performance: Representation and Invention in Magaña's *Los enemigos,*" 119–130).

7. For summaries in English, see Donald H. Frischmann, "Active Ethnicity: Nativism, Otherness, and Indian Theatre in Mexico," *Gestos* 11 (April 1991): 113–

126; Marilyn Eckdahl Ravicz, *Early Colonial Religious Drama in Mexico: From Tzompantli to Golgotha* (Washington, D.C.: Catholic University of America Press, 1970); Judith A. Weiss, with Leslie Damasceno, Donald Frischmann, Claudia Kaiser-Lenoir, Marina Pianca, and Beatriz J. Rizk, *Latin American Popular Theatre: The First Five Centuries* (Albuquerque: University of New Mexico Press, 1993).

8. María Sten, *Vida y muerte del teatro náhuatl,* 2d ed. (Xalapa: Universidad Veracruzana, 1982), 14.

9. Diana Taylor, "Transculturating Transculturation," 65.

10. See Adam Versenyi, "Getting under the Aztecs' Skin: Evangelical Theatre in the New World," *New Theatre Quarterly* 19 (1989): 217–226; Max Harris, *The Dialogical Theatre: Dramatizations of the Conquest of Mexico and the Question of the Other* (New York: St. Martin's, 1993). The play they discuss is a version of the *Conquest of Jerusalem,* usually credited to the Franciscan, Fray Toribio de Benavente Motolonía, but whose creation as well as execution might have involved native Tlaxcaltecans.

11. Versenyi, "Getting under the Aztecs' Skin," 226.

12. Ibid.

13. Harris, *Dialogical Theatre,* ix.

14. Ibid.

15. See William H. Beezley, Cheryl English Martin, and William E. French, eds., *Rituals of Rule, Rituals of Resistance: Public Celebrations and Popular Culture in Mexico* (Wilmington, Del.: SR Books, 1994).

16. See Victoria Reifler Bricker, *Ritual Humor in Highland Chiapas* (Austin: University of Texas Press, 1973), and her *Indian Christ, Indian King* (Austin: University of Texas Press, 1981).

17. Max Harris, *Aztecs, Moors, and Christians: Festivals of Reconquest in Mexico and Spain* (Austin: University of Texas Press, 2000), 23. Harris is citing terminology introduced by James Scott in his work, *Domination and the Arts of Resistance: Hidden Transcripts* (New Haven: Yale University Press, 1990).

18. Harris, *Aztecs, Moors, and Christians,* 19.

19. Bricker, *Indian Christ;* Gary H. Gossen, "The Other in Chamula Tzotzil Cosmology and History: Reflections of a Kansan in Chiapas," *Cultural Anthropology* 8, 4 (1993): 443–475.

20. Gossen, "The Other in Chamula Tzotzil Cosmology and History," 467. In this passage, Gossen goes on to amend "community" here to "communities," reminding us of the diverse public identities Chamulans may adopt.

21. Thor Andersen's video documentary, *Sacred Games: Ritual Warfare in a Maya Village,* produced in collaboration with Sna Jtz'ibajom (Berkeley: University of California Extension Media Center, 1988; dist. Zeno Production Co.), provides an excellent introduction to contemporary Chamulan Carnaval.

22. Alfonso León de Garay, *Una aproximación a la psicología del mexicano,* cited in Sandra Messinger Cypess, *La Malinche in Mexican Literature: From History to Myth* (Austin: University of Texas Press, 1991), 173n.

23. Cypess, *La Malinche,* 7.

24. This child was not literally the first to be born of a European man and an indigenous woman; Cypess (*La Malinche,* 173n.) cites an early account of a ship-

wrecked Spaniard, Gonzalo Cerrero, who took a Mayan wife and had three children with her before Cortés's arrival. Interestingly, this man "went native," in contrast to his later counterparts, most of whom attempted to maintain and impose European lifestyles.

25. Cited in Cypess, *La Malinche*, 11.

26. Claudio Lomnitz-Adler, *Exits from the Labyrinth: Culture and Ideology in the Mexican National Space* (Berkeley: University of California Press, 1992).

27. Cypess, *La Malinche*, 68.

28. Lomnitz-Adler, *Exits from the Labyrinth*, provides a concise summary of how the "value of whiteness" was maintained in the years between Independence and the Revolution.

29. While a review of the many social, economic, and political histories of Mexico and Latin America is beyond the scope of this book, I would like to mention several works that discuss these histories from the various perspectives of native peoples: Guillermo Bonfil Batalla, *México Profundo: Reclaiming a Civilization*, trans. Philip A. Dennis (Austin: University of Texas Press, 1996; Carlos Montemayor, *Los pueblos indios de México hoy* (México, D.F.: Editorial Planeta Mexicana, 2001); John E. Kicza, ed., *The Indian in Latin American History: Resistance, Resilience, and Acculturation* (Wilmington, Del.: Scholarly Resources, 1993); Greg Urban and Joel Sherzer, eds., *Nation-States and Indians in Latin America* (Austin: University of Texas Press, 1991). A good general introduction is Michael C. Meyer, William L. Sherman, and Susan M. Deeds, *The Course of Mexican History* (New York: Oxford University Press, 1999). By way of contrast, see Enrique Krauze, *Mexico: Biography of Power*, trans. Hank Heifitz (New York: HarperCollins, 1997), which covers political rule in the modern period (1810–1996).

30. Many scholars believe that despite the rhetoric of revolution as an ever-present state suggested by the name of the ruling party, its ideals were betrayed as early as the administration of Miguel Alemán (1946–1952), with successive moves toward increased dependent industrialization and capitalist modernization. As for the ruling party, the PRI remained in power (although not always legitimately) between 1929 and 1997, when it lost the mayorship of Mexico City and its majority in the lower house of Congress. Then, in the presidential elections of 2000, Mexicans elected Vicente Fox Quesada of the conservative National Action Party, making Fox the first non-PRI president since 1929.

31. José Vasconcelos, *La raza cósmica*, trans. Didier T. Jaén (Los Angeles: California State University, Centro de Publicaciones Bilingual Edition, 1979), 38–39.

32. Guillermo Bonfil Batalla, *México Profundo*, 112.

33. Usually left out of the mix by critics and supporters alike are Asian Mexicans, whom latter-day *mestizaje* could never quite contain.

34. "The logic and structure of PRI do not lend themselves to easy explication. The system is esoteric in the extreme, but it can perhaps best be approached as a mechanism for dispensing favors, grand and petty" (Oriol Pi-Sunyer, R. Brooke Thomas, and Magalí Daltabuit, *Tourism and Maya Society in Quintana Roo, Mexico*, Occasional Paper No. 17 [Amherst: Latin American Studies Consortium of New England, September 1999], 10). George Baker and Alfonso Galindo suggest

it is "more accuratre to call the PRI a coalition of competing, centrist forces, than to think of it as a single party with a narrowly defined ideological framework," there being within it forces that lean rather more left, right, or center. See Baker and Galindo, "PRI Victory?" *Documents on Mexican Politics* (http://db.uwaterloo .ca/~lopez-o/politics/privictory.html.

35. For an interesting brief history of the tensions between tradition and modernity in the context of Mexican nationalism, see Claudio Lomnitz, "Nationalism's Dirty Linen," 132–136.

36. See also Michael Taussig, *Mimesis and Alterity: A Particular History of the Senses* (New York: Routledge, 1993), for an interesting and wide-ranging discussion of the instability of both categories in the history and ethnography of European colonialism.

37. Bonfil Batalla, *México Profundo*, 115.

38. My thanks to Mark Pedelty for making me aware of this part of Las Casas's work and to Fr. Miguel Rolland, O.P., for helping me to understand the context for Las Casas's changing views. For more about Las Casas in English, see Helen Rand Parish, *Bartolomé de Las Casas: The Only Way* (Mahwah, N.J.: Paulist Press, 1992); Benjamin Keen, *Bartolomé de Las Casas in History* (DeKalb: Northern Illinois University Press, 1971); and André Collard's translation of Las Casas's work, *History of the Indies* (New York: Harper and Row, 1971). In Spanish, see Bartolomé de Las Casas, *Historia de las Indias,* ed. André Saint-Lu (Caracas: Biblioteca Ayacucho, 1986). For a history of the changing ideology of Mexican indigenismo, from colonial times to the formation of the Instituto Nacional Indigenista in 1948, see Luis Villoro, *Los grandes momentos del indigenismo en México,* 2d ed. (México, D.F.: SEP, 1987). Gonzalo Aguirre Beltrán's *Regiones de refugio* (México, D.F.: Instituto Internacional Indigenista, 1967) elaborates on INI's role in official indigenismo.

39. For critiques of the official line, see Francisco Rojas Aravena, ed., *América Latina: Etnodesarrollo y etnocidio* (San José, Costa Rica: Ediciones FLACSO, 1982); and the Instituto Indigenista Interamericano anthology, *Indianidad, etnocidio e indigenismo en América Latina* (México, D.F., 1988). Cynthia Hewitt de Alcántara traces the development of that critique in her *Anthropological Perspectives on Rural Mexico* (New York: Routledge, 1984); for a summary of the positions, see R. A. M. van Zantwijk's "*Indigenismo:* A Philosophy and a Method of Guided Development of the Aboriginal Minorities in Mexico: Historical Background and Actual Orientations," *Plural Societies* 7 (1976): 95–103.

40. Lomnitz-Adler, *Exits from the Labyrinth,* 280.

41. Cited in Joanna O'Connell, *Prospero's Daughter: The Prose of Rosario Castellanos* (Austin: University of Texas Press, 1995), 54.

42. Cited in Urban and Sherzer, *Nation-States and Indians,* 6.

43. Again, see Hewitt de Alcántara, *Anthropological Perspectives,* for an overview of this activity.

44. See Evon Z. Vogt's retrospective, *Fieldwork among the Maya* (Albuquerque: University of New Mexico Press, 1994).

45. "De la consecución de estas metas depende en gran parte la integración de tzotziles y tzeltales a la vida nacional" (Gonzalo Aguirre Beltrán and Ricardo

Pozas Arciniega, *La política indigenista en México: Métodos y resultados,* vol. 2: *Instituciones indígenas en el México actual,* 2d ed. [México, D.F.: Instituto Nacional Indigenista y Secretaria de Educación Pública, 1973], 245).

46. Aguirre Beltrán and Pozas Arciniega, *La pólitica indigenista,* 201–216.

47. "Si para los manipuladores del guiñol era impreciso el límite entre lo real y lo imaginario, mucha más tenía que serlo para el auditorio. A nosotros (¿quienes éramos, después de todo, sino una ladina, una enemiga por su raza, y sus renegados de la suya?) era posible vernos con desconfianza y tratarnos con reticencia. Pero cuando reflexionaban en el que éramos también los portadores de Petul, se les borraba el ceño y se volvían hospitalarios y amables" (Rosario Castellanos, cited in Mary Seale Vásquez, "Rosario Castellanos, Image and Idea," in *Homenaje a Rosario Castellanos,* ed. Maureen Ahern and Mary Seale Vásquez [Valencia, Spain: Albatros Hisponofila, 1980], 23). "Ladina" is a term used in Chiapas and Guatemala to refer to a nonindigenous woman (that is, it identifies a woman of sociocultural privilege in the dominant culture).

48. Gary H. Gossen, "From Olmecs to Zapatistas: A Once and Future History of Souls," *American Anthropologist* 96, 3 (1994): 567.

49. ". . . abierto a las noticias que le traen sus amigos mestizos o blancos, gracias a cuya intervención el desenlace resulta siempre un triunfo de la inteligencia sobre las supersticiones, del progreso sobre la tradición, de la civilización sobre la barbarie" (Rosario Castellanos, cited in Vásquez, "Rosario Castellanos," 23).

50. This is in addition to thousands of open-air theatres constructed on schoolgrounds in the 1930s. See Donald H. Frischmann's *El nuevo teatro popular en México* (México, D.F.: INBA, 1990).

51. Elena Garro, *La dama boba,* in *Un hogar sólido y otras piezas* (Xalapa: Universidad Veracruzana, 1983), 171–246; all quotations in English are my translation.

52. Elena Garro, "The Author Speaks . . . ," interview with Michèle Muncy, *A Different Reality: Studies on the Work of Elena Garro,* ed. Anita Stoll (London and Toronto: Associated University Presses, 1990), 33.

53. While in Mexico I heard many stories about the rumored sexual depravity of rural schoolteachers in this period of educational reform. Engracia Loyo covers the problematic nature of relations between maestros and communities in her "Popular Reactions to the Educational Reforms of Cardenismo."

54. O'Connell, *Prospero's Daughter,* 52. O'Connell traces the roots of this literature to the nineteenth century, in work labeled by others as "indianista" for its tendency to romanticize and exoticize its subject.

55. Sandra Messinger Cypess, "The Figure of La Malinche in the Texts of Elena Garro," 119, 133.

56. INI, Mexico's great national symbol of indigenismo, became decentralized in December 1996 and dismantled altogether in April 2003. It has been replaced by a new organization, the National Commission for the Development of Indigenous Peoples, which many feel simply puts a new face on an old, indigenistic institution.

57. O'Connell, *Prospero's Daughter,* 57.

58. Conasupo is an acronym for the state-subsidized food, clothing, and shelter agency that in the early 1990s would come under scrutiny for its role in the laundering of drug profits in the Salinas Gortari administration (1988–1994).

59. ". . . llevar al campo buenas obras del repertorio universal" (Frischmann, *El nuevo teatro*, 53). Interestingly, Teatro Conasupo was headed by Eraclio Zepeda, who along with Rosario Castellanos was a leading writer of indigenista fiction in the 1960s.

60. ". . . participar activamente en la actividad teatral como forma de denunciar y de contribuir a la transformación de realidades represivas" (Frischmann, *El nuevo teatro*, 291).

61. ". . . la tradición cultural (el silencio de la mujer), su situación social (el peso del machismo) y el complejo racial (exponerse a los ojos de los mestizos)" (Frischmann, *El nuevo teatro*, 81).

62. ". . . la liberación de la mujer del peso de la tradición paternalista" (Frischmann, *El nuevo teatro*, 292).

63. Alicja Iwańska, *The Truths of Others: An Essay on Nativistic Intellectuals in Mexico* (Cambridge, Mass.: Schenkman, 1977), 1.

64. A flyer advertising Ruíz's visit to Arizona State University (ASU) labeled his deacons an "army," alluding to the connection between consciousness-raising and revolution. The deacons were ordained locally—"neither by Rome nor in rebellion against it"—which has caused the Vatican to put a halt to further ordinations. Although several of the Zapatista leaders had been ordained by Ruíz and he has been called "El comandante Sam" by his opponents, he has never advocated armed rebellion. After the Zapatista uprising, he became a key mediator between the EZLN and the Mexican government and has been nominated several times for the Nobel Peace Prize. My discussion of Ruíz's work is drawn from his comments during the ASU presentation, "La iglesia autóctona en Chiapas: Una experiencia pastoral indígena" (Phoenix, April 25, 2002); from Jean Meyer, with Federico Anaya Gallardo and Julio Ríos, *Samuel Ruíz en San Cristóbal, 1960–2000* (México, D.F.: Tusquets, 2000); and Gary MacEoin, *The People's Church: Bishop Samuel Ruíz of Mexico and Why He Matters* (New York: Crossroad/Herder and Herder, 1996). See also Carlos Fazio, *Samuel Ruíz, el caminante* (México, D.F.: Espasa Calpe, 1994).

65. Although labeled a "first," a similar congress had in fact been held in the late 1930s in Michoacán. Jesús Morales Bermúdez, one of the organizers of this congress, chronicles its successes and limitation from the perspective of twenty years after the fact in his 1995 essay, "El Congreso Indígena de Chiapas: Un testimonio," *América Indígena* 55, 1–2 (1995): 305–340.

66. Yves Materne, ed., *The Indian Awakening in Latin America* (New York: Friendship Press, 1980), 51. The speaker was not identified by name.

67. In Mexico, "neoliberalism" refers to a program of economic reform, begun in the 1980s, that can be loosely but validly translated as "Reaganomics" for U.S. readers: a commitment to an economy based on free enterprise rather than state control, legalized by constitutional reforms passed during the Salinas Gortari administration (1988–1994).

68. Marcos has subsequently been "unmasked" by the Mexican government as Rafael Sebastián Guillén Vicente, a former professor of Marxist theory and communications at the Xochimilco campus of the Universidad Autónoma Metropolitana (UNAM). Ilan Stavans, a student there while Guillén was teaching (but not one of his students), finds the claim credible. But, as he writes, this was "a reve-

lation, indeed, which El Sup [Marcos] immediately disputed . . . before vanishing into the night. . . . In Mexico, of course, the government is always wrong; that is, since it promotes itself as the sole owner of the Truth, nobody believes it. . . . So what if he is Guillén, and vice versa? Simply that his unmasking has served its purpose: El Sup has faded away from public attention. His once-omnipresent visage now appears infrequently, if at all, a haggard reminder of the still miserable conditions in the South." This was written in 1996; although Marcos addresses the press even less frequently today, Zapatistas still draw thousands of marchers in street protests of new federal trade and human rights policies. See Ilan Stavans, "Unmasking Marcos," in Tom Hayden, ed., *The Zapatista Reader* (New York: Thunder's Mouth Press/Nation Books, 2002), 386–395.

69. See, for example, Rosalva Aida Hernández Castillo, "Entre el etnocentrismo feminista y el esencialismo étnico: Las mujeres indígenas y sus demandas de género," *Debate Feminista* 12, 24 (October 2001): 206–229; Rosalva Aida Hernández Castillo, ed., *The Other Word: Women and Violence in Chiapas Before and After Acteal* (Copenhagen: International Work Group for Indigenous Affairs, 2001); June Nash, ed., *Crafts in the World Market: The Impact of Global Exchange on Middle American Artisans* (Albany: State University of New York Press, 1993).

70. Although he does not address the question of women specifically, Bishop Ruíz describes an emergent pastoral process in his diocese, one that draws on and from the lived experiences of the faithful as participants in local history. This new method, *tijuanej* (Tzeltal for "to vibrate," connoting also "to disturb" or "to bother"), is based on "asking questions to stimulate participatory discussion" during Bible study. Thus, rather than impose church doctrine from without, his diocese began to "grow" it from within, using a dialogic process. In this environment, the experiences of women also began to be taken into consideration in a new way. See Michel Andraos, ed. and trans., *Seeking Freedom: Bishop Samuel Ruíz in Conversation with Jorge S. Santiago* (Toronto: Toronto Council—Development and Peace, 1999); and Ruíz's *Mi trabajo pastoral* (México, D.F.: Ediciones Paulinas, 1999).

71. A particularly gruesome example of how such "customary law" can work against the human rights of women was related to me by several U.S. anthropologists working in Chiapas in the 1990s. There, a husband has the right to take a warm tortilla from the cooking fire and apply it to his wife's forearm for as long as he deems it necessary to teach her a lesson in her domestic duties. Depending on his estimate of her learning curve, the results range from first- to third-degree burns. Another example, equally disturbing on a symbolic level, was an oral story circulating in the 1990s among Tzotzil women, documented by the anthropologist Kathleen Sullivan. Its moral, passed along from mother to daughter, is this: Don't ask too many questions of your husband, or he can and will beat you. Here, a survival strategy unfortunately also does the work of silencing women.

72. ". . . si se va a legislar el reconocimiento de los usos y costumbres, son las propias mujeres quienes deberán decidir cuáles permanecen y cuáles se tienen que cambiar por ser lesivos a sus derechos humanos" (Rosa Rojas, *Del dicho al hecho: Reflexiones sobre la ampliación de la ley revolucionaria de mujeres del EZLN* [México, D.F.: Ediciones del Taller Editorial La Correa Feminista, 1996], n.p.).

73. *A Place Called Chiapas,* dir. Nettie Wild (Canada Wild Production, 1998).

As early as February 8, 1994, less than a month after the fighting in Chiapas had stopped, Tim Golden of the *New York Times* wrote, "Among leftist intellectuals, Marcos has already established himself as the region's first postmodern guerrilla hero" (Tim Golden, "The Voice of the Rebels Has Mexicans in His Spell," *New York Times,* February 8, 1994, A3).

74. Victor Ballinas, Programas antipobreza en Chiapas, estrategia contrainsurgente: observadores internacionales, *La Jornada* on-line: July 30, 2002. URL: www.jornada.unam.mx. "War of attrition" (*guerra de desgaste*) is a term coined by the authors of a recent study published by two Mexican nongovernmental organizations to distinguish the Mexican situation from "low intensity warfare" in other countries. Such a war is characterized not only by military and paramilitary action but also by economic actions, information control, intelligence operations, and political initiatives. The study, published by Grupo de Acción Comunitaria and the Centro de Derechos Humanos Miguel Agustín Pro Juárez in 2002, was also discussed by Ballinas in *La Jornada,* June 18, 2002, 9.

75. This initiative, a development agreement between Mexico and the seven Central American countries, will expand the number of transoceanic canals for East-West shipping and improve the overland infrastructure for transporting goods between North and South America. Because it also allows for private interests to gain greater access to natural resources in Mexico and Central America, many indigenous communities are justifiably concerned about its effects. On August 16, 2002, some fifteen thousand Mayans from Chiapas demonstrated in the streets of San Cristóbal against this initiative, and on January 1, 2003, more than twenty thousand marched there again, to mark the ninth anniversary of the uprising.

76. See, for example, Roberto Blancarte, *Cultura e identidad nacional* (México, D.F.: Consejo Nacional para la Cultura y las Artes, 1994).

77. "Este engullir los productos indianos es un acto simbólico que refleja la verdadera intención de tragarse al pueblo indio" (Jacinto Arias, "Mucha semilla desparramada," *Hojarasca* 8 [May 1992]: 28). "Indianness" (*indianidad*) is the term he prefers to "ethnicity," because in his view the two are not coterminous; his preference is to preserve the unique position of Native Americans who, unlike other ethnic groups in the Americas, have occupied the same lands for thousands of years. Arias himself is not immune to critique for his own involvement as a member of the PRI; for example, he was implicated in the December 1997 massacre of thirty-two women and thirteen men praying inside a church in the village of Acteal in Chiapas, which was carried out by a PRI-supported paramilitary organization.

2. "Más que una noticia . . ."

1. Louis Montrose, "The Work of Gender in the Discourse of Discovery," in *New World Encounters,* ed. Stephen Greenblatt (Berkeley: University of California Press, 1993), 177–217. José Rabasa characterizes the engraving, which was printed as a wall hanging and as an illustration in a book on modern discoveries called *Nova reperta* in 1638, as having "monumental import" because it was later included in many other texts on the exploration of the New World. See his *Invent-*

ing America: Spanish Historiography and the Formation of Eurocentrism (Norman: University of Oklahoma Press, 1993).

2. At least in its modern incarnation she is industrious. Rabasa, *Inventing America*, suggests that the sleeping America of the van der Straet engraving contributed to the image of native Americans as slothful.

3. June C. Nash explores this in more detail in *Mayan Visions: The Quest for Autonomy in an Age of Globalization* (New York: Routledge, 2001). According to Nash, one of the most important differences between the logic of indigenous movements for autonomy and that of the global free market is the former's emphasis on the collectivity over the individual, the principal subject in free market democracies.

4. Christine Eber and Brenda Rosenbaum provide a fascinating study of the effects of women's weaving production on household relations in Chiapas in "'That we may serve beneath your hands and feet': Women Weavers in Highland Chiapas, Mexico." In addition to Nash's recent study cited above, see also Brenda Rosenbaum, *With Our Heads Bowed: The Dynamics of Gender in a Maya Community* (Albany Institute for Mesoamerican Studies, State University of New York, 1993); Kathleen Sullivan, "Protagonists of Change," *Cultural Survival Quarterly* 16, 4 (winter 1992): 38–40; Elizabeth Kadetsky, "The Human Cost of Free Trade," *Ms.* 4, 4 (February 1994): 10–15.

5. Nash, *Mayan Visions,* 25.

6. Ibid., 50.

7. Mary Jordan, "In Mexico, an Unpunished Crime: Rape Victims Face Widespread Cultural Bias in Pursuit of Justice," *Washington Post,* June 30, 2002, A1.

8. Cynthia Steele, "A Woman Fell into the River: Negotiating Female Subjects in Contemporary Mayan Theatre," in *Negotiating Performance: Gender, Sexuality, and Theatricality in Latin/o America,* ed. Diana Taylor and Juan Villegas (Durham: Duke University Press), 239–256.

9. Kathleen Sullivan, "Religious Change and the Recreation of Community in an Urban Setting among the Tzotzil Maya of Highland Chiapas, Mexico" (Ph.D. diss., City University of New York, 1998), 185–190.

10. I use the abbreviation "Sna" to refer to the organization as a whole and "Lo'il Maxil" to refer to the theatre troupe specifically.

11. La Fomma operates with a core staff of four to six permanent employees and several interns and offers programs for up to twenty-five women, plus children. The women receive a small stipend to offset their lost wages. In summer 2002, Lo'il Maxil featured an ensemble of eight: three women and five men. All receive full-time salaries for their participation as actors, writers, teachers, and photographers. Another woman works full time in Sna's photography area.

12. According to the 2000 Mexican national census, Tzeltal and Tzotzil speakers together total slightly more than half a million people (582,387) in a state whose population is estimated at close to 4 million. Of the total, roughly 1.5 million, or 37 percent, speak an indigenous language. That estimate is probably very conservative, given the difficulties of gathering census data there. Although the census reports roughly the same number of Tzeltal speakers as Tzotzil speakers, the latter enjoy slightly more economic power and prestige in the region.

13. Nine of Lo'il Maxil's plays (including one radio-puppet script) have been

anthologized in three volumes of the fifteen-volume series edited by Carlos Montemayor, *Colección letras mayas contemporáneas, Chiapas* (México, D.F.: INI, 1996), published in Spanish and Tzotzil. In Spanish, the title of the three-volume drama series is *Renacimiento del teatro maya en Chiapas.* Subsequent references are identified by volume number. In addition, two short plays by the Lo'il Maxil member Antonio de la Torre López appear in the Sna anthology, *Relatos tseltales y tzotziles* (Tuxtla Gutiérrez: Gobierno del Estado de Chiapas, 1996). Other local stories gathered and written by the group appear in the anthology, *Relatos tzeltales y tzotziles* (México, D.F.: Diana, 1994). An essay recounting Sna's early history by member Manuel Pérez Hernández appears in Montemayor's *Los escritores indígenas actuales,* vol. 2 (México, D.F.: Consejo Nacional para la Cultura y las Artes, 1992). A similar history by Robert M. Laughlin, "En la vanguardia: Sna Jtz'ibajom," appears in Carlos Montemayor, ed., *Situación actual y perspectivas de la literatura en lenguas indígenas* (México, D.F.: Consejo Nacional para la Cultura y las Artes, 1993), 155–172. Robert Laughlin has translated twelve of Lo'il Maxil's plays into English in preparation for a forthcoming book, *The Monkey Business Theatre.*

14. "Unmasking the Maya: The Story of Sna Jtz'ibajom," Smithsonian National Museum of Natural History, Department of Anthropology, www.mnh.si.edu/anthro/maya. For printed accounts, in addition to Steele, "A Woman Fell into the River," see Donald H. Frischmann, "New Mayan Theatre in Chiapas: Anthropology, Literacy and Social Drama," in Taylor and Villegas, *Negotiating Performance,* 213–238; Miriam Laughlin, "The Drama of Mayan Women," *Ms.* 2, 1 (July–August 1991): 88–89; Robert M. Laughlin, "The Mayan Renaissance: Sna Jtz'ibajom, the House of the Writer," *Cultural Survival Quarterly* 17, 4 (winter 1994): 13–15; Robert Laughlin, "Chiapas' Theater of the People," *Cultural Survival Quarterly* 26, 1 (spring 2002): 64–66; and Patrick Breslin, "Coping with Change, the Maya Discover the Play's the Thing," *Smithsonian* 23, 5 (August 1992): 78–87. For an early and much condensed version of the present study, see my "Incidents of Theatre in Chiapas, Tabasco, and Yucatán: Cultural Enactments in Mayan Mexico," *Theatre Journal* 50 (1998): 349–369.

15. Steele, "A Woman Fell into the River," 240.

16. Robert M. Laughlin, E-mail correspondence, March 16, 2003.

17. David Freidel, Linda Schele, and Joy Parker, *Maya Cosmos: Three Thousand Years on the Shaman's Path* (New York: Morrow, 1993).

18. Ralph Lee, telephone interview, November 26, 1996. The play is *Antorchas para amanecer* (Torches for a New Dawn).

19. See the Web site, "Unmasking the Maya," link "Speaking Out," for more information on this visit.

20. Ralph Lee, telephone interview, August 13, 2002.

21. Robert M. Laughlin, E-mail correspondence, August 23, 2002.

22. Although it is a collective, the organization maintains an elected board consisting of president, vice president, secretary, and treasurer; until 2000 the top two posts were held by men.

23. Laughlin was the first to call attention to the women in this way, in his history of Sna, "En la vanguardia."

24. The Laughlins differ in their accounts of Sna's willingness to produce this

play. Robert argues it was performed in full at Texas Christian University; Miriam, that only certain scenes were performed, under protest by the men, at Ohio State University. According to Robert, the men's concern had to do with costuming: several of the men from Zinacantán felt that de la Cruz Cruz, by performing in her own Zinacantecan traje, represented her personal experiences as generalizable to the town as a whole (E-mail communications, March 16 and 17, 2003). For more detail about the reasons for the decision to leave Shan, see Steele's "A Woman Fell into the River" and Harley Erdman's recent interview with the women, "Gendering Chiapas: Petrona de la Cruz and Isabel J. F. Juárez Espinosa of La FOMMA (Fortaleza de la Mujer Maya/Strength of the Mayan Woman)," in Roberta Uno, ed., with Lucy Mae San Pablo Burns, *The Color of Theater: Race, Culture, and Contemporary Performance* (London: Continuum, 2002), 159–170.

25. Doris Difarnecio, telephone interview, August 12, 2002.

26. Petrona de la Cruz Cruz, personal interviews, July 27, 1996, and March 22, 1999, and telephone interview, August 14, 2002.

27. Juárez Espinosa's *Migración* appears in *Cuentos y teatro tzeltales*, 147–163; *La Desconfiada* appears in *Mesoamérica* 23 (June 1992), 135–141; and de la Cruz Cruz's *Una mujer desesperada* appears in Diana Taylor and Roselyn Costantino, eds., *Holy Terrors: Latin American Women Perform* (Durham: Duke University Press, 2003).

28. Miriam Laughlin, "Special Projects Update: Fomma," *Cultural Survival Quarterly* (fall 1996): 14–15.

29. See, for example, Ximena Bedregal, "Fortaleza de la Mujer Maya: Teatreras y escritoras indígenas reconstruyen su mundo," *Triple Jornada* 3 (November 2, 1998): 1 ff.; and Robert Myers, "Mayan Women Find Their Place Is on the Stage," *New York Times*, September 28, 1997, Arts and Leisure, 1.

30. The proceedings were published as *II Encuentro Indígena de las Américas* (San Cristóbal de las Casas: Sna Jtz'ibajom, 2000).

31. The marriage metaphor finds its echo in the two groups' U.S. intermediaries, Robert M. Laughlin, who continues to work with Sna, and Miriam Laughlin, who has helped to arrange La Fomma's U.S. and international grants and bookings.

32. Frischmann, "New Mayan Theatre."

33. The bilingual U.S. production, retitled *The Origin of Corn*, is discussed on La Jolla Playhouse's Web site: http://lajollaplayhouse.com/news/poprel1.htm. Lo'il Maxil's text for this production was developed collectively from a tale related by member Diego Méndez Guzmán, from Tenejapa. It is remarkably consistent with versions of the tale collected by Carlos Navarrete and discussed in his *Relatos mayas de tierras sobre el origen del maíz: Los caminos de Paxil* (Guatemala City: Editorial Palo de Hormigo, 2000). This was not the first U.S. production of a Lo'il Maxil play, but it was the first to use U.S. actors. The group has toured existing work and developed new work in the United States. A recent example is *Trabajadores en el otro mundo* (Workers in the Other World, 1998), developed for a community of Mayan farmworkers in Florida and then adapted and toured in Chiapas (see note 19). Although outside the scope of this chapter, this is an inter-

esting play and an important example of border-crossing exchange, which gave the troupe an opportunity to see how their countrymen fared under the harsh conditions of undocumented farm work in the United States. Perhaps this is why the Mexican version of this play is more didactic than the plays I cover here and less concerned to illustrate the ills of Chiapan and Mexican society that compel people to migrate to the United States in the first place. (Comments based on a typescript and videotaped production in 1999.)

34. "En homenaje a los mártires mayas y zoques caídos en las guerras de Chiapas" (*De todos para todos,* in Vol. 2 of *Renacimiento del teatro maya en Chiapas,* 119). An English translation of this play also appears in Robert M. Laughlin, "From All for All: A Tzotzil-Tzeltal Tragicomedy," *American Anthropologist* 97, 3 (1995): 528–542. The Zoques are another indigenous group resident in Chiapas.

35. Because the precise charge of this insulting term has no equivalent in English, I leave it untranslated here.

36. "¡Indio alzado! ¡Te estoy hablando de las escrituras, porque estas tierras las vinieron a invadir sin permiso de mi familia y ahora van a tener que desocuparlas! ¡Les doy una semana de plazo para que levanten lo que puedan de su cosecha, para que vean que soy buena gente!" (*De todos para todos,* 122).

37. "Quizás porque no sabemos leer ni escribir. Esa fue la única respuesta que me dieron" (*De todos para todos,* 127).

38. A similar theme is explored in a short piece set in the era of Conquest, "Tiempo de los Mayas," in volume 3 of the *Renacimiento* series.

39. Woman-as-sacrifice is also a motif in *Dinastía de jaguares,* a 1992 play that was very popular in its first few years. Steele provides a feminist critique of this motif in "A Woman Fell into the River." Interestingly, as *De todos para todos* was presented again and again in summer 1996, more and more women rebels were added as extras to the final scene, until by August even the troupe's ladina secretary had donned Chamulan traje and taken part in the action.

40. "¡Ésta es una lucha de todos para todos! ¡Aunque caiga nuestra sangre, queremos que nuestros hijos vivan con justicia!" (*De todos para todos,* 141).

41. "¡Retoños de la tierra! ¡Detengan esta matanza! ¡Que no corra más sangre! ¿No ven que todos ustedes son hermanos? Si quieren vivir felices sobre la tierra, deberán aprender a respetarse y a unirse como hermanos y a respetar también a los animales y plantas de la tierra. ¡Que el gran espíritu solar ilumine la verdadera paz, si así lo hacen!" (*De todos para todos,* 141).

42. It is also worth noting that in indigenous communities, the play was performed in Tzotzil; in cities and for international observers, it was performed in Spanish.

43. Ralph Lee, telephone interview, November 26, 1996.

44. Leticia Méndez Intzin, personal interview, June 25, 2002. Robert Laughlin told me that the late Anselmo Pérez Pérez, a founding member of Sna and its resident holy man, had actually seen one, but this is quite rare. Gossen discusses the figure in his 1994 essay, "From Olmecs to Zapatistas." In a more popular venue, Walter F. Morris Jr. discusses these "totally non-Catholic" beings in his *Living Maya* (New York: Harry N. Abrams, 1987), 33.

45. Rosenbaum, *With Our Heads Bowed,* 80.

46. My discussion of this play is based on an unpublished typescript (used with permission) and a videotaped production of a 2001 performance in San Cristóbal.

47. Hernández Castillo, *The Other Word*, 151.

48. Sna's offices have an inside rehearsal space but no open courtyard in which to perform for the public. For this "command performance" for visitors and researchers, they availed themselves of La Fomma's courtyard.

49. Robert M. Laughlin, E-mail correspondence, March 16, 2003.

50. A notable exception is *Herencia fatal* (1991), developed when de la Cruz Cruz and Juárez Espinosa were still both working with Sna. Frischmann discusses this play in some detail in "New Mayan Theatre."

51. *Siempre México con nosotros*, 2–3.

52. For a more detailed discussion of *La migración*, see Underiner, "Incidents of Theatre in Chiapas, Tabasco, and Yucatán." My discussion of the two other migration plays comes from seeing performances of them in spring 1999 and from unpublished manuscripts and typescripts the group has shared with me.

53. "¡Tú tienes que ir a donde yo vaya, quieras o no! ¡Y el terreno, si quiero venderlo, lo vendo! porque es mío" (*Migración*, 154).

54. ". . . aprovechándose del sueldo de los compañeros" (*Migración*, 163).

55. Aleyda Aguirre Rodríguez, "La Vida de las Juanas," *Triple Jornada*, 3 (November 2, 1998): 4.

56. My discussion of *Héchame la mano, La locura de comadres,* and *Conchita desenconchada* is based on interviews with Juárez Espinosa, information and photographs supplied by La Fomma member Faustina López Díaz, and printed English-language summaries archived by La Fomma for grant writing purposes.

57. Nash, *Mayan Visions*.

58. See Bricker, *Ritual Humor in Highland Chiapas.*

59. "Mientras los reflectores iluminan algunos justos sueños hechos altavoz a través de pasa montañas, armas, guerras, comandantes, leyes de comportamiento social y milicianos de algún ya conocido nuevo orden, de manera silenciosa, invisible y pacífica, en una esquina de San Cristóbal de las Casas, Chiapas, un grupo de mujeres indias hace un ruido que pocos oyen pero que cambia las entrañas mismas del sentido del ser y poder de muchas mujeres, crea escenarios a los que pocos llegan pero donde se construyen desconocidos poderes que ninguna derrota política o militar haría retroceder" (Bedregal, "Fortaleza de la Mujer Maya," 1).

60. Loren Kruger, E-mail correspondence, April 1998.

61. Eric van Young, "Conclusion: The State as Vampire—Hegemonic Projects, Public Ritual, and Popular Culture in Mexico 1600–1990," in Beezley, Martin, and French, *Rituals of Rule, Rituals of Resistance,* 366.

62. Grossberg, "Cultural Studies and/in New Worlds," 8.

63. Miriam Laughlin, E-mail correspondence, July 31, 2002.

64. Sántiz Gómez's work is receiving increasing exposure in Mexican art galleries and photo exhibitions, and she has published, with the Indigenous Photo Archive, a collection of her photographs titled *Creencias de nuestros antepasados/Beliefs of Our Ancestors* (1998).

65. Sántiz Gómez, personal interview, August 4, 1996.

66. "Bienvenida a esta casa, a esta vendita tierra, en ella vivirás tu niñez hasta convertirte en mujer."

Tu corazón será guerrero, como el nagual de tu nacimiento curiosa y fuerte.
Volarás disfrutando todo lo que te rodea linda mariposa.
Tu corazón está contento, llevas en ella el fruto de vientre que florece como la
semilla del maíz.
Serás como diosa llena de fortaleza llevada por los pasos de tu hermoso nagual.
No permitas que corten tus alas: saltarás tropiezos y sonríe en tus sueños
deseados.
Con la frente alta seguirás adelante con los ojos fijos y pasos firmes."
La Fomma, unpublished manuscript of "Crecí con el amor de mi madre" (2001)
in author's possession.

3. Transculturation in the Work of Laboratorio de Teatro Campesino e Indígena

1. See the Introduction for more information on transculturation.

2. Patrice Pavis, ed., "Introduction: Towards a Theory of Interculturalism in Theatre?" in *The Intercultural Performance Reader* (London: Routledge, 1996), 1–26.

3. Ibid., 6.

4. In addition to Marranca and Dasgupta, eds., *Interculturalism and Performance*, see Rustom Bharucha, *The Politics of Cultural Practice: Thinking through Theatre in an Age of Globalization* (London: Athlone, 2000).

5. Figures according to the 1990 census; other sources suggest they are higher. The on-line version of the 2000 Mexican census does not quantify the number of Chontal speakers, but according to its figures, 8.5 percent of Tabasco's residents speak Chol as a first language.

6. "Los chontales habían permanecido en la indiferencia durante muchos años atrás, la muestra de la ignorancia de que existían, fue larga, hasta el extremo de declaraciones de que no existían 'Indios' en Tabasco o bien ignorados en algunos de los censos de población (a pesar de documentos de 1933)" (Rubén Vera Cabrera, "Los Chontales de Tabasco: Historia y Desarrollo," *Expresión* 20 [September–October 1987]: 2.

7. Vera Cabrera, "Los Chontales de Tabasco," 6. "Castellano" is a term many indigenous groups use to refer to the Spanish language.

8. Personal interviews with Martínez Medrano and her assistant, Delia Rendón Novelo, July–August 1996.

9. In addition to Vera Cabrera, "Los Chontales de Tabasco," see María del Carmen Rivera Cruz, "Los indígenas Choles de Tabasco," *Expresión* 14 (September–October 1986): 2–5.

10. "Afortunadamente, existen programas desarrollados por el gobierno Estatal y Federal . . . en apoyos para cultivos básicos de autosubsistencia, escuelas para niños y jóvenes así como un proyecto de alfabetización para los adultos. Asimismo destacan la construcción de caminos, viviendas, mejoramiento de la salud y un fuerte impulso para el rescate de sus tradiciones culturales; todo ello en base a la organización comunitaria y la participación de la misma en un proceso de autogestión" (Vera Cabrera, "Los Chontales de Tabasco," 2).

11. Campos's tenure in Tabasco led her to write, in marked contrast to her ex-

perimental novels, a best-selling critique of the history of Mexican social policy, *¿Qué hacemos con los pobres?* (What Do We Do with the Poor?)(México, D.F.: Aguilar, 1995).

12. Seki Sano left Japan in 1930, after he was arrested for Marxist political activism, and spent periods of self-exile in Moscow, Paris, and New York before settling in Mexico City in 1939. While in Moscow he met and studied with both Stanislavsky and Meyerhold and introduced the methods of both to his Mexican students, but he rarely credited the latter in his work. As a result, "The System" in Mexico bears a marked but generally unacknowledged Meyerholdian stamp. See Michiko Tanaka, "Seki Sano and Popular Political and Social Theatre in Latin America," *Latin American Theatre Review* (spring 1994): 53–69.

13. In addition to Oxolotán, the "hub" of the network, the other communities were Mazateupa, Tucta, Simón Sarlat, Los Pájaros, Redención del Campesino, and Villa Quetzalcóatl.

14. María Elena Madrid, Sylvia Sambarino, and Miguel Angel Pineda, eds., *Laboratorio de Teatro Campesino e Indígena* (Villahermosa, Tabasco: DIF, 1987), 1.

15. María Alicia Martínez Medrano, personal interview, August 11, 1996.

16. For photographs of the original production, taken by the Mexican photographer Lourdes Grobet, see the Web site http://www.arts-history.mx/foto/grobet/h2.html.

17. Federico García Lorca, *Bodas de Sangre: Versión oxoloteca de la obra original de Federico García Lorca, Bodas de sangre,* adapted by María Alicia Martínez Medrano (México, D.F.: Gobierno del Estado de Tabasco, 1987).

18. ". . . la overtura presenta a todo el pueblo, en situaciones, trabajos escénicos y papeles que les tocó jugar en la tragedia. Los personajes permanecen en 'estampa' más de quince minutos, con un virtuosismo que solamente logran los buenos y disciplinados actores, aquéllos que saben lo que es y cómo se come la concentración orgánica. Forman un gran mural, cuidado en su composición plástica hasta lo infinito. Música de flauta y tambores chontales . . . detrás irrumpe la muerte a caballo, capa negra, máscara de blancura, cabellera hirsuta, merodea, traza figuras, busca, envuelve al pueblo, rodea a los protagonistas de la pasión. Sale. Con esto ya se tejieron todos los hilos de la trama y se han dada pinceladas de los personajes y símbolos: antes de la entrada de la muerte, aparecieron cuatro 'arlequines,' montados a caballo, vestidos con pantalón de mezclilla, camiseta, paliacate en la cabeza, maquillaje apenas insinuado, son la alegría, la tranquilidad de la vida y de la tierra. En un momento dado la puesta en escena: luchan contra la muerte, la ahuyentan. En este retablo de la vida, María Alicia tiene audacias como la de presentar al novio y al rival juntos sobre una de las estructuras, lo cual resulta intenso y perfecto, pues al final los vuelve a juntar bajo la Tierra" (Tomás Espinosa, "Imágenes del Laboratorio de Teatro Campesino e Indígena," *Expresión* 18 (May–June 1987): 7.

19. Gloria F. Waldman, "Festival Latino Diary," *Latin American Theatre Review* 20, 2 (spring 1997): 102–103.

20. The state of Sinaloa is on Mexico's west coast; its indigenous populations include the Mayo (not to be confused with Maya) and the Yaqui. Although the production originated with the Sinaloan Laboratorio, it included actors from

Tabasco and the Yucatán for the Mayan roles, making it both multicultural and intercultural.

21. Renny Golden, Michael McConnell, Peggy Mueller, Cinny Popper, and Marilyn Turkovitch, *Dangerous Memories: Invasion and Resistance since 1492* (Chicago: Chicago Religious Task Force on Central America, 1992).

22. An interesting side note: Lesvi Vásquez, who played Julieta, and Octavio Cervantes, who played Romeo, were in fact Maya and Mayo, respectively; moreover, they were married to each other in their offstage lives.

23. Elda Maceda, "La repetitiva actuación del Teatro Campesino," review of *Romeo y Julieta*, dir. María Alicia Martínez Medrano, LTCI, Culiacán, Sinaloa, *El Universal*, November 24, 1994, 2.

24. "Una voz, que interrumpe en varias ocasiones el desarrollo de la puesta, anuncia que a los mayos y los mayas no los unió el sentimiento de pertenecer a un país y tampoco los unió la tierra. Los unió—asegura la voz—el odio y el rencor de un cacique: Porfirio Díaz" (ibid., 2).

25. This was the title of Richard F. Shepard's preview article announcing the group's participation in Joseph Papp's 1990 Festival Latino (*New York Times*, September 11, 1990, C15).

26. Wilborn Hampton, "Shakespeare Caliente Is a Visual Spectacle," review of *Romeo y Julieta*, dir. María Alicia Martínez Medrano, Delacorte Theatre, New York (*New York Times*, September 15, 1990, A15).

27. "Rotundo Éxito en Madrid del Grupo Teatral Tabasqueño: Diario 16," review of *Bodas de sangre*, dir. María Alicia Martínez Medrano, LTCI, Spain (photocopy of unidentified newspaper article dated October 18, 1987, in archives of Centro de Investigación Teatral Rodolfo Usigli [CITRU]).

28. "Y la representación se vuelve un ritual y los actores no actúan, se viven a si mismos; sencillos y dignos, dan vida a lo que son. Imaginación, honestidad profesional, alegría. Virtudes que rodean cada expresión, cada diálogo, cada movimiento, cada coro y cada canto. No son actores, son ellos mismos. Marchan, bailan, corren, recitan y, sombreros y faldas que se ponen a jugar con el aire, hacen de la representación un jolgorio" (Arturo García Hernández, "La universalidad de García Lorca, puesta a prueba con el teatro indígena," review of *Bodas de sangre*, dir. María Martínez Medrano, LTCI, Chapultepec Park, Mexico City, *La Jornada* 31 [March 1987]).

29. "Muchos críticos piensan . . . que el indígena es incapaz de representar bien una obra teatral, porque afirman que 'los indios no saben nada de teatro.' Nosotros consideramos esta situación como una ventaja, ya que los entrenamos sin el obstáculo de malos hábitos como los que muchos otros actores tienen y son difíciles de modificar. Esta gente está 'fresca,' son materia tierna, sin pretensiones mayores que la de convivir y defender su cultura; se les puede moldear y educar sin malos hábitos" (Delia Rendón Novelo, "Califican al teatro indígena y campesino de Yucatán como uno de los mejores del país," *Diario Yucatán*, June 24, 1994, 2).

30. Gerardo Albarrán de Alba, "Julieta Campos rememora con nostalgia el Teatro Campesino e Indígena de Oxolotán," *Proceso* 1008 (February 26, 1996): 52–58.

31. ". . . este grupo amorfo que amparado en una supuesta actividad cultural

'para rescatar valores en manos de los campesinos,' se han hecho cómplices en mal uso de los presupuestos y degeneración, incluso, de grupos campesinos de Oxolotán, Tabasco. . . . El caso es que el grupo LTCI se gastó más de 500 millones de pesos en el montaje de una obra 'bodas de sangre' y en el viaje—hasta con caballos—a España para montar la obra con 'actores campesinos,' que no son otra cosa que habitantes de Oxolotán que a cambio de un poco de comida hacen lo que los 'intelectuales del teatro campesino' les piden" (Reynaldo Zúñiga, "'Teatro Campesino,' cortina de humo de corruptelas, malversación y degeneración," n.p., April 24, 1990, 48). The sum of 500 million pesos in 1987 would have been roughly equivalent to U.S. $135,000. Rendón has told me also that they did not ship horses to Spain for the trip but hired them from Spanish ranchers.

32. "'¿Bueno . . . a ustedes quién los engaño con que son artistas? Ustedes lo que necesitan es ir a echar machete al campo y sembrar la tierra.'

"Entre burlas compartidas por el secretario particular y el secretario general de Gobierno de Neme, Francisco Garrido todavía les dijo que necesitaba 20 peones para sus ranchos y les ofreció 10,000 viejos pesos de jornal . . ." as told to Albarrán de Alba by LTCI participant Auldárico Hernández Gerónimo (Albarrán de Alba, "Julieta Campos rememora," 53–54). The wages would have been the equivalent of U.S. $3–$4.

33. Personal interview, Mérida, August 26, 1996.

34. Trinh T. Minh-ha, *Woman, Native, Other,* 89.

35. Auldárico Hernández Gerónimo, Eutimio Hernández Román, Martha Alicia Trejo Espinoza, and María Alicia Martínez Medrano, *La tragedia del jaguar* (Villahermosa: Instituto de Cultura de Tabasco, 1989), 15–16.

36. ". . . dicen que mataron los conquistadores a todos los jaguares" (ibid., 48).

37. My discussion of *El árbol de la vida* comes from my observation of the event in May 2000. The Concheros are a familiar sight in the Zócalo, where they perform in elaborate costumes with feather headdresses, beads, and bells to the insistent and dramatic beat of several drums. Their link to an "authentic" performance tradition is both presumed and tenuous, the result a newly invented tradition that presents an ambivalent spectacle to tourists and passersby. The Concheros appeal to the past as a source of ethnic and Mexican pride, but they are also viewed skeptically by many as a symbol of ethnic resistance. Very recently, my own local public television station featured a tribute to Mexican mariachi music in which the Concheros also performed. Mariachi music is as different in style and apparent ideology from the Concheros as it is possible to be, but in this case I read the Concheros' involvement as an authenticating device, linking mariachi to the deep roots of Mexican indigeneity. Nancy Lee Ruyter provides an accessible introduction to the Concheros in "Ancient Images: The Pre-Cortesian in 20th-Century Dance Performance," *Gestos* 21 (April 1996): 145–155. My thanks also to Patricia Ybarra for her insights about the Concheros.

38. For Sayers's comments and a photograph of an elaborate Tree of Life by the contemporary artist Tiburcio Soteno, see http://www.mexicanceramic.com/folk/folk1.htm.

39. Martínez Medrano had also developed a play in memory of the victims of the 1997 Acteál massacre in Chiapas, which I have not yet seen.

40. I saw the performance of *Moctezuma II* by the Laboratorio de Teatro Comunitario Iztapalapa on November 2, 2000.

41. I saw *Los 72 Banda en concierto: Homenaje a Dámaso Pérez Prado* in an open-air theatre outside the Instituto Nacional de Bellas Artes in Mexico City on November 1, 2000. This production was reprised the following summer in Valladolid, at the same time the *Vaquería* was premiering in nearby X'ocen.

42. "Mayan Theatre," http://www.yucatantoday.com/events/eng-teatro-indigena.htm.

43. My discussion here is based on a production of *Siete momentos* I attended on March 22, 2003; interviews and correspondence with Delia Rendón between 1996 and 2002; a professionally edited videotape of the X'ocen performance; programs and promotional materials given me by Rendón; and two newspaper reviews: Lorenzo Salas González, "El alma colectiva de un pueblo recupera su esencia" (*Por Esto!* September 5, 2001), 12–14; and Mary J. Andrade, "La Vaquería: fiesta autóctona (*La Oferta*, April 12, 2002), 10–11.

44. Feliciano Sánchez Chan, personal interview, Mérida, June 15, 2002.

45. María Alicia Martínez Medrano, "Información sobre los Laboratorios de Teatro Campesino e Indígena," internal document, undated, 1.

46. Grossberg, "Cultural Studies and/in New Worlds," 12.

47. Martín Pérez Dzul, personal interview, Mérida, August 29, 1996.

48. Carl Weber, "AC/TC: Currents of Theatrical Exchange," in Marranca and Dasgupta, eds., *Interculturalism and Performance*, 34.

49. In Western theatre history, samplings and borrowings probably go back as far as the Greeks and are, arguably, fundamental processes at work in all creative endeavor. But my concern here is less to trace their history than to briefly describe their dynamic.

50. Laura Bohannan, "Shakespeare in the Bush," in *Every Man His Way: Readings in Cultural Anthropology*, ed. Alan Dundes (Englewood Cliffs, N.J.: Prentice-Hall, 1968), 477–486.

4. Theatre and Community on the Yucatán Peninsula

1. Fernando Muñoz, *El teatro regional de Yucatán* (Mérida: Grupo Editorial Gaceta), 1987.

2. ". . . aunque intervienen alguna vez en la acción personas de más elevada categoría social, los verdaderos héroes de la farsa pertenecen al pueblo, son indios de las haciendas y 'mestizos' de las pobalciones del interior del Estado o de los barrios de Mérida. Otros personajes que figuran en las representaciones son chinos y árabes, estos últimos designados con el nobre de 'turcos.' Parece cosa inusitada que en un teatro esencialmente regional, tengan cabida personajes de nacionalidad extranjera, pero en el caso presente no debe causar extrañeza, ya que los extranjeros de que se trata desde hace muchísimos años radican en Yucatán y se han mezclado, aunque sin confundirse, a las masas populares. A estos personajes siempre se les dibuja por el lado cómico y con las exageraciones de la caricatura" (Arturo Gamboa Garibaldi, "Historia del teatro y de la literatura dramática," *Enciclopedia yucatanense*, vol. 1, 2d ed. (1977), 286–287.

3. For a brief summary of nineteenth-century Yucatecan regionalism and nationalistic movements, see Castañeda, *In the Museum of Maya Culture*.

4. See, for example, Fernando Benítez, *Ki: El drama de un pueblo y una planta*, 2d ed. (México, D.F.: SEP, 1985); Miguel Alberto Bartolomé, *La dinámica social de los mayas de Yucatán* (México, D.F.: INI, 1988).

5. See Grant D. Jones, *Maya Resistance to Spanish Rule* (Albuquerque: University of New Mexico Press, 1989).

6. Recent studies of the relationship between television and cultural identity in rural Yucatán include Cynthia J. Miller, "The Social Impacts of Televised Media among the Yucatec Maya," *Human Organization* 57, 3 (fall 1998): 307–314; Henry Geddes Gonzales, "Mass Media and Cultural Identity among the Yucatec Maya: The Constitution of Global, National, and Local Subjects," *Studies in Latin American Popular Culture* 15 (1996): 131–153.

7. "Así fue cómo resolví el enigma de ese fenómeno biológico; escribiendo estas obritas i otras que publico en este folleto llevando como argumentos primordiales las campañas; antialcohólica, alfabetizante i de castellanización mismas que empeñosamente está deseando realizar la Secretaría de Educación" (Santiago Pacheco Cruz, *Teatro Maya*, 1st ed. [Mérida: Campaña Indigenista Pro-Educación, 1940], afterword). Photocopy available at the Library of the Universidad Autónoma de Yucatán in Mérida.

8. Although Teatro Communitario translates literally as "community theatre," it is different from community theatre in the United States that stages local renditions of famous plays (often Broadway hits). For example, Weiss et al., *Latin American Popular Theatre*, uses "grassroots theatre" as a more accurate translation of the term. I use "community-based theatre" in the same spirit.

9. Donald H. Frischmann, "Contemporary Mayan Theatre and Ethnic Conflict: the Recovery and (Re)Interpretation of History," in Gainor, ed., *Imperialism and Theatre*, 73–74.

10. The following information is based on interviews I had with Sánchez Chan between July 1996 and July 1999.

11. ". . . cobrar cierta fama, interpretando a los grandes personajes del teatro universal" (Alejandro Ortíz B., "Teatro popular y educación," paper presented at the first Encuentro Nacional de Teatro Popular, Nuevo León, October 1985; cited in Feliciano Sánchez Chan, *Manual de Teatro Comunitario* [México, D.F.: Dirección General de Culturas Populares, 1992], 37). Sánchez Chan also cites René Acuña, *Farsas y representaciones escénicas de los mayas antiguos* (México, D.F.: UNAM, 1978).

12. "Entendemos por teatro comunitario, aquel que hacen aquellos grupos que no se ciñen a los espacios convencionales, con grandes escenografías, utilerías, iluminación y vestuarios especiales, ni se expresan necesariamente a través de obras escritas por grandes autores, sino con textos creados en función a sus necesidades y a partir de su propia problemática y realidad, sean estos grupos indígenas, campesinos, populares o comunitarios. . . . Es una actividad artístico-cultural que un determinado grupo de personas desarrolla, en base a su propia realidad y creatividad, utlizando para ello, elementos que forman parte de su vida común, para expresar su punto de vista sobre determinada situación de su misma comunidad,

con el cual se invita a las demás personas a reflexionar sobre el tema expuesto. En el Teatro Comunitario, que normalmente es hablado en la lengua materna (maya), se muestra nuestra forma de vida, señalando en ocasiones lo que nos gusta y lo que no nos gusta, hasta se propone la forma como queremos cambiar las cosas" (Sánchez Chan, *Manual*, 5, 9).

13. MacAloon, *Rite, Drama, Festival, Spectacle*, 1.

14. Sánchez Chan, *Manual*, 18.

15. Ibid., 20–24.

16. I base this observation on personal experience of such dances and note there are two exceptions: when they are performed for tourist groups and when they themselves tour to regional festivals, where they must accommodate urban tastes or performance time limits.

17. Góngora Pacheco's work has been published in several anthologies and individual printings, including Montemayor's *Los escritores indígenas actuales* ("X-ootzilil/La Pobreza/The Poor Woman" and "U suumil k'i'ik mani/La soga de la sangre/Blood Ties," 1992). Her "Monografía de Oxkutzcab" (Monograph on Oxkutscab) was published in Spanish in 1983. Her "Utzikbaliloób Oxkutzcab yéetel Maní/Cuentos de Oxkutzcab y Maní/Tales from Oxkutzcab and Maní" appears in the series *Maya dziibo'ob bejla'e/Letras mayas contemporáneas*, vols. 3 and 4 (México, D.F.: INI and SEDESOL, 1994).

18. I am very grateful to Wendy Cruz and William May Itzá for the simultaneous Spanish-language translation they provided at the time and to Góngora Pacheco for later helping me to clarify points of plot and theme (personal interview, June 27, 2002).

19. Feliciano Sánchez Chan, *Baldzamo'ob/Teatro maya contemporáneo*, vols. 1 and 2 (México, D.F.: INI and SEDESOL, 1994).

20. Personal interviews, June 10 and 15, 2002, Mérida.

21. Personal interview, June 30, 1997.

22. "Es que he estado soñando que mi señor Jobnil Bakab viene a visitarnos, y que todas mis compañeras lo agarran y lo comen. Yo salgo de mi Jobón y veo el campo todo seco, con sus árboles muertos, y como de la nada surgen unas abejas grandes que me persiguen. Yo me encierro en mi Jobón y cuando siento que voy a morir de asfixia, despierto. Yo no sé por qué sueño cosas horribles" (Feliciano Sánchez Chan, *Las abejas*, 44).

23. My thanks to Sarah Bryant-Bertail for pointing out this similarity, especially as it regards the dramatic exploration of alternatives as an intervention against history's retrospectively perceived inevitability.

24. "Esta historia que les vamos a contar, comienza a principios de los años 40 y llega hasta nuestros días. Se las contaremos tal y como lo viven los habitantes de las zonas rurales del estado de Yucatán" (Feliciano Sánchez Chan, *Las langostas*, 41).

25. "Entran dos Langostas muy misteriosamente y empiezan a hacer gestos y pases mágicos alrededor de los niños, como en una danza de encantamiento en la que emiten sonidos distintos . . ." (Sánchez Chan, *Las langostas*, 48).

26. 1. "UN PUEBLO QUE PRODUCE LO QUE COME, JAMÁS SERÁ MANIPULADO" (Sánchez Chan, *Las langostas*, 61).

27. Castañeda, *In the Museum of Maya Culture,* 37.

28. Ibid.

29. Ibid.

Epilogue

1. Matthew Restall, *Maya Conquistador* (Boston: Beacon, 1998), 40.

2. Juan Balboa, "Celebra el EZLN sus 15 años," *La Jornada,* November 18, 1998 (taken from the *Jornada* Web version), n.p.

3. *Municipios* are the most local form of government in Mexico, similar in function (if not size and population) to U.S. counties. I should point out, however, that local control is not the same thing as the autonomy argued for by the Zapatistas, since it will still be up to the states to enact local customs. Zapatistas demand instead a regional autonomy independent of state legislatures.

4. "¿Zapatur? Ni modo. Marcos pierde imagen, pero los indígenas ganan seguridad. Es lo que importa. Tendrán más probabilidad de comer, y menos amenazas encima. Así que bienvenidos los famosos" (Marcos, quoted in Regis Debray, "Régis Debray subraya la advertencia del 'profeta' Marcos . . . ," *Proceso* 1019 [May 13, 1996]: 7).

5. Guillermo Gómez-Peña, "From Chiapas to Wales," *Performance Research* 2, 2 (1997): 66.

6. Ibid., 69.

7. Bob Frissel, "Nothing to Something at the Prophets Conference—Tulum/ Caribbean," on-line posting, prophets@maui.net, January 20, 1999. See also Quetzil Castañeda's documentary film, *Incidents of Travel in Chichén Itzá* (Watertown, Mass.: Documentary Educational Resources, 1997).

BIBLIOGRAPHY

Abercrombie, Thomas. "To Be Indian, to Be Bolivian: 'Ethnic' and 'National' Discourses of Identity." In Urban and Sherzer, 95–130.

Abreu Gómez, Ermilo. *Leyendas y consejos del antiguo Yucatán.* México, D.F.: Biblioteca Joven, 1985.

Acuña, René. *Farsas y representaciones escénicas de los mayas antiguos.* México, D.F.: UNAM, 1978.

———. *El teatro popular en Hispanoamérica: Una bibliografía anotada.* México, D.F.: UNAM, 1979.

Adams, Richard N. "Strategies of Ethnic Survival in Central America." In Urban and Sherzer, 181–206.

Aguirre Beltrán, Gonzalo. *Regiones de refugio.* México, D.F.: INI, 1967.

Aguirre Beltrán, Gonzalo, and Ricardo Pozas Arciniega. *La política indigenista en México: Métodos y resultados,* 2d ed. Vol. 2: *Instituciones indígenas en el México actual.* México, D.F.: INI and Secretaria de Educacíon Publica, 1973.

Ahern, Maureen, and Mary Seale Vásquez, eds. *Homenaje a Rosario Castellanos.* Valencia, Spain: Albatros Hispanofila, 1980.

Albarrán de Alba, Gerardo. "Julieta Campos rememora con nostalgia el Teatro Campesino e Indígena de Oxolotán." *Proceso* 1008 (February 26, 1996): 52–58.

Alberto Bartolomé, Miguel. *La dinámica social de los mayas de Yucatán.* México, D.F.: INI, 1988.

Anderson, Thor, dir. *Sacred Games: Ritual Warfare in a Maya Village.* Berkeley: University of California Extension Media Center, 1988. Dist. Zeno Production Company.

Andrade, Mary J. "La Vaquería: Fiesta autóctona." *La Oferta,* April 12, 2002, 10–11.

Argueta, Arturo, and Arturo Warman, eds. *Nuevos enfoques para el estudio de las etnias indígenas en México.* México, D.F.: Centro de Investigaciones Interdisciplinarias en Humanidades, UNAM, 1991.

Arias, Jacinto. "Mucha semilla desparramada." *Hojarasca* 9 (May 1992): 24–31.

Arróniz, Othón. *Teatro de Evangelización en Nueva España.* México, D.F.: UNAM, 1979.

Austin, Gayle. *Feminist Theories for Dramatic Criticism.* Ann Arbor: University of Michigan Press, 1990.

Baker, George, and Alfonso Galindo. "PRI Victory?" *Documents on Mexican Politics.* http://db.uwateerloo.ca/~lopez-o/politics/privictory.html.

Balboa, Juan. "Celebra el EZLN sus 15 años." *La Jornada,* on-line posting, November 18, 1998.

Ballinas, Victor. "En Chiapas hay una *guerra integral* o de desgaste, sostienen Acción Comunitaria y el Centro Pro." *La Jornada,* June 18, 2002, 9.

———. "Programas antipobreza en Chiapas, estrategia contrainsugente: Observadores internacionales." *La Jornada,* on-line posting, July 30, 2002, www.jornada.unam.mx.

Barrera Vásquez, Alfredo. *El libro de los cantares de Dzitbalché.* México, D.F.: Instituto de Antropología e Historia, 1965.

Bedregal, Ximena. "Fortaleza de la Mujer Maya: Teatreras y escritoras indígenas reconstruyen su mundo." *Triple Jornada* 3 (November 2, 1998): 1 ff.

Beezley, William H., Cheryl English Martin, and William E. French, eds. *Rituals of Rule, Rituals of Resistance: Public Celebrations and Popular Culture in Mexico.* Wilmington, Del.: SR Books, 1994.

Benítez, Fernando. *Ki: El drama de un pueblo y una planta.* 2d ed. México, D.F.: SEP, 1985.

Benser, Caroline Cepin. *Egon Wellesz: Chronicle of a Twentieth-Century Musician.* New York: Peter Lang, 1985.

Behar, Ruth, and Deborah Gordon, eds. *Women Writing Culture.* Berkeley: University of California Press, 1995.

Beverley, John, José Oviedo, and Michael Aronna, eds. *The Postmodernism Debate in Latin America.* Durham: Duke University Press, 1995.

Bhabha, Homi K. "The Postcolonial and the Postmodern: The Question of Agency." In *The Location of Culture,* 171–197. London: Routledge, 1994.

———. "Translator Translated." *Artforum* (March 1995): 80 ff.

Bharucha, Rustom. *The Politics of Cultural Practice: Thinking through Theatre in an Age of Globalization.* London: Athlone, 2000.

Blancarte, Roberto, ed. *Cultura e identidad nacional.* México, D.F.: Consejo Nacional para la Cultura y las Artes, 1994.

Bohannan, Laura. "Shakespeare in the Bush." In *Every Man His Way: Readings in Cultural Anthropology,* ed. Alan Dundes, 477–486. Englewood Cliffs, N.J.: Prentice-Hall, 1968.

Boling, Becky. "Language and Performance: Representation and Invention in Magaña's *Los enemigos.*" *Gestos* (April 1995): 119–130.

Bonfil Batalla, Guillermo. "Lo propio y lo ajeno: Una aproximación al problema del control cultural." In *Pensar nuestra cultura: Ensayos,* 49–57. México, D.F.: Alianza, 1991.

———. *México Profundo: Reclaiming a Civilization.* Trans. Philip A. Dennis. Austin: University of Texas Press, 1996.

Boone, Elizabeth Hill, and Walter D. Mignolo, eds. *Writing without Words: Alternative Literacies in Mesoamerica and the Andes.* Durham: Duke University Press, 1994.

Breslin, Patrick. "Coping with Change, the Maya Discover the Play's the Thing." *Smithsonian* 23, 5 (August 1992): 78–87.

Bricker, Victoria Reifler. *Ritual Humor in Highland Chiapas.* Austin: University of Texas Press, 1973.

———. *Indian Christ, Indian King.* Austin: University of Texas Press, 1981.

Bruna, Dick. *Kitten Nell.* Trans. Sandra Greifenstein. Chicago: Follett, 1963.
"Califican al teatro indígena y campesino de Yucatán como uno de los mejores del país." *Diario Yucatán,* June 24, 1994, 2 ff.
Camargo Breña, Angelina. "'Labor de arqueología, básica en el teatro.'" *Excelsior,* January 23, 1990, C2–3.
———. "Menosprecio por el Arte Indígena en Todo México: Uriarte." *Excelsior,* September 14, 1990, C1–2.
———. "Teatro Off Broadway, Alternativa en EU." Review of *Romeo y Julieta,* dir. María Alicia Martínez Medrano. LTCI. Delacorte Theatre, New York. *Excelsior,* September 19, 1990, C4.
Campos, Julieta. *¿Qué hacemos con los pobres?* México, D.F.: Aguilar, 1995.
Cardona, Patricia. "Una creación del Alma." Review of *Bodas de Sangre,* dir. María Alicia Martínez Medrano. LTCI. *El Público* (Madrid) (October 1987): 7–8.
Caso, Alfonso, Silvio Zavala, José Miranda, and Moisés González Navarro. *La política indigenista en México: Métodos y resultados,* vol. 1. 2d ed. México, D.F.: INI and Secretaría de Educación Publica, 1973.
Castañeda, Quetzil E. *In the Museum of Maya Culture: Touring Chichén Itzá.* Minneapolis: University of Minnesota Press, 1996.
———. *Incidents of Travel in Chichén Itzá.* Watertown, Mass.: Documentary Educational Resources, 1997.
Castellanos, Rosario. "Petul en la Escuela Abierta." In *Teatro Petul,* 42–65. México, D.F.: Instituto Nacional Indigenista, 1962.
———. "Teatro Petul." *Revista de la Universidad de México* (January 1965): 30–31.
Ceballos, Edgar. *Diccionario enciclopédico básico de teatro mexicano.* México, D.F., 1996.
Chanady, Amaryll, ed. *Latin American Identity and Constructions of Difference.* Minneapolis: University of Minnesota Press, 1994.
Cisneros, Ulises. "Los yoremes y el teatro." Review of *Romeo y Julieta,* dir. María Alicia Martínez Medrano. LTCI. *Excelsior,* April 19, 1990, C6.
Clark, VeVe, Ruth-Ellen B. Joeres, and Madelon Sprengnether, eds. *Revising the Word and the World: Essays in Feminist Literary Criticism.* Chicago: University of Chicago Press, 1993.
Clifford, James. *The Predicament of Culture: Twentieth-Century Ethnography, Literature and Art.* Cambridge, Mass.: Harvard University Press, 1988.
———. *Routes: Travel and Translation in the Late Twentieth Century.* Cambridge, Mass.: Harvard University Press, 1997.
Clifford, James, and George Marcus, eds. *Writing Culture: The Poetics and Politics of Ethnography.* Berkeley: University of California Press, 1986.
Conquergood, Dwight. "Performance Studies: Interventions and Radical Research." *TDR: The Drama Review* 46, 2 (summer 2002): 145–156.
Cypess, Sandra Messinger. *La Malinche in Mexican Literature: From History to Myth.* Austin: University of Texas Press, 1991.
———. "The Figure of La Malinche in the Texts of Elena Garro." In Stoll, 117–135.

Debray, Régis. "Régis Debray subraya la advertencia del 'profeta' Marcos . . ." *Proceso* 1019 (May 13, 1996): 6–11.

de Certeau, Michel. *Heterologies.* Trans. Brian Massumi. Minneapolis: University of Minnesota Press, 1986.

———. "The Politics of Silence: The Long March of the Indians." In *Heterologies,* 225–233.

de la Vega, Miguel. "El grupo teatral indígena Sna Jtz'Ibajom, de Chiapas, recoge la tradición de la cultura maya . . ." *Proceso* 901 (January 7, 1994): 70–71.

Deleuze, Gilles, and Félix Guattari. *A Thousand Plateaus: Capitalism and Schizophrenia.* Trans. Brian Massumi. London: Athlone, 1987.

Deloria, Philip J. *Playing Indian.* New Haven: Yale University Press, 1998.

Di Leonardo, Micaela, ed. *Gender at the Crossroads of Knowledge: Feminist Anthropology in the Postmodern Era.* Berkeley: University of California Press, 1991.

Díaz Polanco, Héctor. *Indigenous Peoples in Latin America.* Trans. Lucia Rayas. Boulder, Colo.: Westview, 1997.

Diskin, Martin. "Ethnic Discourse and the Challenge to Anthropology: The Nicaraguan Case." In Urban and Sherzer, 156–180.

Eber, Christine E. "Three Women's Experience of the Zapatista Uprising." Unpublished essay, 1996.

Eber, Christine, and Brenda Rosenbaum. "'That we may serve beneath your hands and feet': Women Weavers in Highland Chiapas, Mexico." In Nash 1993, 155–180.

Elmendorf, Mary Lindsay. *Nine Mayan Women: A Village Faces Change.* Rochester, Vt.: Schenkman, 1991.

Erdman, Harley. "Gendering Chiapas: Petrona de la Cruz and Isabel J. F. Juárez Espinosa of La FOMMA (Fortaleza de la Mujer Maya/Strength of the Mayan Woman)." In Uno, 159–170.

Espinosa, Tomás. "Imágenes del Laboratorio de Teatro Campesino e Indígena." *Expresión* 18 (May–June 1987): 6–9.

———. "Laboratorios de Teatro Campesino e Indígena de México: Tabasco, Yucatán y Sinaloa: el Renacimiento." *Conjunto* 88 (July–September 1991): 85–89.

Fane, Diana, ed. *Converging Cultures: Art and Identity in Spanish America.* New York: Brooklyn Museum and Harry Abrams, 1996.

Favorini, Attilio. "Ophelia's Coiffure: Observations on Shakespeare and Interculturalism." Intercultural Theatre Seminar, ASTR Conference. Doubletree Plaza Hotel, Pasadena, November 16, 1996.

Fazio, Carlos. *Samuel Ruíz, el caminante.* México, D.F.: Espasa Calpe, 1994.

Fernández Retamar, Roberto. *Caliban and Other Essays.* Trans. Edward Baker. Minneapolis: University of Minnesota Press, 1989.

"Fine Mexican Ceramics Art Gallery." Web site http://www.mexicanceramic.com/folk/folk1.htm.

Fischer, Edward F. *Cultural Logics and Global Economies: Maya Identity in Thought and Practice.* Austin: University of Texas Press, 2001.

Fomma, La. *FOMMA* (promotional brochure). 1996.

———. "Víctimas del engaño." 1998–1999. Typescript in author's possession.

———. "La vida de las Juanas." 1999. Typescript in author's possession.
———. "Crecí con el amor de mi madre." 2001. Typescript in author's possession.
Freidel, David, Linda Schele, and Joy Parker. *Maya Cosmos.* New York: Morrow, 1993.
Friede, Juan, and Benjamin Keen. *Bartolomé de Las Casas in History.* DeKalb: Northern Illinois University Press, 1971.
Friedlander, Judith. *Being Indian in Hueyapan: A Study of Forced Identity in Contemporary Mexico.* New York: St. Martin's, 1975.
Frischmann, Donald H. *El nuevo teatro popular en México.* México, D.F.: INBA, 1990.
———. "Active Ethnicity: Nativism, Otherness, and Indian Theatre in Mexico." *Gestos* 11 (April 1991): 113–126.
———. "Misiones Culturales, Teatro Conasupo, and Teatro Comunidad: The Evolution of Rural Theatre." In Beezley, Martin, and French 285–306.
———. "New Mayan Theatre in Chiapas: Anthropology, Literacy, and Social Drama." In Taylor and Villegas, 213–238.
———. "Contemporary Mayan Theatre and Ethnic Conflict: The Recovery and (Re)Interpretation of History." In Gainor, 71–84.
———. "La construcción del sujeto poscolonial en el discurso escénico maya contemporáneo de México." Paper presented at the meeting of the Asociación Mexicana de Investigación Teatral, UNAM, Mexico City, March 25–27, 1999.
Frissel, Bob. "Nothing to Something at the Prophets Conference—Tulum/Caribbean." On-line posting. prophets@maui.net. January 20, 1999.
Frye, David. *Indians into Mexicans: History and Identity in a Mexican Town.* Austin: University of Texas Press, 1996.
Gainor, J. Ellen, ed. *Imperialism and Theatre: Essays on World Theatre, Drama, and Performance.* New York: Routledge, 1995.
Gamboa Garibaldi, Arturo. "Historia del teatro y de la literatura dramática." In *Enciclopedia yucatanense,* vol. 1, 109–316. 2d ed. 1977.
García Canclini, Néstor. *Hybrid Cultures: Strategies for Entering and Leaving Modernity.* Trans. Christopher L. Chiappari and Silvia L. López. Minneapolis: University of Minnesota Press, 1995.
García Hernández, Arturo. "La universalidad de Lorca, puesta a prueba con el teatro indígena." Review of *Bodas de sangre,* dir. María Alicia Martínez Medrano. LTCI. Chapultepec Park, Mexico City. *La Jornada,* March 31, 1987.
García Lorca, Federico. *Bodas de sangre: Versión oxoloteca de la obra original de Federico García Lorca.* Adapted by María Alicia Martínez Medrano. Villahermosa, Tabasco: Gobierno del Estado de Tabasco, 1986.
———. *Bodas de sangre.* México, D.F.: Editores Mexicanos Unidos, 1993.
Garro, Elena. *La dama boba.* In *Un hogar sólido y otras piezas,* 171–246. Xalapa: Universidad Veracruzana, 1983.
———. "The Author Speaks . . ." Interview with Michèle Muncie. In Stoll, 23–37.
Geertz, Clifford. *The Interpretation of Cultures: Selected Essays.* New York: Basic Books, 1973.
Gilbert, Adrian G., and Marice M. Cotterell. *The Mayan Prophecies: Unlocking the Secrets of a Lost Civilization.* Rockport, Mass.: Element Books, 1995.

Golden, Renny, Michael McConnell, Peggy Mueller, Cinny Poppen, and Marilyn Turkovitch. *Dangerous Memories: Invasion and Resistance since 1492.* Chicago: Chicago Religious Task Force on Central America, 1992.

Golden, Tim. "The Voice of the Rebels Has Mexicans in His Spell," *New York Times,* February 8, 1994, A3.

Gómez-Peña, Guillermo. "From Chiapas to Wales." *Performance Research* 2, 2 (1997): 64–75.

Gonzales, Henry Geddes. "Mass Media and Cultural Identity among the Yucatec Maya: The Constitution of Global, National, and Local Subjects." *Studies in Latin American Popular Culture* 15 (1996): 131–153.

Gonzales, Patrisia, and Roberto Rodriguez. "Mexico: The Indian and the Mestizo." *Native Americas* 19, 1–2 (spring–summer 2002): 37–39.

González Angulo, Gildo. "Comienzan a despuntar los talentos." Review of *De todos para todos,* Lo'il Maxil. Mérida, Yucatán. *¡Por Esto!* September 4, 1996.

Gossen, Gary H. "The Other in Chamula Tzotzil Cosmology and History: Reflections of a Kansan in Chiapas." *Cultural Anthropology* 8, 4 (1993): 443–475.

———. "From Olmecs to Zapatistas: A Once and Future History of Souls." *American Anthropologist* 96, 3 (1994): 553–570.

———. "Maya Zapatistas Move to the Ancient Future." *American Anthropologist* 98, 3 (1996): 528–538.

Graham-White, Anthony. "The Characteristics of Traditional Drama." *Yale/Theatre* 8, 1 (fall 1976): 11–24.

Greenblatt, Stephen, ed. *New World Encounters.* Berkeley: University of California Press, 1993.

Grossberg, Lawrence. "Cultural Studies and/in New Worlds." *Critical Studies in Mass Communication* 10 (1993): 1–22.

Hahner, June E., ed. *Women in Latin American History: Their Lives and Views.* Rev. ed. Los Angeles: UCLA Latin American Center Publications, 1980.

Hampton, Wilborn. "Shakespeare Caliente Is a Visual Spectacle." Review of *Romeo y Julieta,* dir. María Alicia Martínez Medrano. LTCI. Delacorte Theatre, New York. *New York Times,* September 15, 1990, A15.

Harding, Susan, ed. *Feminism and Methodology: Social Science Issues.* Bloomington: Indiana University Press, 1987.

Harris, Max. *The Dialogical Theatre: Dramatizations of the Conquest of Mexico and the Question of the Other.* New York: St. Martin's, 1993.

———. *Aztecs, Moors, and Christians: Festivals of Reconquest in Mexico and Spain.* Austin: University of Texas Press, 2000.

Hayden, Tom, ed. *The Zapatista Reader.* New York: Thunder's Mouth Press/Nation Books, 2002.

Heath, Shirley Brice. *La política del lenguaje en México.* 3d ed. México, D.F.: INI, 1992.

Heilbrun, Carolyn. *Writing a Woman's Life.* New York: Norton, 1988.

Hernández Castillo, Rosalva Aída. "Entre el etnocentrismo feminista y el esencialismo étnico: Las mujeres indígenas y sus demandas de género." *Debate Feminista* 12, 24 (October 2001): 206–229.

Hernández Castillo, Rosalva Aída, ed., *The Other Word: Women and Violence in*

Chiapas before and after Acteal. Copenhagen: International Work Group for Indigenous Affairs, 2001.

Hernández Gerónimo, Auldárico, Eutimio Hernández Román, Martha Alicia Trejo Espinoza, and María Alicia Martínez Medrano. *La tragedia del jaguar.* Villahermosa, Tabasco: Instituto de Cultura de Tabasco, 1989.

Herron Gallant, Ruth. "Tradition in Transition: Women in Chiapas Search for Their Place in a Changing Society." *The Pacific* (summer 1996): 20 ff.

Hewitt de Alcántara, Cynthia. *Anthropological Perspectives on Rural Mexico.* New York: Routledge, 1984.

Hill, Jane H. "In Neca Gobierno de Puebla: Mexicano Penetrations of the Mexican State." In Urban and Sherzer, 72–94.

Hobsbawm, Eric, and Terence Ranger, eds. *The Invention of Tradition.* Cambridge: Cambridge University Press, 1983.

Horcasitas, Fernando. *El Teatro Náhuatl: Épocas novohispana y moderna.* México, D.F.: UNAM, 1974.

Instituto Nacional Indigenista. *Teatro Petul.* México, D.F.: INI, 1962.

Instituto Indigenista Interamericano. *Indianidad, etnocidio, e indigenismo en América Latina.* México, D.F., 1988.

Iwaŋska, Alicja. *The Truths of Others: An Essay on Nativistic Intellectuals in Mexico.* Cambridge, Mass.: Schenkman, 1977.

Jones, Grant D. *Maya Resistance to Spanish Rule.* Albuquerque: University of New Mexico Press, 1989.

Jones, Willis Knapp. *Behind Spanish American Footlights.* Austin: University of Texas Press, 1966.

Jordan, Mary. "In Mexico, an Unpunished Crime: Rape Victims Face Widespread Cultural Bias in Pursuit of Justice," *Washington Post,* June 30, 2002, A1.

José Gurrola, Juan. "¡Angel! . . . ¡Te estoy hablando, chingaos!" *Uno más Uno,* March 29, 1989, 23.

Joseph, Gilbert M., and Daniel Nugent, eds. *Everyday Forms of State Formation: Revolution and the Negotiation of Rule in Modern Mexico.* Durham: Duke University Press, 1994.

Juárez Espinosa, Isabel. *Migración.* In *Cuentos y Teatro Tzeltales,* 143–164. México, D.F.: Editorial Diana, 1994.

Kadetsky, Elizabeth. "The Human Cost of Free Trade." *Ms.* 4, 4 (February 1994): 10–15.

Kadir, Djelal. *The Other Writing: Postcolonial Essays in Latin America's Writing Culture.* West Lafayette, Ind.: Purdue University Press, 1993.

Katzenberger, Elaine. *First World, Ha Ha Ha! The Zapatista Challenge.* San Francisco: City Lights, 1995.

Keen, Benjamin. *Essays in the Intellectual History of Colonial Latin America.* Boulder, Colo.: Westview, 1998.

Kelly-Gadol, Joan. "The Social Relation of the Sexes: Methodological Implications of Women's History." In *Feminism and Methodology: Social Science Issues,* ed. Susan Harding, 15–18. Bloomington: Indiana University Press, 1987.

Kicza, John E., ed. *The Indian in Latin American History: Resistance, Resilience, and Acculturation.* Wilmington, Del.: Scholarly Resources, 1993.

King, Linda. *Roots of Identity: Language and Literacy in Mexico*. Stanford: Stanford University Press, 1994.

Klor de Alva, J. Jorge. "The Postcolonization of the (Latin) American Experience: A Reconsideration of 'Colonialism,' 'Postcolonialism,' and 'Mestizaje.'" In Prakash, 241–278.

Krauze, Enrique. *Mexico: Biography of Power*. Trans. Hank Heifetz. New York: HarperCollins, 1997.

"Laboratorio de Teatro Campesino e Indígena." *Expresión* 2 (September–October 1984): 3–9.

Laboratorio de Teatro Campesino e Indígena. Internal documents archived in the group's Mérida, Yucatán, offices.

Lafaye, Jacques. *Quetzalcóatl and Guadalupe: The Formation of Mexican National Consciousness, 1531–1813*. Trans. Benjamin Keen. Chicago: University of Chicago Press, 1974.

Las Casas, Bartolomé de. *History of the Indies*. Trans. Andrée Collard. New York: Harper and Row, 1971.

———. *Historia de las Indias*. Ed. André Saint-Lu. Caracas: Biblioteca Ayacucho, 1986.

Laughlin, Miriam. "The Drama of Mayan Women." *Ms.* 2, 1 (July–August 1991): 88–89.

———. "Mayan Women Playwrights." *Belles Lettres* 7, 2 (winter 1991–1992): 45, 47.

———. "Special Projects Update: La Fomma." *Cultural Survival Quarterly* 20, 3 (fall 1996): 14–15.

Laughlin, Robert M. *Of Cabbages and Kings: Tales from Zinacantán*. Washington, D.C.: Smithsonian Institution Press, 1977.

———. "The Mayan Renaissance: Sna Jtz'ibajom, the House of the Writer." *Cultural Survival Quarterly* 17, 4 (winter 1994): 13–15.

———. "En la vanguardia: Sna Jtz'ibajom." In Montemayor, *Situación actual*, 155–172.

———. "From All for All: A Tzotzil-Tzeltal Tragicomedy." *American Anthropologist* 97, 3 (1995): 528–542.

———. "Chiapas' Theater of the People." *Cultural Survival Quarterly* 26, 1 (spring 2002): 64–66.

Laughlin, Robert M., trans., and Carol Karasik, ed. *Mayan Tales from Zinacantán: Dreams and Stories from the People of the Bat*. Washington, D.C.: Smithsonian Institution Press, 1988.

Lechuga, Ruth D. *El traje de los indígenas de México*. México, D.F.: Panorama, 1991.

Leinaweaver, Richard E. "Rabinal Achí." *Latin American Theatre Review* 1–2 (spring 1968): 3–53.

Lenkersdorf, Carlos. *Los hombres verdaderos: Voces y testimonios tojolobales*. México, D.F.: Siglo XXI, UNAM, 1996.

———. *Cosmovisiones*. México, D.F.: UNAM, 1998.

Leñero, Estela. "Teatro indígena en los altos de Chiapas." *Uno más Uno*, February 25, 1990, S4.

León-Portilla, Miguel. *Pre-Columbian Literatures of Mexico*. Trans. Grace Lobanov and Miguel León-Portilla. Norman: University of Oklahoma Press, 1969.

———. *Endangered Cultures*. Trans. Julie Goodson-Lawes. Dallas: Southern Methodist University Press, 1990.

———. *Literaturas indígenas de México*. México, D.F.: Editorial MAPFRE, 1992.

León-Portilla, Miguel, ed. *The Broken Spears: The Aztec Account of the Conquest of Mexico*. Trans. Angel Maria Garibay K. and Lysander Kemp. Boston: Beacon, 1962.

Lerner, Gerda. *Why History Matters*. London: Oxford University Press, 1997.

Lomnitz, Claudio. *Deep Mexico, Silent Mexico: An Anthropology of Nationalism*. Minneapolis: University of Minnesota Press, 2001.

———. "Nationalism's Dirty Linen: 'Contact Zones' and the Topography of National Identity." In *Deep Mexico, Silent Mexico*, 125–144.

Lomnitz-Adler, Claudio. *Exits from the Labyrinth: Culture and Ideology in the Mexican National Space*. Berkeley: University of California Press, 1992.

Loyo, Engracia. "Popular Reactions to the Educational Reforms of Cardenismo." In Beezley, Martin, and French, 247–260.

MacAloon, John, ed. *Rite, Drama, Festival, Spectacle: Rehearsals toward a Theory of Cultural Performance*. Philadelphia: Institute for the Study of Human Issues, 1984.

Mace, Carroll E. "New Information about the Dance-Dramas of Rabinal and the Rabinal-Achi." *Xavier University Studies* 6, 1 (1967): 1–19.

Maceda, Elda. "La repetitiva actuación del Teatro Campesino." Review of *Romeo y Julieta*, dir. María Alicia Martínez Medrano. LTCI. Culiacán, Sinaloa. *El Universal*, November 24, 1990, C2.

MacEoin, Gary. *The People's Church: Bishop Samuel Ruíz of Mexico and Why He Matters*. New York: Crossroad/Herder and Herder, 1996.

Madrid, María Elena, Sylvia Sabarino, and Miguel Angel Piñeda, eds. *Laboratorio de Teatro Campesino e Indígena*. Villahermosa, Tabasco: DIF, 1987.

Magaña, Sergio. *Los enemigos*. México, D.F.: Editores Mexicanos Unidos, 1990.

Marcos, Subcomandante. *Shadows of Tender Fury: The Letters and Communiqués of Subcomandante Marcos and the Zapatista Army of National Liberation*. New York: Monthly Review Press, 1995.

———. "Marcos visto por Marcos." Interview with Dauno Tótoro. *Este Sur*, August 5, 1996, 13 ff.

———. *Our Word Is Our Weapon: Selected Writings*. Ed. Juana Ponce de Leon. New York: Seven Stories Press, 2001.

Marranca, Bonnie, and Gautam Dasgupta, eds. *Interculturalism and Performance*. New York: PAJ, 1991.

Martin, David. *Tongues of Fire: The Explosion of Protestantism in Latin America*. Oxford: Basil Blackwell, 1990.

Martínez Medrano, María Alicia. "La sociedad, empeñada en matar amor." Interview with Angelina Camargo Breña. *Excelsior*, September 12, 1990, C3.

———. "Información sobre los Laboratorios de Teatro Campesino e Indígena." Internal document, undated.

Matadamas, María Elena. "El teatro campesino bajo la lluvia." Review of *Romeo y Julieta,* dir. María Alicia Martínez Medrano. LTCI. Delacorte Theatre, New York. *El Universal,* September 18, 1990, C1+.

———. "El teatro campesino reinvindica nuestras raíces y cultura." *El Universal,* September 18, 1990, C1 ff.

Magaña, Sergio. *Los enemigos.* México, D.F.: Editores Mexicanos Unidos, 1990.

Materne, Yves, ed. *The Indian Awakening in Latin America.* New York: Friendship Press, 1980.

McGee, R. Jon. *Life, Ritual, and Religion among the Lacandon Maya.* Belmont, Calif.: Wadsworth, 1990.

Menchú, Rigoberta. *I, Rigoberta Menchú.* Trans. Elizabeth Burgos-Debray. London: Verso, 1987.

Meyer, Jean, with Federico Anaya Gallardo and Julio Ríos. *Samuel Ruíz en San Cristóbal, 1960–2000.* México, D.F.: Tusquets, 2000.

Meyer, Michael C., William L. Sherman, and Susan M. Deeds. *The Course of Mexican History.* New York: Oxford University Press, 1999.

Miller, Cynthia J. "The Social Impacts of Televised Media among the Yucatec Maya." *Human Organization* 57, 3 (fall 1998): 307–314.

Monsiváis, Carlos. "De algunos problemas del término 'Cultura Nacional' en México." *Revista Occidental. Estudios Latinoamericanos* 2, 1 (1985): 37–48.

Montemayor, Carlos, coord. *Maya dziibo'ob bejla'e/Letras mayas contemporáneas.* México, D.F.: INI and SEDESOL, 1994.

———. *Collección letras mayas contemporáneas, Chiapas.* México, D.F.: INI, 1996.

Montemayor, Carlos, ed. *Los escritores indígenas actuales.* Vol. 2. México, D.F.: Consejo Nacional para la Cultura y las Artes, 1992.

———. *Situación actual y perspectivas de la literatura en lenguas indígenas.* México, D.F.: Consejo Nacional para la Cultural y las Artes, 1993.

———. *Los pueblos indios de México hoy.* México, D.F.: Editorial Planeta Mexicana, 2001.

Monterde, Francisco. *Teatro indígena prehispánico.* México, D.F.: UNAM, 1955.

Montrose, Louis. "The Work of Gender in the Discourse of Discovery." In Greenblatt, 177–217.

Moore-Gilbert, Bart. *Postcolonial Theory: Contexts, Practices, Politics.* London: Verso, 1997.

Morales Bermúdez, Jesús. "El Congreso Indígena de Chiapas: Un testimonio." *América Indígena* 55, 1–2 (January–June 1995): 305–340.

Morris, Walter F., Jr. *Living Maya.* New York: Harry N. Abrams, 1987.

Muñoz, Fernando. *El teatro regional de Yucatán.* Mérida: Grupo Editorial Gaceta, 1987.

Myers, Robert. "Mayan Women Find Their Place Is on the Stage." *New York Times,* September 28, 1997, Arts and Leisure, 1 ff.

Nash, June C. *Mayan Visions: The Quest for Autonomy in an Age of Globalization.* New York: Routledge, 2001.

Nash, June, ed. *Crafts in the World Market: The Impact of Global Exchange on Middle American Artisans.* Albany: State University of New York Press, 1993.

Navarrete, Carlos. *Relatos mayas de tierras altas sobre el origen del maíz: Los caminos de Paxil.* Guatemala City: Editorial Palo de Hormigo, 2000.

O'Connell, Joanna. *Prospero's Daughter: The Prose of Rosario Castellanos.* Austin: University of Texas Press, 1995.

O'Gorman, Edmundo. *La invención de América: El universalismo de la cultura del Occidente.* México, D.F.: Fondo de Cultura Económica, 1958.

Oppenheimer, Andres. *Bordering on Chaos: Guerrillas, Stockbrokers, Politicians, and Mexico's Road to Prosperity.* Boston: Little, Brown, 1996.

Ortiz, Fernando. "Del fenómeno social de la transculturación y de su importancia en Cuba." *Revista Bimestre Cubana* 46 (1940): 272–278.

Ortiz, Teresa. Comments made during a visit to my seminar, "Theatre of the Americas," University of Minnesota, Minneapolis, April 30, 1999.

Ortíz B., Alejandro. "Teatro popular y educación." Paper presented at first Encuentro Nacional de Teatro Popular, Nuevo León, October 1985.

Pacheco Cruz, Santiago. *Teatro Maya.* 1st ed. Mérida: Campaña Indigenista Pro-Educación, 1940. Photocopy available at the Library of the Universidad Autónoma de Yucatán, Mérida.

Padial, Anita L. "American Pre-Columbian Drama: The Rabinal Achi." Ph.D. diss., University of Tennessee, 1981.

Padial, Anita L., and A. M. Vázquez-Bigi. "Estudio comparativo del Rabinal-Achi y la tragedia clásica griega." *Cuadernos Americanos* 249, 4 (July–August 1983): 159–189.

Parish, Helen Rand. *Bartolomé de Las Casas: The Only Way.* Mahwah, N.J.: Paulist Press, 1992.

Partida Tayzan, Armando. "Interculturalidad: Deconstrucción de un texto y construcción escénica del *Rabinal-Achí-Los enemigos.*" *Gestos* 19 (April 1995): 101–117.

Pavis, Patrice, ed. "Introduction: Towards a Theory of Interculturalism in Theatre?" In *The Intercultural Performance Reader,* 1–26. London: Routledge, 1996.

Perales, Rosalina. *Teatro hispanoamericano contemporáneo, 1967–1987.* Vol. 1. México, D.F.: Grupo Editorial Gaceta, 1993.

———. *Teatro hispanoamerico contemporáneo, 1967–1987.* Vol. 2. México, D.F.: Grupo Editorial Gaceta, 1993.

Pérez Hernández, Manuel. "Vivencias de nuestra palabra: El resurgimiento de la cultura maya en Chiapas." In Montemayor, *Los escritores indígenas actuales,* vol. 2, 83–101.

Peters, Julie Stone. "Intercultural Performance, Theatre Anthropology, and the Imperialist Critique: Identities, Inheritances, and Neo-Orthodoxies." In Gainor, 199–213.

Phelan, Peggy. *Unmarked: The Politics of Performance.* London: Routledge, 1993.

Pierce, Donna. Catalog notes. In *Converging Cultures: Art and Identity in Spanish America,* ed. Diana Fane. New York: Brooklyn Museum and Harry N. Abrams, 1996.

Pi-Sunyer, Oriol, R. Brooke Thomas, and Magalí Daltabuit. *Tourism and Maya Society in Quintana Roo, Mexico.* Occasional Paper No. 17. Amherst: Latin American Consortium of New England, September 1999.

A Place Called Chiapas. Dir. Nettie Wild. Canada Wild Productions, 1998.

Poniatowska, Elena. "No More Fiesta of Bullets." *The Nation,* July 28–August 4, 1997, 23–24.

Potter, Robert. "Abraham and Human Sacrifice: The Exfoliation of Medieval Drama in Aztec Mexico." *New Theatre Quarterly* 2, 8 (1986): 306–312.

Pozas, Ricardo. *Juan the Chamula.* Trans. Lysander Kemp. Berkeley: University of California Press, 1962.

Prakash, Gyan, ed. *After Colonialism: Imperial Histories and Postcolonial Displacements.* Princeton: Princeton University Press, 1994.

"Proyecto Fotográfico Chiapas." Archivo Fotográfico Indígena. www.chiapas photo.org.

Rabasa, José. *Inventing America: Spanish Historiography and the Formation of Eurocentrism.* Norman: University of Oklahoma Press, 1993.

Rao, Diane. "Reconciliation and Baptism in Sixteenth-Century Aztec Didactic Dramas." Paper presented at the ATHE Conference, Philadelphia, August 1993.

Ravicz, Marilyn Eckdahl. *Early Colonial Religious Drama in Mexico: From Tzompantli to Golgotha.* Washington, D.C.: Catholic University of America Press, 1970.

Reed, Nelson. *The Caste War.* Stanford: Stanford University Press, 1964.

Restall, Matthew. *Maya Conquistador.* Boston: Beacon, 1998.

"Report from Chiapas." Multiple authors. *Cultural Survival Quarterly* 17, 1 (spring 1994): 9–34.

Ricard, Robert. *The Spiritual Conquest of Mexico.* Trans. Leslie Byrd Simpson. Berkeley: University of California Press, 1966.

Rivera Cruz, María del Carmen. "Los indígenas Choles de Tabasco." *Expresión* 14 (September–October 1986): 2–5.

Rojas, Rosa. *Chiapas ¿y las mujeres qué?* México, D.F.: Ediciones La Correa Feminista, 1995.

———. *Del dicho al hecho: Reflexiones sobre la ampliación de la ley revolucionaria de mujeres del EZLN.* México, D.F.: Ediciones del Taller Editorial La Correa Feminista, 1996.

Rojas Aravena, Francisco, ed. *América Latina: Etnodesarrollo y etnocidio.* San José, Costa Rica: Ediciones FLASCO, 1982.

Root, Deborah. *Cannibal Culture: Art, Appropriation, and the Commodification of Difference.* Boulder, Colo.: Westview, 1996.

Rosales Ayala, Héctor, ed. *Cultura, sociedad civil y proyectos culturales en México.* México, D.F.: Consejo Nacional para la Cultura y las Artes, 1994.

Rosenbaum, Brenda. *With Our Heads Bowed: The Dynamics of Gender in a Maya Community.* Albany: Institute for Mesoamerican Studies, State University of New York, 1993.

"Rotundo Éxito en Madrid del Grupo Teatral Tabasqueño: Diario 16." Review of *Bodas de sangre,* dir. María Alicia Martínez Medrano. LTCI. Spain. Photocopy of unidentified newspaper article dated October 18, 1987, in archives of Centro de Investigación Teatral Rodolfo Uisgli, Instituto Nacional de Bellas Artes, Mexico City.

Rowe, William, and Vivian Schelling. *Memory and Modernity: Popular Culture in Latin America.* London: Verso, 1991.

Ruíz, Samuel García. *Mi trabajo pastoral.* México, D.F.: Ediciones Paulinas, 1999.

———. *Seeking Freedom: Bishop Samuel Ruíz in Conversation with Jorge S. Santiago.* Ed. and trans. Michel Andraos. Toronto: Toronto Council/-Development and Peace, 1999.

———. "La iglesia autóctona en Chiapas: Una experiencia pastoral indígena." Paper presented at Arizona State University, Phoenix, April 25, 2002.

Ruyter, Nancy Lee. "Ancient Images: The Pre-Cortesian in 20th-Century Dance Performance." *Gestos* 21 (April 1996): 145–155.

Salas González, Lorenzo. "El alma colectiva de un pueblo recupera su esencia." *¡Por Esto!* September 5, 2001, 12–14.

Sánchez Chan, Feliciano. *Manual de Teatro Comunitario.* México, D.F.: Dirección General de Culturas Populares, 1992.

———. *Teatro maya contemporáneo.* Vols. 1 and 2. México, D.F.: INI and SEDESOL, 1994.

Sangari, Kumkum. "The Politics of the Possible." *Cultural Critique* 7 (1987): 157–185.

Schaefer, Claudia. *Danger Zones: Homosexuality, National Identity, and Mexican Culture.* Tucson: University of Arizona Press, 1996.

Schmidt, Henry C. "The Search for National Identity in Mexico, 1900–1934." Ph.D. diss., University of Texas, 1972.

Scott, James. *Domination and the Arts of Resistance: Hidden Transcripts.* New Haven: Yale University Press, 1990.

Scott, Joan Wallach. *Gender and the Politics of History.* New York: Columbia University Press, 1988.

Seminar on Feminism and Culture in Latin America. *Women, Culture, and Politics in Latin America.* Berkeley: University of California Press, 1990.

Shepard, Richard F. "Shakespeare in Tongues He Surely Never Heard." Review of *Romeo y Julieta,* dir. María Alicia Martínez Medrano. LTCI. Delacorte Theatre, New York. *New York Times,* September 11, 1990, C15.

Simpson, Leslie Byrd. *Many Mexicos.* New York: Putnam, 1966.

Sna Jtz'ibajom. *Relatos tzeltales y tzotziles.* México, D.F.: Diana, 1994.

———. *Relatos tseltales y tzotziles.* Tuxtla Gutiérrez: Gobierno del Estado de Chiapas, 1996.

———. *Renacimiento del Teatro Maya en Chiapas.* Vols. 1–3. México, D.F.: INI, 1996.

———. *De todos para todos.* In Sna Jtz'ibajom, *Renacimiento,* vol. 2, 119–142.

———. "Trabajadores en el otro mundo." 1998–1999. Typescript in author's possession.

———. *II Encuentro Indígena de las Américas: Memoria 1999.* San Cristóbal de las Casas: Sna Jtz'ibajom, 2000.

———. "El origen del maíz." 2000. Typescript in author's possession.

———. "Siempre México con nosotros." 2002. Typescript in author's possession.

———. "Proyectos para el mantenimiento y expansión de las actividades . . ."

Report. Archives of Centro de Investigación Teatral Rodolfo Usigli, Instituto Nacional de Bellas Artes, Mexico City, n.d.

Soyinka, Wole. "Art, Exile, and Resistance." *American Theatre* 14, 1 (January 1997): 26–29.

Spivak, Gayatri. "Can the Subaltern Speak?" In *Marxism and the Interpretation of Culture*, ed. Cary Nelson and Lawrence Grossberg, 271–313. Champaign: University of Illinois Press, 1988.

Stavans, Ilan. "'Romeo y Julieta' del LTC, otro punto de vista." Review of *Romeo y Julieta*, dir. María Alicia Martínez Medrano. LTCI. Delacorte Theatre, New York. *El Universal*, September 18, 1990, C1.

———. "Unmasking Marcos." In Hayden, 386–395.

Stavenhagen, Rodolfo, and Margarita Nolasco, eds. *Política cultural para un país multiétnico: Coloquio sobre problemas educativos y culturales en una sociedad multiétnica*. México, D.F.: SEP, 1988.

Stayton, Kevin L. "The Algara Romero de Terreros Collection: A Mexican Aristocratic Family in the Colonial Era." In Fane, 69–74.

Steele, Cynthia. "Indigenismo y posmodernidad: narrativa indigenista, testimonio, teatro campesino y video en el Chiapas finisecular." *Revista de Crítica Literaria Latinoamericana* 19, 38 (1993): 249–260.

———. "A Woman Fell into the River: Negotiating Female Subjects in Contemporary Mayan Theatre." In Taylor and Villegas, 239–56.

———. Introduction to graduate seminar, "Travelers, Ethnographers, Guerrillas, and Priests: Conflicts over Narrative Authority in Chiapas, Mexico." University of Washington, fall 1995.

Sten, María. *Vida y muerte del teatro náhuatl*. 2d ed. Xalapa: Universidad Veracruzana, 1982.

Stephen, Lynn. *¡Zapata Lives! Histories and Cultural Politics in Southern Mexico*. Berkeley: University of California Press, 2002.

Stoll, Anita, ed. *A Different Reality: Studies on the Work of Elena Garro*. London: Associated University Presses, 1990.

Stoll, David. *Rigoberta Menchú and the Story of All Poor Guatemalans*. Boulder, Colo.: Westview, 1999.

Sullivan, Kathleen. "Protagonists of Change." *Cultural Survival Quarterly* 16, 4 (winter 1992): 38–40.

———. "Religious Change and the Recreation of Community in an Urban Setting among the Tzotzil Maya of Highland Chiapas, Mexico." Ph.D. diss., City University of New York, 1998.

Sullivan, Paul. *Unfinished Conversations: Mayas and Foreigners Between Two Wars*. Berkeley: University of California Press, 1991.

Tanaka, Michiko. "Seki Sano and Popular Political and Social Theatre in Latin America." *Latin American Theatre Review* 27, 2 (spring 1994): 53–69.

Taylor, Diana. "Transculturating Transculturation." In Marranca and Dasgupta, 60–74.

Taylor, Diana, and Roselyn Costantino, eds. *Holy Terrors: Latin American Women Perform*. Durham: Duke University Press, 2003.

Taylor, Diana, and Juan Villegas, eds. *Negotiating Performance: Gender, Sexuality, and Theatricality in Latin/o America*. Durham: Duke University Press, 1994.

Tedlock, Barbara. *Time and the Highland Maya*. Rev. ed. Albuquerque: University of New Mexico Press, 1992.

Tedlock, Dennis. *Popul Vuh*. New York: Simon and Schuster, 1985.

———. *Breath on the Mirror: Mythic Voices and Visions of the Living Maya*. San Francisco: Harper, 1993.

———. "The *Rabinal Achi*: Continuity and Change in a Mayan Dance Drama." Paper presented at the University of Minnesota, Minneapolis, October 8, 1998.

———. *"The Rabinal Achi": A Mayan Drama of War and Sacrifice*. New York: Oxford University Press, 2003.

Testimonios de Culturas Populares. México, D.F.: SEP, 1988.

Trinh, T. Minh-ha. *Woman, Native, Other*. Bloomington: Indiana University Press, 1989.

Turner, Victor. *Dramas, Fields and Metaphors: Symbolic Action in Human Society*. Ithaca: Cornell University Press, 1974.

———. *From Ritual to Theatre: The Human Seriousness of Play*. New York: PAJ, 1982.

Underiner, Tamara L. "Incidents of Theatre in Chiapas, Tabasco, and Yucatán: Cultural Enactments in Mayan Mexico." *Theatre Journal* 50 (1998): 349–369.

"Unmasking the Maya: The Story of Sna Jtz'ibajom." Smithsonian Museum of Natural History, Department of Anthropology. http://www.mnh.si.edu/an thro/maya.

Uno, Roberta, with Lucy Mae San Pablo Burns. *The Color of Theater: Race, Culture, and Contemporary Performance*. London: Continuum, 2002.

Urban, Greg, and Joel Sherzer, eds. *Nation-States and Indians in Latin America*. Austin: University of Texas Press, 1991.

van den Berghe, Pierre L. *The Quest for the Other: Ethnic Tourism in San Cristóbal, Mexico*. Seattle: University of Washington Press, 1994.

van Young, Eric. "Conclusion: The State as Vampire—Hegemonic Projects, Public Ritual, and Popular Culture in Mexico, 1600–1900." In Beezley, Martin, and French, 343–374.

van Zantwijk, R. A. M. *"Indigenismo:* A Philosophy and a Method of Guided Development of the Aboriginal Minorities in Mexico: Historical Background and Actual Orientations." *Plural Societies* 7 (1976): 95–103.

Vasconcelos, José. *La raza cósmica*. Trans. Didier T. Jaén. Los Angeles: California State University Centro de Publicaciones, Bilingual Edition, 1979.

Vásquez, Mary Seale. "Rosario Castellanos, Image and Idea." In Ahern and Vásquez, 15–40.

Vera Cabrera, Rubén. "Los Chontales de Tabasco: Historia y desarrollo." *Expresión* 20 (September–October 1987): 2–7.

Versenyi, Adam. "Searching for El Dorado: Ritual in Early Latin America." *New Theatre Quarterly* 16 (1988): 330–334.

———. "Getting under the Aztecs' Skin: Evangelical Theatre in the New World." *New Theatre Quarterly* 19 (1989): 217–226.

———. "Ritual Meets the Postmodern: Contemporary Mexican Theatre." *New Theatre Quarterly* 31 (August 1992): 221–225.

———. *Theatre in Latin America: Religion, Politics, and Culture from Cortes to the 1980s*. Cambridge: Cambridge University Press, 1993.

Vicente Mosquete, José L. "Un Lorca indígena, ritual y campesino." Review of *Bodas de sangre*, dir. María Alicia Martínez Medrano. LTCI. Chapultepec Park, Mexico City. *El Público* (Madrid) 44 (May 1987): 57–63.

Villoro, Luis. *Los grandes momentos del indigenismo en México*. 2d ed. México, D.F.: SEP, 1987.

Vogt, Evon Z., Jr. *Fieldwork among the Maya*. Albuquerque: University of New Mexico Press, 1994.

Waldman, Gloria F. "Festival Latino Diary." *Latin American Theatre Review* 20, 2 (spring 1987): 99–105.

Warren, Kay B. *Indigenous Movements and Their Critics: Pan-Maya Activism in Guatemala*. Princeton: Princeton University Press, 1998.

Watanabe, John M. *Maya Saints and Souls in a Changing World*. Austin: University of Texas Press, 1992.

Wearne, Philip. *Return of the Indian: Conquest and Revival in the Americas*. London: Cassel, 1996.

Weber, Carl. "AC/TC: Currents of Theatrical Exchange." In Marranca and Dasgupta, 27–37.

Weil, James. Discussant's Comments. Sociocultural Formations panel, North Central Council of Latin Americanists Conference, Ripon, Wisc., October 28, 1995.

Weiss, Judith A., with Leslie Damasceno, Donald Frischmann, Claudia Kaiser-Lenoir, Marina Pianca, and Beatriz J. Rizk. *Latin American Popular Theatre: The First Five Centuries*. Albuquerque: University of New Mexico Press, 1993.

Williams, Jerry M. *El teatro del México colonial: Época misionera*. New York: Peter Lang, 1992.

Williams, Michael. Comments during graduate seminar in Comparative Religion, University of Washington, December 1993.

Wolf, Margery. *A Thrice-Told Tale: Feminism, Postmodernism, and Ethnographic Responsibility*. Stanford: Stanford University Press, 1992.

Ximenez Estrada, Carlos. "Festival Scheduled to Support Campesino Theatre." *The News*, June 30, 1989, 18.

XII censo general de población y vivienda de los Estados Unidos Mexicanos. México, D.F.: INEGI, 2000. http://www.inegi.gob.mx/difusion/espanol/fpobla.html

Yanagisako, Sylvia, and Jane Collier, eds. *Gender and Kinship: Essays toward a Unified Analysis*. Stanford: Stanford University Press, 1987.

Yurchenco, Henrietta. *Music of the Maya-Quiches of Guatemala: The Rabinal Achí and Baile de las Canastas*. Sound recording, with notes. Folkways Records, New York, 1978.

Zuñiga, Reynaldo. "'Teatro Campesino,' cortina de humo de corruptelas, malversación y degeneración," *La Tribuna*, April 24, 1990, 48.

INDEX